Tourism Ethnographies

How is ethnography practiced in the context of tourism? As a multi- and interdisciplinary area of academic enquiry, the use of ethnography to study tourism is found in an increasingly diverse number of situations.

This book is a collection of essays that discuss the practice of ethnography in tourism settings. Scholars from different countries share their work. Reflecting on their experiences, each author presents an individual insight into the complexities of ethnographic practice in destinations from around the globe, including Amsterdam, Angola, Bali, Greece, India, Namibia, Portugal, Spain and the UK. The book explores a range of themes, including obtaining institutional ethical approval; the ethics of fieldwork in situ; the use of oral histories; the role of memory; and empowerment and disempowerment in field relations. It looks at gender issues in negotiating entrance to the field, the use of collaborative fieldwork in teaching, team ethnographies, and reflections on writing up.

This is the first book to bring together several tourism scholars using ethnography as their research method. It gives insight into the experience of this unique technique and will be a useful guide for those new to the field, as well as the more seasoned ethnographer who may recognise similar experiences to their own.

Hazel Andrews is Reader in Tourism, Culture & Society at Liverpool John Moores University.

Takamitsu Jimura is Programme Leader for MSc International Tourism Management at Liverpool John Moores University. His primary research interest is heritage tourism.

Laura Dixon is Programme Leader in Events Management at Liverpool John Moores University. Her primary research interest is British tourism in Spain.

Routledge Advances in Tourism and Anthropology: People, Place and World

Series Editors:
Dr Catherine Palmer (University of Brighton, UK) C.Palmer3@brighton.ac.uk
Dr Jo-Anne Lester (University of Brighton, UK) J.Lester@brighton.ac.uk

To discuss any ideas for the series please contact Faye Leerink, Commissioning Editor: faye.leerink@tandf.co.uk or the Series Editors.

This series draws inspiration from anthropology's overarching aim to explore and better understand the human condition in all its fascinating diversity. It seeks to expand the intellectual landscape of anthropology and tourism in relation to how we understand the experience of being human, providing critical inquiry into the spaces, places, and lives in which tourism unfolds. Contributions to the series will consider how such spaces are embodied, imagined, constructed, experienced, memorialized and contested. The series provides a forum for cutting-edge research and innovative thinking from tourism, anthropology, and related disciplines such as philosophy, history, sociology, geography, cultural studies, architecture, the arts, and feminist studies.

The Affective Negotiation of Slum Tourism
City Walks in Delhi
Tore Holst

Tourism and Ethnodevelopment
Inclusion, Empowerment and Self Determination
Edited by Ismar Borges de Lima and Victor King

Everyday Practices of Tourism Mobilities
Packing a Bag
Kaya Barry

Tourism and Indigenous Heritage in Latin America
As Observed through Mexico's Magical Village Cuetzalan
Casper Jacobsen

Tourism and Embodiment
Edited by Catherine Palmer and Hazel Andrews

Tourism Encounters and Imaginaries: The Front and Back Stage of Tourism Performance
Edited by Frances Julia Riemer

For more information about this series please visit: www.routledge.com/Routledge-Advances-in-Tourism-and-Anthropology/book-series/RATA

Tourism Ethnographies

Ethics, Methods, Application and
Reflexivity

**Edited by
Hazel Andrews, Takamitsu Jimura and
Laura Dixon**

LONDON AND NEW YORK

First published 2019
by Routledge
2 Park Square, Milton Park, Abingdon, Oxon OX14 4RN

and by Routledge
52 Vanderbilt Avenue, New York, NY 10017

Routledge is an imprint of the Taylor & Francis Group, an informa business

British Library Cataloguing in Publication Data
A catalogue record for this book is available from the British Library

Library of Congress Cataloging-in-Publication Data
A catalog record has been requested for this book

ISBN: 978-1-138-06176-7 (hbk)
ISBN: 978-0-367-58208-1 (pbk)
ISBN: 978-1-315-16216-4 (ebk)

Typeset in Times New Roman by
Taylor & Francis Books

Contents

Illustrations

Figures

Boxes

Contributors

Dr Hazel Andrews is a social anthropologist and Reader in Tourism, Culture and Society at Liverpool John Moores University. With a particular focus on practices of embodiment, consumption, habitus and place, Hazel's research and publications have examined social and symbolic constructions of national, regional and gendered identities in the context of British tourists to Mallorca. Hazel is the author of numerous texts on her work in Mallorca including *The British on Holiday. Charter Tourism, Identity and Consumption* (2011). Other publications include *Tourism & Violence* (2014) and *Liminal Landscapes. Travel, experience and spaces in-between* (2012).

Dr Fiona Eva Bakas is a critical tourism researcher with 20 years of industry and academic work experience. She is currently a postdoctoral researcher in a nationwide project creating a network of creative tourism offers in rural areas and small cities (CREATOUR), at Coimbra University, Portugal. Before this, 2014-2016, Fiona worked in Aveiro University on GENTOUR II, a project investigating gender roles and the Portuguese tourism workforce. She gained her PhD Tourism in Otago University, NZ and has published in peer-reviewed journals on aspects of creative and cultural tourism, gender in tourism labour, qualitative methodologies, handicrafts, entrepreneurship, rural tourism, ecotourism, and feminist economics. She is an Associate of Equality in Tourism, an NGO that researches and highlights gender equality issues in tourism.

Dr Laura Dixon is a social anthropologist and Senior Lecturer in Tourism and Leisure Management and Events Management at Liverpool John Moores University. Her publications to date focus on recognition, cosmopolitanism, gender and sexuality amongst elite British 'lifestyle migrants' in the tourist town of Sitges, in Spain. She is currently working on exploring ideas of temporality and spatialisation in relation to Britons who have recently returned to the UK from Spain.

Dr Claudia Dolezal is a Lecturer in Tourism at the University of Westminster and editorial board member of the Austrian Journal of South-East Asian Studies (ASEAS). Her background is in tourism, international development and social anthropology, with a geographical focus on the region of South-east Asia. Claudia's research interests focus on tourism for development and community-based tourism, in specific tourism encounters, social inequalities, power relations and people's empowerment. Her PhD investigated power dynamics between the actors involved in CBT to ultimately identify possibilities for residents' empowerment through tourism, and further made use of the practice of reflexivity to gain insights into fieldwork practices.

Dr Filipa Fernandes is an anthropologist, she holds a PhD in Tourism from the University of Évora. She is Assistant Professor at the Institute of Social and Political Science – University of Lisbon since 2013. She is senior researcher at the Centre of Administration and Public Policies from the University of Lisbon. She is Visiting Academic at Multidimensional Tourism Institute, University of Lapland. Filipa has done fieldwork in Madeira Island (Portugal) on heritage, memory and tourism, and in Rovaniemi (Finland) on the production of Christmas tourism imaginaries. She is the author of several articles and a book. Recently she co-authored the book Antropologia e Turismo: teorias, métodos e praxis (Anthropology and Tourism: theories, methods and praxis). Her current research interests focus on the production of tourism imaginaries in Finnish Lapland; and touristification, tourism impacts and new hospitalities in the city of Lisbon, Portugal. Her other research interests include: heritage, anthropology and tourism, tourism imaginaries, hospitality, sharing economy, touristification, climate change and tourism.

Dr Pamila Gupta is Associate Professor at WISER (Wits Institute for Social and Economic Research) at the University of Witwatersrand in Johannesburg, South Africa. She holds a PhD in Socio-cultural Anthropology from Columbia University. She writes about Lusophone India and Africa, Portuguese colonial and missionary history, decolonization, heritage tourism, visual cultures and islands in the Indian Ocean. She has published in Interventions, South African Historical Journal, African Studies, Journal of Asian and African Studies, Critical Arts, Ler História, Ecologie & Politique, and Public Culture, and is the co-editor of Eyes Across the Water: Navigating the Indian Ocean with Isabel Hofmeyr and Michael Pearson (UNISA, 2010). Her first monograph entitled The Relic State: St. Francis Xavier and the Politics of Ritual in Portuguese India was published by Manchester University Press (2014). Her second monograph entitled Portuguese Decolonization in the Indian Ocean World: History and Ethnography was recently published with Bloomsbury Academic Press (2018).

Dr Martín Gómez-Ullate is researcher in the University of Extremadura, Spain. Martin has a Ph.D. in Social Anthropology from the University Complutense of Madrid, he has lectured in public universities and research centres in Portugal, France, Mexico and Spain where he has developed research in a number of areas, including identity, social representations and intercultural relationships, cultural heritage, qualitative methodology and shared musical heritage and cultural tourism. He has written in Spanish on visual anthropology and counterculture. He won the Fernán Caballero Prize in Short Essays on Social Sciences. He is coordinating the project Cultour+, an Erasmus+ Strategic Partnership involving six countries in the research and promotion of European Cultural Routes, mostly those dealing with pilgrimage and religious tourism. He is now conducting fieldwork in pilgrimage and cultural tourism in the Via de la Plata and the Caminho Interior de Santiago.

Dr Takamitsu Jimura is Programme Leader for MSc International Tourism Management and Senior Lecturer in Tourism at Liverpool John Moores University. Takamitsu holds a PhD in Tourism and Cultural Heritage Management and an MSc in Tourism, Conservation and Sustainable Development. His key research interests include cultural heritage and tourism, tourism marketing and sustainable tourism. Takamitsu is especially interested in exploring the impacts of World Heritage Site (WHS) designation on tourism development, local communities, and heritage management and conservation activities. He is the author of several journal articles and book chapters and has presented his research outputs regularly at international conferences. Many of them were developed from his fieldwork in the UK and Japan. His latest journal article examines the WHS management at Sacred Sites and Pilgrimage Routes in the Kii Mountain Range in Japan. He is currently working on two monographs: One focuses on WHSs, tourism, local communities and conservation activities, and the other looks at cultural heritage and tourism in Japan.

Burcu Kaya Sayarı is a Ph.D. candidate and a research assistant in Tourism at Anadolu University. She is taking social anthropology courses from METU University in Ankara. She has conducted research about social memory and national identity and participated in an oral history project about tourism. She is currently conducting more research that aims at modelling the relationship between places, narratives, identities, commemoration and performances. Her research interests are discourses, space and place, rituals, social memory, identity, narratives and performances.

Dr Danielle Kelly works at the Yunus Centre for Social Business and Health at Glasgow Caledonian University. Her work focuses on the health and wellbeing impact and development of grassroots community initiatives, such as social enterprises and Men's Sheds. In particular, her work uses participatory methods, such as action research and ethnography. She graduated from the University of Edinburgh with an MA in Social Anthropology in 2008. Following this, she went on to study a PhD in Public Health at Liverpool John Moores University, focusing on young people's substance use, sexual health and utilisation of health services during periods of travel. The project involved mixed methods, including periods of ethnographic fieldwork in the resort of Ibiza, Spain, studying young British casual workers. During her PhD studies, Danielle worked at the Centre for Public Health, LJMU on projects relating to communities, health and environment.

Dr Stasja Koot (stasjakoot.com) works as an assistant professor at Wageningen University, the Netherlands. He is an ecological anthropologist with a specific interest in political ecology. Before this he lived with Bushmen hunter-gatherers in Namibia from 2002 until 2007, working on a community-based tourism project (Treesleeper Camp). He has spent several periods of fieldwork among the Bushmen in southern Africa since 1999. His research focused on indigenous people, nature conservation, tourism, land conflicts and natural resource management. He is currently working on new research in the Kruger to Canyon biosphere next to the Kruger National Park, South Africa, where he is investigating how the tourism industry is being affected by the (rhino) poaching crisis, and how they respond to it. Moreover, he is exploring wildlife estates, which is a new tourism and nature conservation model that currently thrives in South Africa.

Diana Loutfy is a graduate of the M.A. Management Masters Program at Karlshochschule International University. Her two concentrations were 'Branding' and 'Creativity and Innovation'. Her research focus is on creativity techniques, cultural diversity and integration. This was reflected in her Masters Thesis about the effect of physical spaces on individual creativity: she studied the relationship between physical structures and their impacts on achieving individual creativity flow. Currently, she is working as a Startup Consultant at the CyberForum e.V. in Karlsruhe where she supports startups in IT security as part of the CyberLab's IT Accelerator Program.

Dr Xerardo Pereiro works at the University of Trás-os-Montes and Alto Douro (UTAD), Portugal. Xerardo holds a European PhD in Social Anthropology from the University of Santiago de Compostela (Galicia – Spain) and another international PhD in Tourism from the University of La Laguna (Canarias – Spain). His research is about the anthropology of tourism and cultural heritage in CETRAD (Centre for Transdiciplinary Development Studies) of UTAD. He has undertaken fieldwork in Asturias and Galicia (Spain), Portugal and in Panama about indigenous guna tourism. He was the Head of the Applied Anthropology Degree of UTAD, and visiting lecturer in the universities of Vigo, Coruña, Santiago de Compostela, Pablo Olavide (Seville), Salamanca, Panamá, "Universidade Nova de Lisboa". He was awarded, in 1994, the Vicente Risco Award for Social Anthropology and Social Sciences, 2007 FITUR in research tourism and 2011 Sol-Meliá – University of Balears Islands Awards for Tourism Research. He is also a member of the editorial board of the journal PASOS. His current research focuses on the Portuguese routes of the Santiago de Compostela.

Professor Francisco Martins Ramos (1943–2017). Francisco was raised in the Alentejo, a southern rural area of Portugal. He lived in Africa and travelled extensively in the United States and Europe. He received his BA in Anthropology from the ISCSP - Technical University of Lisbon (1978) and earned his doctorate in Anthropology at the University of Évora in 1992. He was Professor of Anthropology until 2009 when he retired. In 2010, he was nominated Professor Emeritus and continued his work at the university. He published nine books and dozens of articles in Portugal and abroad. He taught tourism courses at the Methodist University of Angola. His areas of interest included community studies, nicknames, Alentejo, tourism and Africa.

Dr Jonathan Skinner is Reader in Anthropology in the Department of Life Sciences, University of Roehampton, UK. He is also Chair of TECHNE (AHRC Doctoral Training Programme) Training Group. He has a particular interest in interviewing skills and qualitative research methods. He has undertaken fieldwork in the Eastern Caribbean on the island of Montserrat (tourism and trauma, colonial relations and disaster recovery) and in the US/UK (social dancing, arts health, contested heritage). He is currently an Adjunct Fellow of the Centre for Cosmopolitan Studies, University of St Andrews, co-edits the book series 'Movement and Performance Studies' for Berghahn Publishers with Professor Helena Wulff (University of Stockholm) and is advisor to the arts health charity Arts Care.

Karolin Stuke is a graduate of the M.A. Management Master's Program at Karlshochschule International University specialising in 'Brand' and 'Creativity and Innovation'. With a Bachelor degree in Asian Studies and Management, she approaches management from a cultural science and holistic perspective in her fields of research; fair trade, CSR, sustainability and innovation. In her Master's thesis, she analysed and developed the concept of Responsible Innovation in the fashion industry. Currently, she is working as a Project Management Trainee at the CSR and Sustainability department at Arthen Kommunikation GmbH in Karlsruhe. There, she develops and implements CSR-related projects and communication strategies for dm drogerie-markt GmbH & Co. KG.

Dr J. M. Trapp-Fallon is Principal Lecturer in the Welsh Centre of Tourism Research based in Cardiff School of Management at Cardiff Metropolitan University, UK. She has a background of working in the tourism industry including for Thomas Cook in the UK and Sunmed Holidays in Greece. Over thirty years she has taught tourism at home in the UK and overseas on a range of courses and has been both a postgraduate Programme lead and Head of Department for Tourism and Leisure Programmes. She is on the editorial advisory board for the Journal of Culture, Hospitality and Tourism and is a visiting professor for doctoral students at Assumption University, Bangkok, Thailand and University of West of Scotland. Her interest in oral history started with her doctoral research into leisure activity on the canals in South Wales when she also became a regional networker for the Oral History Society. Her research interests are wide-ranging and include publications on oral history as research technique, mobilities and canals, international students' learning experiences and place marketing.

Dr Desmond Wee has a Professorship for Tourism and is currently Dean of International Tourism Management at the Cologne Business School in Germany. His passion lies in creating projects merging teaching, research and learning, encouraging students to venture outside the classroom through 'feeldwork' to study tourism through tourism. One such inter-disciplinary project is the HOTEL Business Simulation in which students and coaches from partner universities collaborate to conceptualise a hotel from scratch. His research interests explore contemporary tourism theories in the social sciences and centres on visual, reflexive and embodied methodologies in the making of everyday spaces and identities in cities

Dr Medet Yolal is Professor of Marketing in the Faculty of Tourism at Anadolu University, Turkey, where he mainly teaches about issues related to destination management and marketing, tourism marketing and consumer behaviour. In 2003, he received his PhD in Tourism Management from Anadolu University, Turkey. He has worked on several research projects related to small and medium sized enterprises and family businesses in tourism. He worked for one year as a visiting scholar at Washington State University, USA. His research interests mainly focus on tourism marketing, consumer behaviour, tourists' experiences, event management, tourism development and quality of life research in tourism.

1 Doing tourism ethnography

Hazel Andrews, Takamitsu Jimura and Laura Dixon

This book is a collection of essays that consider the experience of undertaking ethnography within the subject field of tourism. As will be discussed later in this introduction, ethnography is closely associated with the academic discipline of social anthropology. The study of tourism is also part of the anthropology canon as it can yield many insights about the nature of the social world, questions of identity, host–guest relationships, development and sociality, which are all subjects at the heart of anthropological enquiry. However, this book is not intended to be restricted to anthropology because, as we shall see, ethnography is used by an increasingly diverse range of academic disciplines. The 'rolling out' of ethnography beyond the boundaries of social anthropology has continued the discipline's self-examination, as we will outline in this introduction. So, we proceed with caution in terms of not wishing to plant our flag firmly within the boundaries of the discipline of anthropology wherever they might be drawn; nevertheless, we cannot be (and nor should we be) completely de-coupled from the anthropological context. It is with this that we begin.

Commenting on a number of papers first submitted to the Association of Social Anthropologists annual conference in 2007 and later written as a special issue of the *Journal of Tourism Consumption and Practice* (Andrews and Gupta 2010), which considered reflexivity and gender within the context of tourism ethnography, Marilyn Strathern argued in relation to the stories that the writers laid out 'so many of the issues ... are generic to social anthropology' (2010: 80). That is, reflecting on the practice and being aware of the emotional investment that fieldwork requires 'forces us to think through the consequences of our relations with others' (ibid: 82). However, as Pamila Gupta argued in her reflection on the 'dilemmas' of her position in the field as an Indian American scholar (raised in the United States by parents of Indian descent), these dilemmas were not seen as problems to be addressed but as ways of accessing 'domains of knowledge' that could be used as ethnographic data in their own right and bring insight into the nature of social relations. This present volume is in many ways a continuation of that project; although not focused on gender, it nevertheless invites reflexivity, the recounting of dilemmas and the experiences of undertaking this type of research, and in so doing gives voice to a group of people who would identify their research practice as being ethnography.

This opening chapter will continue by briefly outlining the practice of ethnography in general. From there it will consider this practice in the very specific field of the study of tourism. This will then be followed by an outline of the book, and the chapter's closing remarks.

Ethnography

As noted, the collection of data through ethnography has long been associated with the discipline of social anthropology. As the subject moved from the 'armchair' anthropology of James Frazer to an arguably more engaged practice of living among the subjects of enquiry, ethnography became established practice for anthropologists. Moreover, as Jon P. Mitchell attests, 'anthropologists defend it as a method that generates theoretical insights that could not have been generated in any other way' (2010: 1). It is the obtaining and processing of these insights that make an anthropological contribution to knowledge so unique. However, and especially since the publication in 1967 of the private fieldwork diaries of Bronisław Malinowski – the early pioneer of the method – the use of ethnography has been the subject of much scrutiny and analysis within anthropology, especially in relation to the role of the ethnographer and her/his fieldwork relationships. This was not least because the diaries revealed a tension between his desire to claim ethnographic (and therefore anthropological) objectivity and his struggle with his own subjective antipathy towards the people and society he was studying.

One concern is the question of how knowledge is produced through the chosen data collection instrument. As Collins and Gallinat point out, in the early days of anthropology the discipline was seen as a science characterised by objectivity and detachment in which the anthropologist as person was little considered. They argue that 'the anthropological endeavour gained legitimacy from "being there" so long as evidence of "doing there" was eradicated' (2010: 2). As noted, the exposure of Malinowski's thoughts about his research informants in his diaries brought reflection on the questions of 'who' the anthropologist is and how she/he relates to the field and those who inhabit it into sharper focus. This reflection began in the 1970s with the 'growing recognition ... that the anthropologist can never be an entirely neutral "device" for describing and explaining other cultures' (Collins and Gallinat, 2010: 3). The need for reflexivity was also illuminated by the highly influential book *Writing Culture* by James Clifford and George Marcus. First published in 1986, the book critically examined the way in which representations of other cultures were written as part of ethnographic accounts based on the 'authoritative' voice of the fieldworker. Chapter 11 in the current volume, by Burcu Kaya Sayari and Medet Yolal, picks up the theme of the writing of ethnographic accounts in the context of tourism. Their work, like that of Clifford and Marcus, shows that the writing is as much a part of the craft of ethnography as the fieldwork itself.

However, this still does not get to the nub of what ethnography is. Mitchell states that it 'means, literally, "writing people" and is therefore rooted in the notion of description' (2010: 2). Tim Ingold echoes this definition, arguing, 'quite literally, *it means writing about the people*' (2014: 2, emphasis in original). We will return to Ingold's discussion of what ethnography is in due course; but for the present we can say ethnography is closely connected with doing fieldwork that mainly involves (but is not restricted to) spending a lengthy period of time living among the people of the community under study, with the idea that it will allow for deeper social relationships with community members to be developed and thus a more in-depth understanding of the social life therein. In terms of the timeframe, a lengthy period is of course relative, ranging from several months to years. This need not be in one 'chunk' of time, but may be spread out over a course of time. Even short-term or micro-ethnographies can prove insightful; see, for example, Passariello's (1983) 'micro-ethnography' of Mexican city dwellers' touristic practices at rural beaches during the weekends. Once 'in the field', the ethnographer may use a variety of methods to collect data (Mitchell, 2010), perhaps the best known being participant observation. Participant observation exists on a continuum that includes other forms of participation, including complete participant; complete observer; and observer as participant. The time in the field is likely to comprise all these states of participation and observation as the fieldworker ethnographer responds to the field (Hammersley and Atkinson 1995: 104). Before moving on, it is worth noting that the field need not be one place or space, and that it can now also be virtual. Indeed, as George Marcus (1995) identified, the emergence of multi-sited ethnographies that cut across traditional disciplinary boundaries and utilised a variety of techniques for collecting data meant that data could be collected from a variety of sources. For example, Trapp-Fallon (Chapter 9 in this volume) argues the case for the use of oral histories alongside ethnography.

At this juncture, it is worth pausing to consider the notion of 'the field'. The traditional view of the field is about the idea of a bounded space, a locus of action in which we can find a community or specific culture. In the Malinowskian take on the field, we have a bounded space which the anthropologist arrives at, enters and takes up their position as fieldworker to observe (with or without participation) what happens. We then discuss 'our time in the field' and our number of 'field visits', we reflect on 'the field' both as a source of data and as a form of practice. In Low and Lawrence-Zúñiga's (2003) work, they discuss the idea of 'locating' culture. With this goes the baggage of effectively fixing or tying cultural practices to a place. In our locating of a field in which we gather the data, we serve to also *make* that space and often give categorisation to different types of space – see for example Appadurai's (1996) identification of different types of 'scapes' including, for example, ethnoscapes, mediascapes and technoscapes; and Ingold's (2000) taskscapes. However, tying culture or cultural practices to a bounded location, as Low and Lawrence-Zúñiga seem to imply, becomes problematic in as much as life is practised in a world increasingly infused by networks, flows and various forms of mobility. In addition, 'the field' where ethnography takes place also comprises what we as ethnographers take to it, how we remember it, and how we 'write it' as it is composed of those who are the 'objects' of our enquiry. Stasja Koot (Chapter 4 in this volume) draws our attention to this. Indeed, as Tilley and Cameron-Daum (2017: 5) note in a discussion of landscape (a term that might be substituted for field as it also contains notions of a backdrop against which, or within which, action might take place), 'landscape is part of ourselves, a thing in which we move and think … It is not a blank slate for conceptual or imaginative thought.'

Equally, in the case of a tourism ethnography, the idea of *locating the field*, to borrow from Coleman and Collins (2006), must also recognise the 'leaky' nature of location. Where does tourism exactly take place? Is it the site of the holiday – the beach, the hotel – or does it start even before the tourist has left home as the imagination of the prospective tourist is infused with destination images, prior experiences and their own sense of habitus in relation to their gendered, sexual and class identities? (see for example Andrews 2009, 2017). Les Roberts in his book *Spatial Anthropology* explores, in much more detail, the idea that 'Space [should be] understood as a performative field rather than a container of social action' (2018: 27). Moreover, he argues that 'Whatever the nature of the relationship between the body-subject and the space "being framed", it is not one that can be characterised as mute or static' (ibid: 29). He goes onto to argue that the relationship between ourselves and space is dialectical. In acknowledging the leaky porosity of 'the field', we follow Roberts's call for the fieldwork location of tourism ethnographies to go beyond the location of where the action of tourism is thought to be located, whether that be places of transit or the holiday destination, and to consider how 'the "why" is held together by the "what" and the "where"; [in which] the underlying "where" is thus by no means inconsequential to the positing of both the object of study (the "what") and the case for study (the "why")' (2018: 21).

The idea of being responsive to the field brings into focus one of the difficulties associated with ethnography. That is, it is difficult to equip the first-time fieldworker with a 'tool kit' for exactly 'how to do' ethnography. As Hammersley and Atkinson argue 'no set of rules can be devised which will produce good field relations. All that can be offered is discussion of some of the main methodological and practical considerations surrounding ethnographers' relations in the field' (1995: 80). The reasons why there is no certainty of method attached to ethnography is because, as was highlighted by George Dearborn Spindler (1970), each fieldwork place is different, and each fieldworker is different. As with life *anywhere*, there are no certainties to a given situation, or formulas for ways of doing or ways of being, that can be carried from one context to the next (Collins and Gallinat 2010: 12).

Without being able to equip ourselves with the implements of the trade, what might we learn from each other? We might take comfort from being able to identify similar experiences. As Filipa Fernandes explores, in her chapter with Francisco Martins Ramos (Chapter 6), she struggled with her role in the field in part because of 'mistaken' identity, a situation not unknown in tourism ethnography, as she draws on personal communications with both Dixon and Andrews to make her point, but also a situation not unfamiliar within other fieldwork settings. For example, Mitchell (2010) reminds us of Jeremy Boissevain's (1970) experience of being mistaken as a spy when showing interest in the complex political entanglements of the Maltese village in which Boissevain's fieldwork took place. But, perhaps most of all, we can return to the lessons from Spindler's edited collection that through the presentation of several fieldwork settings, the need for 'a flexibility of approach and a willingness to respond to the constraints and possibilities of the field' (Mitchell 2010: 5) is what becomes important. From this comes the need to reflect on how our flexibility and willingness, and conversely our own limits in the field, influence our knowledge production. Further, if there is no certainty of doing fieldwork, how can those of us who teach (and teach within the increasingly rigid formulaic demands of neoliberalism-infused higher education institutions) bring that understanding to our students? Diana Loutfy, Karolin Stuke and Desmond Wee (Chapter 10 in this volume) bring insight to the value of collaborative ethnography in teaching.

Another issue that emerges from the unpredictability and uncertainty of the field, and the perhaps haziness of the individual ethnographer's craft, is in relation to ethics, or perhaps more appropriately the institutional ethics board or ethics committee. Sharon Macdonald (2010) points out that the Association of Social Anthropologists and the American Anthropological Association have long had codes of ethics, and that the ethics of ethnographic research have long been the subject of scrutiny and debate within the discipline. However, more recently there has been a 'move towards increasing codification and bureaucratisation of ethics, especially by universities' (ibid.: 80), in which institutions develop a code of ethics that needs to cover a range of activities and academic disciplines, and is not only used to give approval to the research, but may also be ways by which the research is monitored, controlled and completed. It is worth noting that some applications for ethical approval require the applicant to say how long they will store their 'data sets' following the completion of data collection. As we will discuss, there are several issues relating to ethnography and ethics committees. As Skinner's Chapter 2 highlights, this is particularly the case when the topic of study is deemed to be contentious (here, 'suicide tourism'), revealing a tension between university ethics procedures and the complex reality of the ethnographic pursuit, but an issue that is perhaps less obvious is where the data are held. Given that ethnography is a practice in which the ethnographer is the data-collection instrument, embodying her/his findings as much as recording them in note form and later recalling the experience to analyse notes, write papers and so on (see for example Okely 1994, 2010), how should the ethics applicant respond to the question of how long the data will be kept for? And if it is until 'death us do part', then what are the implications for the permissions of each use?

It is clear and without doubt that we should take care of those who contribute to our research endeavours: they have a right to anonymity, to be not caused harm by our work, to not take part, and so on. We should all be aware of what we do, but the problem is that without a solidly definable field, or solidly definable fieldwork relationships, it is harder to prove to an ethics committee that duty of care and ethical standards will be met and maintained. Part of the going to look, understand and learn in the field is that it is not *pre*-scribed, we cannot *fore*see exactly what or who we will encounter, we cannot *pre*-determine situations or reactions, we cannot even expect that the people in 'our' field will want to speak to us about what we want to speak to them about. But increasingly ethics committees want to know all of this in detail before they give sanction to research taking place. Careful crafting of the ethics application may be required, but equally ethics committees (if the professional judgement of the academic really cannot be trusted) need also to be carefully composed, to be less positivistic in stance, and to have at least some understanding of what ethnography is and how it is practised. One colleague based at a UK university reported on the difficulties of getting ethical clearance for a piece of undergraduate student research using auto-ethnography because the researcher had not indicated on the form that consent from the participant would be received before the data were collected.

This example illustrates exactly the issues to which Tim Ingold (2014) draws attention in his insightful essay 'That's enough about ethnography!', in which he notes 'those who assess our own proposals demand of us, in the name of ethnography, the same slavish adherence to the protocols of positivist methodology' (ibid.: 2). In his essay, Ingold notes that the term '"ethnographic" has become the most overused term in the discipline of anthropology' (ibid.: 1). He raises concerns that the spread of the use of ethnography beyond anthropology as a discipline dilutes the work of anthropology itself; that the term is too readily used as a synonym for qualitative, which undermines the very nature of anthropological inquiry. Ingold goes on to argue that it is *participant observation* that is key to the anthropological endeavour, and that this is not necessarily the same as ethnography.

As Ingold attests, participant observation involves the watching, listening and feeling of what is taking place. In this, as we noted earlier, it is not much different from what it is to live a life. It is important because knowledge emerges as part of a process of an embodied engagement with the world in which we do not stand outside activities and collect 'data', but engage in an 'ontological commitment' (ibid.: 5). In this respect, the participant observer is not bound by a set way of doing or observing, but must respond to the conditions of the places and peoples in which they work, which allow knowledge to unfold with us in the *doing*: the practice of *being there*.

With such an approach, the idea and use of the word 'data' also becomes problematic, although we acknowledge our own use of it in this introduction because in many ways we are confined by the language that communicates shared ideas. 'Data' has the whiff of positivism associated with it. It implies a final outcome, a bounded set of information that can be analysed to provide 'results'. And yet, as noted in the comments above on the embodied experience of ethnography and the role of memory, ethnographic projects are not finite. There will always be room for new understanding and development of ideas.

Ingold's concern for what is meant by ethnography and its relationship to anthropology is in part fuelled by its use in other disciplines. He cites sociology, social policy, social psychology and education as arenas that increasingly lay claim to the use of ethnography. To this could be added human/cultural geography, and business and management studies. Similarly, Mitchell (2010: 1) notes that ethnography can be used in a number of interdisciplinary contexts including what he describes as 'mobile fields', whereby the object of study (for example, corporate social responsibility – see Garsten 2010) appears in several different locations: the boardroom, the office, the conference. A point to bear in mind is that as each discipline uses ethnography or refers to ethnographic techniques, it will bring its own epistemological inflections to what it is and how it is practised. Thus undertaking ethnography does not mean that the resulting work is anthropology; for those involved in the field of tourism studies and concerned with the epistemological foundations of research outputs, this needs to be borne in mind. This is particularly so for the study of tourism, as it is a subject that lends itself to both multi- and interdisciplinary research.

Given the complexity of what tourism is and the multi- and interdisciplinary approach to its study we are not (and perhaps cannot) make claims in this volume about anthropology and ethnography *per se*, but are reflecting on what researchers (some anthropologist, some not) call ethnography in the context of tourism. In the next section we consider briefly the idea of 'tourism ethnography'.

Tourism ethnography

Tourism is not *an* industry, it is not one place or one group of people. Rather, it is composed of numerous different industries and economic sectors including, for example, various forms of transport, museums, festivals, hotels and restaurants, and the supporting infrastructure. The list could go on – and where tourism ethnographies could take place is potentially inexhaustible. As technology has developed, working with the internet and considering the role of social media becomes more important; and potentially, as there are more technological advances, off-planet tourism ethnographies may well be on the horizon (Mann, 2017). What, then, is a tourism ethnography? We define it here simply as that which takes place within the context of tourism or with people who identify themselves as tourists. But this is also a self-definition by the researcher. All the main contributors to this volume responded to a call for work on tourism ethnography, recognising something in the label with which they could identify. There are many fine considerations of settings that could fall under the remit of tourism; see Marc Augé's (1995) *Non-Places*, and for more detail on this point see Roberts and Andrews (2013). However, the researchers themselves have not called their work 'tourism ethnography'. Nevertheless, some of the early foundations for work on the study of modern-day tourism were laid by anthropologists. This follows a trajectory of interest that is echoed elsewhere in the discipline, for example relating to pilgrimage, nomadism and various forms of migration. Given these roots, it is worth sketching out in brief what the early contributions have been.

As some authors in this volume note, Theron A Nuñez Jr's work, published in the journal *Ethnology* in 1963, is often cited as the earliest publication of anthropological work in tourism and thus of the use of ethnography to elucidate theory. In Nuñez's case he was drawn to the issue of acculturation in a Mexican village. Part of his conclusion is that tourism can be an agent of change and as such is 'a legitimate and necessary area of culture change research' (ibid.: 352). The idea that tourism presented conditions for cultural change was furthered in Valene Smith's (1977) influential edited collection *Host and Guests: The Anthropology of Tourism* and Jeremy Boissevain's (1977) paper of the same year regarding tourism development in Malta.

In Malcolm Crick's (1994) ethnography of tourism in Kandy, Sri Lanka, he considers the changes brought to the socio-cultural dynamics of Kandy by the presence of international tourism. However, prior to this he had reflected on his experience of conducting this type of research in a tourism setting, and in an insightful essay (Crick 1985) he asks us to reflect on the parallels of being an ethnographer and being a tourist (building further on the insights of Dumont 1977 and Mintz 1977). This developed anthropologists' interest in the anthropological self that began in the 1970s (Collins and Gallinat 2010). Questions that we might want to ask include: In what ways does the presence of the researcher influence the research setting? How are fieldwork relationships between the self and the other formulated? What is the influence of the personality of the ethnographer on how they conduct themselves in the relationships they negotiate and the activities in which they take part? Does all of this involve some kind of game-playing that is a characteristic of both ethnographic and touristic endeavour?

The entanglement of anthropologists and tourists brought about by seeming to share similar practices was further highlighted by Frederick Errington and Deborah Gewertz (1989), who acknowledged that they inhabited much of the same terrain as tourists when conducting their fieldwork in Papua New Guinea. They nevertheless argued that the endeavour of the fieldworker is characterised by a much more serious one than that of tourists, and that tourists bring little understanding or show little real interest in the cultures that form part of the holiday destination. Indeed, in writing of the witnessing of a Chambri hazing initiation ceremony, Errington and Gewertz argue 'the tourists …were more aware than the Chambri that the tourist trade was an important component in change. However, they lacked sufficient knowledge of both cultural particulars and cross-cultural patterns to understand in any sort of detail either the process or the effect of change', noting further that 'they were, in most cases, uninterested in oversimplified explanation of even the most noticeable events' (ibid.: 51).

In demarcating the differences that they perceived between anthropologist and tourist, Errington and Gewertz indicate what for them is the serious nature of their work, and a rebuttal to Crick's call for a more ludic approach. Although commenting on the presence of tourists, their work is not directly about tourism. Nuñez's and Smith's work testifies that much of the early anthropology of tourism was concerned with change wrought by tourism activities and underpinned with earnest concerns about, for example, power relations, changing cultural practices and so on.

The study of tourism and touristic practice continues apace, and since the work of the aforementioned writers there have been numerous publications by anthropologists that continue the discussions and forge new directions. Examples include Boissevain (1996), Selwyn (1996), Waldren (1996), Abram et al. (1997), Löfgren (1999), O'Reilly (2000), Harrison (2003), Ness (2003), Tucker (2003), Bruner (2005), Salazar (2010), Scott and Selwyn (2010), Andrews (2011), Skinner and Theodossopoulos (2011) and Palmer (2018), among many others too numerous to list or to consider in detail here. Drawing our attention back to some of the earlier work is valuable in allowing us to re-anchor the theoretical lineage on which subsequent scholarship should be built, but which is often lost as disciplinary boundaries are crossed.

As discussed above, we have problematised the notion of 'the field' as a space in which we conduct our research. At the same time, we might also problematise the idea of field in terms of practice. Simon Coleman asks 'whether we can discern continuities of approach across varied projects' (2010: 169) that would apply to the case of ethnography (understood as participant observation) by both anthropologists and those outside the discipline. He argues that 'it may be that we are facing the development of forms of "adjectival ethnography"' in which both those within anthropology and from other disciplines 'react to shifting, increasingly hard-to-encapsulate "fields" by deploying practices that evoke some of the elements of ethnographically oriented fieldwork … Such work may seem to be more ethnograph*ic* than ethnography' (ibid.). In our argument that the location of the field in tourism is not a clearly bounded entity, and noting that the study of tourism by means of ethnography is not limited to the anthropologist, we suggest that 'tourism ethnography' understood as a form of 'adjectival ethnography' might prove useful when the method is discussed within the arena of tourism studies (however that is delineated). The remainder of this introduction offers an outline of the chapters that follow, before a few closing remarks.

This book

It is useful not only to say what the book is, but also to reiterate what it is not. As noted, it is not based exclusively within the discipline of anthropology. It is not an examination of tourism – that is, what tourism is, how it is practised and what impacts it has. Nor does the book claim to be an instruction manual of how to 'do ethnography'. This is not to say that it cannot be instructive: the issues and examples raised in the chapters can, nevertheless, be reflected upon to inform future research and debate. Additionally, some of the 'dilemmas' presented in the volume's chapters are not necessarily new to the practice of ethnography. However, in their appearance as seemingly perennial issues, the re-presentation of these dilemmas stands as a testament to a form of 'wayfinding' (Ingold 2011) to human relations as they unfold in the present. This book is about providing a space to voice experiences and to explore what doing ethnography in the context of tourism has been like for the authors who share their stories. Its significance is in wishing to draw attention to and highlight the 'method', however we might define it, in a world increasingly dominated by metrics; and in a subject area too often seen in terms of business.

We have tried to include in this book the processual nature of undertaking a research project, although as much as the field is porous, so too is the start and end of our research endeavours. Of course, research begins with ideas, reading and developing proposals, and, in most cases, before it can go anywhere, it needs to be approved (certainly within the UK) by a university research ethics committee or some form of internal review panel. Equally, what (if any) is the end point? If ethnography is writing about people, then writing up must also be part of the process of doing research. We have therefore not sought in this book to bind ethnography to what happens in the field; rather, by 'topping and tailing' the book with what might be the start of at least the formal process (ethics) and the 'end' (the writing), we acknowledge not only the complexities of undertaking ethnography, but also its making through its doing.

Before we continue, we would like to take the opportunity to highlight the contribution made by Filipa Fernandes to this collection. Filipa's chapter is presented as a co-authored piece with Professor Francisco Martins Ramos. Sadly, during the writing of the work Professor Ramos passed away. We pay tribute to Filipa for remaining committed to the chapter and to wanting to give voice to Professor Ramos's work, which, following his death, she had to interpret for herself. We are honoured to have been able to include the insights they both share into the ephemeral nature of fieldwork relations. While the unreliable and fleeting nature of such relations is not unique to the setting of tourism (see, for example, Mitchell's comments; 2010: 6), it perhaps feels heightened within what is supposed to be an inherently temporary experience – that of being on holiday. The passing of Professor Ramos highlights the stresses and strains that we probably all face at times in our academic endeavours, of balancing professional commitments with the other practical and emotional realities of our daily lives. What follows is an overview of the order of the book.

In Chapter 2 Jonathan Skinner explores the issues in trying to achieve university ethical approval for research relating to suicide tourism, currently an illegal activity in the UK. The proposed project included various stake-holders with different interests in the research project. The difficulties encountered by Skinner as part of the ethics review and approval activity are illustrative of problems faced when wanting to obtain approval for ethnography in a process set within the framework of a neoliberal audit culture.

Danielle Kelly continues the discussion of ethics in Chapter 3 as she explores the dilemmas faced in undertaking ethnographic work in the party tourism resorts of Ibiza, Spain, in which she must engage with tourists who have been taking drugs and drinking alcohol. As she points out, it is not unknown for fieldworkers both within and outside tourism settings to participate in these activities. Kelly considers whether controlled measures around alcohol use by researchers could potentially be facilitated. She argues that this may be a way of understanding how ethnographic research can move forward ethically within this type of tourism arena.

In Chapter 4, Stasja Koot provides a methodological and epistemological examination of his fieldwork and data. By doing so he reflects on his long-itudinal relation with the indigenous Hai//om Bushmen in Namibia, where his research takes place. Using autoethnography, he investigates his changing positions of power in relation to the people he worked with, during and after collaborating with them to initiate a community-based tourism project. The chapter explores three important and connected, yet underanalysed, elements of autoethnography: unawareness, memory and power. He argues that even when there is a lack of awareness of 'doing research', knowledge is acquired which can still be used during analysis. How he has then remembered this 'research' serves to reinforce the power of the researcher in the subsequent representation and interpretation of events and experiences.

Moving to Greece, in Chapter 5 Fiona Bakas aims to advance understanding of the influence of gender in fieldwork. She explores the way in which gender affected how she developed and maintained access to the field, highlighting their continued negotiation. In reflecting on the socially embedded practices involved in building and maintaining relationships in fieldwork, she argues that the gendered positionalities of both researcher and informants need consideration. Working within the context of a critical feminist tourism ethnography and subsequent knowledge production, Bakas highlights that long and unsocial hours combined with gender roles and ideas of femininity present researchers with unique problems in gaining and maintaining access to complete participant observation. This, she notes, is further exacerbated by time constraints and a lack of understanding of the technique by gatekeepers and informants.

In Chapter 6, Filipa Fernandes and Francisco Martins Ramos use their different experiences of conducting ethnographic research in Portugal (Fernandes and Ramos) and Angola (Ramos) to examine the difficulties encountered when trying to interact with informants whose presence is, in their words, 'ephemeral in the field'. The chapter shows that some of the problems encountered in the early days of 'tourism ethnographies' remain in the fields of the present and across different cultural contexts.

Claudia Dolezal, in Chapter 7, provides a reflexive account of her experience of conducting ethnographic fieldwork in Bali, Indonesia, conducted as part of her research into issues relating to empowerment in community-based tourism. She reflects on challenges and limitations while entering, being in and leaving the field. By making use of the practice of reflexivity, she analyses how the intersubjectivities between her interlocutors and herself shaped their behaviour towards each other and in turn the data she then collected.

Team ethnography is the focus of Chapter 8, as Xerardo Pereiro and Martín Gómez-Ullate discuss the experience of putting together a team and setting goals in observing, sharing and collaborating on an anthropological research of pilgrimage tourism. The work is based on research in Portugal and Spain, integrated in an Erasmus+ project titled 'Innovation and capacity building in higher education for cultural management, hospitality and sustainable tourism in European cultural routes'. The chapter explores the advantages and disadvantages of doing ethnography in multidisciplinary teams composed of members with different understandings of tourism and tourism research.

In Chapter 9, Julia Trapp-Fallon explores the value of using oral history for ethnographic research and the significance of the recorded voice in tourism anthropology. The chapter highlights both the importance of voice in understanding tourism and its worthiness as an ethnographic research tool. In this chapter there is an encouragement for tourism ethnographers to engage in oral history research.

Diana Loutfy, Karolin Stuke and Desmond Wee's Chapter 10 takes us to the use of ethnography in teaching. It proposes engaging students in a collaborative field, as reflexive researcher-students spanning the role of the anthropologist, the tourist and the local, and using contemporary technologies such as modern mobilities and social media to build on cultural knowledge. The collaboration Loutfy, Stuke and Wee identify is constitutive of the field, encompassing the multiple actors, and provides a mediation between self and other in the way in which fields within the field develop and evolve.

In Chapter 11, Burcu Kaya Sayari and Medet Yolal, taking their cue from the work of Clifford and Marcus (1986), consider that the dominant discourses identified as part of representation are also rooted in the notion of culture. There is still a need for critical studies that focus on solutions to this issue, rather than the problems and their associated identification causes. In so doing, they discuss that the ways to overcome these problems are intrinsically rooted in the idea of culture itself.

Chapter 12 is an elegantly written Afterword by Pamila Gupta. She notes that although tourism is underwritten by ideas of pleasure, researching it by use of ethnography does not necessarily follow the same path. Gupta identifies three themes to emerge from the chapters, which she calls 'wild zones'; 'the ongoing epistemic'; and 'team research'. She uses these headings to show not only their significance, but how they might inform the future direction of tourism research.

The studies presented in this book were selected from a response to a call for papers, which was circulated through established JISCMAIL discussion lists (for example, TRINET and Anthropology Matters). Together, these lists have global reach and potentially can be read by over 3,000 individuals. In response to the call we received more than 50 submissions, all interesting, and many exciting in the rich insights they wanted to share about their research. It is notable that the majority of the submissions were from Western-based academics, which poses the question of where are the voices from those not based in the West? The answer is that they did not respond to the call. Similarly, the submissions from Europe were from the West, despite the growing voice of Eastern European anthropologists (see Owsianowska and Banaszkiewicz 2018). We can only speculate on how the pattern of responses emerged and reflect on how future calls for submissions, on whatever subject, could be crafted to attract a more worldwide submission base. Nevertheless, the case studies in this volume still provide invaluable insight into issues relating to undertaking ethnography in the context of tourism. It is hoped that with such discussions, dialogue will continue to flourish on the use of ethnography for researching tourism, and in so doing pave the way for a truly global set of voices to be heard.

References

Abram, S., Waldren, J. and Macleod, D. (eds) (1997) *Tourists and Tourism: Identifying with People and Places*. Oxford: Berg.

Andrews, H. (2009) Tourism as a 'Moment of Being'. *Suomen Antropologi*, 34 (2): 5–21.

Andrews, H. (2011) *The British on Holiday: Charter Tourism, Identity and Consumption*. Bristol: Channel View.

Andrews, H. (2017) Becoming through tourism. imagination in practice. *Suomen Antropologi*, 42: 31–44.

Andrews, H. and Gupta, P. (2010) Researching tourism: reflexive practice and gender. *Journal of Tourism Consumption and Practice*, 2 (2): 1–14. Available at https://pearl.plymouth.ac.uk/handle/10026.1/11520

Appadurai, A. (1996) *Modernity at Large Cultural Dimensions of Globalisation*. Minneapolis: University of Minnesota Press.

Augé, M. (1995) *Non-Places: Introduction to an Anthropology of Supermodernity*. London: Verso.

Boissevain, J. (1970) Fieldwork in Malta, in G. D. Spindler (ed.) *Being an Anthropologist: Fieldwork in Eleven Cultures*. New York: Holt, Rinehart & Winston, pp 58–84.

Boissevain, J. (1977) Tourism and development in Malta. *Development and Change*, 8: 523–538.

Boissevain, J. (ed.) (1996) *Coping with Tourists: European Reactions to Mass Tourism*. Oxford: Berghahn Books.

Bruner, E. M. (2005) *Culture on Tour. Ethnographies of Travel*. Chicago: Chicago University Press.

Clifford, J. and Marcus, G. (1986) *Writing Culture. The Poetics and Politics of Ethnography*. Berkeley: University of California Press.

Coleman, S. (2010) Representing anthropology, in M. Melhuus, J. P. Mitchell and H. Wuff (eds) *Ethnographic Practice in the Present*. Oxford: Berghahn Books, pp. 169–175.

Coleman, S. and Collin, P. (eds) (2006) *Locating the Field: Space, Place and Context in Anthropology*. Oxford: Berg.

Collins, P. and Gallinat, A. (2010) The ethnographic self as resource: an introduction. In P. Collins and A. Gallinat (eds) *The Ethnographic Self as Resource. Writing Memory and Experience into Ethnography*. Oxford: Berghahn Books, pp. 1–22.

Crick, M. (1985) 'Tracing' the anthropological self: quizzical reflections on field work, tourism, and the ludic. *Social Analysis*, 17 August, pp. 71–92.

Crick, M. (1994) *Resplendent Sites, Discordant Voices: Sri Lankans and International Tourism*. Reading: Harwood Academic.

Dumont, J.-P. (1977) Review of D. MacCannell: *The tourist. A new theory of the leisure class*. New York: Schoken Books, 1976. *Annals of Tourism Research*, 4: 223–225.

Errington, F. and Gewertz, D. (1989) Tourism and anthropology in a post-modern world. *Oceania*, 60 (1): 37–54.

Garsten, C. (2010) Ethnography at the interface: 'corporate social responsibility' as an anthropological field of enquiry, in M. Melhuus, J. P. Mitchell and H. Wuff (eds) *Ethnographic Practice in the Present*. Oxford: Berghahn Books, pp. 56–68.

Gupta, P. (2010) "I thought you were one of those modern girls from Mumbai": Gender, reflexivity, and encounters of Indian-ness in the field. *Journal of Tourism Consumption and Practice*, 2 (2): 59–79.

Hammersley, M. and Atkinson, P. (1995) *Ethnography Principles in Practice*, 2nd edn. London: Routledge.

Harrison, J. (2003) *Being a Tourist. Finding Meaning in Pleasure Travel*. Vancouver: University of British Columbia Press.

Ingold, T. (2000) *The Perception of the Environment. Essays in Livelihood: Dwelling and Skill*. London: Routledge.

Ingold, T. (2011) *Being Alive: Essays on Movement, Knowledge and Description*. London: Routledge.

Ingold, T. (2014) That's enough about ethnography! *HAU: Journal of Ethnographic Theory*, 4 (1): 383–395.

Löfgren, O. (1999) *On Holiday. A History of Vacationing*. Berkeley: University of California Press.

Low, S. and Lawrence-Zúñiga, D. (eds) (2003) *The Anthropology of Space and Place. Locating Culture*. Oxford: Blackwell.

Macdonald, S. (2010) Making ethics, in M. Melhuus, J. P. Mitchell and H. Wuff (eds) *Ethnographic Practice in the Present*. Oxford: Berghahn Books, pp. 80–94.

Mann, A. (2017) So you want to be a space tourist? Here are your options, *MACH (NBC News)*, 21 July. https://www.nbcnews.com/mach/science/so-you-want-be-spa ce-tourist-here-are-your-options-ncna784166

Marcus, G. E. (1995) Ethnography in/of the world system: the emergence of multi-sited ethnography. *Annual Review of Anthropology*, 24: 95–117.

Mintz, S. M. (1977) Infant, victim and tourist: the anthropologist in the field. *John Hopkins Magazine*, 27: 54–60.

Mitchell, J. P. (2010) Introduction, in M. Melhuus, J. P. Mitchell and H. Wuff (eds) *Ethnographic Practice in the Present*. Oxford: Berghahn Books, pp. 1–15.

Ness, S. A. (2003) *Where Asia Smiles. An Ethnography of Philippine Tourism*. Philadelphia: University of Pennsylvania Press.

Nuñez, T. A. Jr (1963) Tourism, tradition, and acculturation: *weekendismo* in a Mexican village. *Ethnology*, 2 (3): 347–352.

Okely, J. (1994) Thinking through fieldwork, in A. Bryman and R. G. Burgess (eds) *Analysing Qualitative Data*. London: Routledge, pp. 18–34.

Okely, J. (2010) Fieldwork as Free Association and Free Passage, M. Melhuus, J. P. Mitchell and H. Wuff (eds) *Ethnographic Practice in the Present*. Oxford: Berghahn Books, pp. 28–41.

O'Reilly, K. (2000) *The British on the Costa Del Sol: Transnational Identities and Local Communities*. London: Routledge.

Owsianowska, S. and Banaszkiewicz, M. (eds) (2018) *Anthropology of Tourism in Central and Eastern Europe. Bridging Worlds*. London: Lexington.

Palmer, C. (2018) *Being and Dwelling Through Tourism. An Anthropological Perspective*. London: Routledge.

Passariello, P. (1983) Never on Sunday? Mexican tourists at the beach. *Annals of Tourism Research*, 10: 109–122.

Roberts, L. (2018) *Spatial Anthropology. Excursions in Liminal Space*. London: Rowman & Littlefield.

Roberts, L. and Andrews, H. (2013) (Un)doing tourism anthropology: outline of a field of practice. *Journal of Tourism Challenges and Trends*, VI (2): 13–38.

Salazar, N. (2010) *Envisioning Eden. Mobilizing Imaginaries in Tourism and Beyond*. Oxford: Berghahn Books.

Scott, J. and Selwyn, T. (2010) *Thinking Through Tourism*. Oxford: Berghahn Books.

Selwyn, T. (ed.) (1996) *The Tourist Image: Myths and Myth Making in Tourism*. Chichester: John Wiley and Sons.

Skinner, J. and Theodossopoulos, D. (eds) (2011) *Great Expectations, Imagination and Anticipation in Tourism*. Oxford: Berghahn Books.

Smith, V. (ed.) (1977) *Hosts and Guests: The Anthropology of Tourism*. Oxford: Blackwell.

Spindler, G. D. (ed.) (1970) *Being an Anthropologist: Fieldwork in Eleven Cultures*. New York: Holt, Rinehart & Winston.

Strathern, M. (2010) Afterword. *Journal of Tourism Consumption and Practice*, 2 (2): 80–82.

Tilley, C. and Cameron-Dunn, K. (2017) *An Anthropology of Landscape: The Extraordinary in the Ordinary*. London: UCL Press.

Tucker, H. (2003) *Living with Tourism: Negotiating Identities in a Turkish Village*. London: Routledge.

Waldren, J. (1996) *Insiders and Outsiders. Paradise and Reality in Mallorca*. Oxford: Berghahn Books.

2 "This research project is not ready"

Ethics and institutional hurdles in a neoliberal era

Jonathan Skinner

Introduction

This chapter is an examination of getting a contentious research project off the ground. It is about experiences facing research and ethics clearance, as well as those of the researcher coming to terms with the nature and problematics of research – both professional and personal. Ultimately, it is about the formation, deformation, and attempted reformation of research. I hope that it does not appear reckless in its revelations, nor undermines my work as a researcher, or my colleagues and line managers. It has been approved for publication with the proviso that I note that the research proposal was vetted formally at a university research management level, but at a stage prior to submission to the university's ethics committee. The intention is to show the importance of being ready for the field, as far as that is possible. As such it is an 'entering the field' narrative with reactions to the research grant application, or rather attempted entry, as you shall find out.

Whilst it can be said that one can never really be ready for the field, nor that one should in that the fieldworker's sense of 'displacement' – what Angela Bammer (1994: xii) characterises as an interrogation of the modern – is to the advantage of the research, there is a mental, physical and material cultural preparation for the research. This is the more so when fieldwork is taking place 'away from home' such that there is a clear separation between research time and place (space) and non-research time and place (cf. Amit 2000). These distinctions are increasingly moot in our social media-mediated environments, and with the acceptance of an anthropology at home (cf. Rapport 2002) and an austerity in funding research overseas, with impact being more removed from the international common wealth of nations.

On not being ready

Monday 10 August 2015

This afternoon was supposed to be a late-summer excursion to the coast with my dog and my fiancée. In my imagination it was to be a relaxed visit to a new part of the English coast for us. With my work cap on, it was also a visit to a site that I had read a little about and was starting to develop an academic interest in. Editing a book on the relationship with leisure and death with my colleague Adam Kaul, I had been struck by his chapter on the Cliffs of Moher (Kaul 2018), a tourist attraction and physical and existential borderland. It was not just a stark dividing line between land and non-land, between life and almost certain death, but could also be seen as a life-affirming place as every step back from the cliff face had a non-suicidal quality to it. 'Here, you can look at the end of the world and turn away from it', as the journalist Fintan O'Toole (2007: 16) expresses it. Working with this suggested interpretation, I wanted to re-appraise the cliffs of Beachy Head similarly. This would link to my work on dark tourism. There might even be a comparison and contrast between those who visit Dignitas in Zurich, an assisted suicide organisation that provides a clinical but calm end-of-life 'experience', and those who visit Beachy Head to dramatically jump to their death from this natural cliff face. I was tentatively in communication with the organisations at Beachy Head, with the potential view towards spending my forthcoming sabbatical alongside them, the Beachy Head Chaplaincy Team in particular.

It is a cold afternoon, foggy and spooky as we park at the cliff car park. There is an obvious Samaritans' sign present. Little else can be seen through the drizzle. We visit the Beachy Head Visitor Centre: there are displays about the local ecology as well as World War II memorabilia. I had not expected the war nostalgia: the cliffs would have been the first sight of Great Britain for returning flying crews, rather like the White Cliffs near Dover. It was important to visit this potential fieldsite so that I could talk to people about my project and refine it for funding and ethical practice. It was very much early days, and the project was just one idea piling up in my head alongside a number of others. At present, I was only partially invested in it but I recognised that it fitted the trajectory of my research on difficult travel and the problems articulating that travel (cf. Skinner 2012).

Walking along the cliffside, inland a bit, the slope of the ground slipped towards the cliffs and the sea below. This sight was revealed in the occasional clearing of the fog. People came out of nowhere and disappeared into nowhere, eerily. I was already feeling queasy and was reminded of my father's vertigo. I didn't like heights, but I had been able to clean the gutters on the house when I visited him. But I had once had an ear infection that made my balance slip and left me feeling like I was slipping to the left side all the time. Walking along the coast with the slopes giving way to the left, I was strongly reminded of that slipping sensation and my imagination started working up a slipping and sliding narrative that left me hanging from the cliff top unable to counter the sensations I was creating but experiencing. Tom Hunt felt the draw of the cliffs, practically hypnotic such that when he visited to research for his book *The Cliffs of Despair* (2006), he feared that he might have 'an aptitude' for suicide. Vertigo, for him, is the cliff-edge of the soul (Hunt 2000).

It is this sensationalism and suicide that I was subsequently asked to avoid by colleagues working on the same subject.

Further along the cliffs, walking on the inside to my partner, the fog lifted and the over 500 foot (152 metre) chalk drop became visible. Just across from the path, small wooden crosses perched just out of reach. They were at angles to be seen. Someone had gone over and stuck them in the ground. More disturbingly, someone had gone over. They were commemorative warnings (see Figure 2.1).

I felt a loss for them, but also a growing fear for myself. This was not the place for me, my fiancée or my dog. One push. One pull. One gust of wind. One cliff break and a tumbling freefall and a personal 9/11. Would I fly or would I tumble? My mind started doing somersaults. I start taking photographs as a distraction. Through my lens, I am not there. In retrospect, the photos frame the narrative of our visit, and come to tell a story just as eerie as the cliffs themselves.

***

Suicide tourism: from Beachy Head to Dignitas

Abstract: (max. 100 words)

In the UK, close to 6,000 – predominantly male – adults die by suicide every year. This project looks at the relationship in the UK between leisure and death and how tourism features in the context of this dramatic last act. Specifically, this project seeks to understand the new niche tourism practice

Figure 2.1 Beachy Head cliff drop and commemorative crosses
Source: J. Skinner, August 2015

'suicide tourism' – the movements and last journeys taken by the suicidal as final last tourists. It does so by researching two *zeitgeist* tourist destinations associated with tourism and suicide: the iconic Beachy Head cliffs in Sussex, and the controversial Dignitas association's premises in Zurich, Switzerland.

Places where you will carry out the proposed research (max. 100 words)

This project will be carried out in two locations: Beachy Head, England and Zurich, Switzerland.

Relevant experience/skills/training (max. 100 words)

I am an expert in the field of sensitive and contentious forms of niche tourism (disaster tourism on Montserrat, dark tourism at the Maze Prison in Belfast), and very experienced in qualitative interview methods having worked with former paramilitaries turned tour guides. These areas of strength are needed for this project. I have also edited and co-edited three books on tourism and one on interviewing, and so shall be building on my previous research expertise and methods training in this project.

Detailed statement of proposed research (scope and importance; objectives, methodology and outcome, e.g. publication plans)

Death by suicide – globally (1 million per year) or in the UK (6,000 per year) – is a traumatic act for the individual involved, bystanders, as well as relatives and the wider community. The last UK Government prioritised the prevention of suicide as a cross-government initiative (HMG 2012) and the current government recently debated an Assisted Dying Bill on 11 September 2015. There is public and political recognition and concern for the rising suicide levels, and lobbying and campaigning on the right to death and the right to life (Dignity in Dying, Living and Dying Well, Care Not Killing). Hanging and strangulation, self-poisoning, and jumping from high-risk locations are the most common death by suicide practices in the UK. It is the result of complex factors from illness, bereavement, mental health factors and post-traumatic trauma disorder to austerity and privatisation. Little is known, however, about the category of 'nonresidential suicide' (Gross et al. 2007) and the characteristics of people who travel substantial distances to die by suicide. This project seeks to alter this deficit by examining in detail the sites of 'suicide tourism' or 'death tourism' (Srinivas 2009).

This project investigates death by suicide in two contrasting locations: the iconic Beachy Head cliffs in Sussex, and the controversial Dignitas premises in Zurich, Switzerland. Beachy Head is a high-risk – high-fatality rate – location for suicide. Sublimely beautiful and seductively deadly, Beachy Head is a 530 foot chalk sea cliff close to the tourist seaside town of Eastbourne. Its vertical white cliffs are a tourist attraction for viewing, but it is also one of the world's most notorious suicide hotspots, averaging one death by suicide every fortnight and so considered to necessitate round-the-clock suicide prevention patrols by the Beachy Head Chaplaincy Team that specialises in crisis intervention and search and rescue. Their vision is to proactively end suicide at Beachy Head, a landscape that has been turned into a 'black spot' (Rojek 1993) site of death through the numbers of death by suicide, and its cultural and national significance in various media (from online 'suicide selfies' and newspaper-reported 'celebrity copycat' attempts to music video backdrops and popular movie settings). Beachy Head is iconic as both a condensed symbol of Britishness and a suicide landmark, and appeals to generation after generation of visitors: first-time tourists, return tourists and, as this pioneering study will investigate, last-visit 'suicide tourists' – a one-way visit that undermines the classic definition of tourism which typically holds on to the notion of 'return' (Burkart and Medlik 1981).

Whereas Beachy Head is a 'natural' and very public destination visited by both pleasure seekers and those in despair, Dignitas – one of six assisted-dying organisations in Switzerland – maintains a private building in an industrial park on the outskirts of Zurich. Deliberately assisting a suicide is illegal in most of the UK[1] and many other EU countries, whereas assisted suicide legislation is unclear in Switzerland, resulting in an influx of international visitors intent upon death by assisted suicide. This has resulted in a new category of medical tourism that Gauthier et al. (2015) refer to as 'suicide tourism'. On average, a British citizen undertakes a one-way journey to Dignitas every fortnight, constituting 14% of all international visitors (Dignitas 2015). Between 2008 and 2012, 611 people 'visited' from over 31 countries, with 44% coming from Germany and 21% from the UK. They are drawn to the right to die, visit alone or with friends and/or family and, if they can prove mental competence and determination to die, and typically a terminal illness and/or unendurable incapacitation or unbearable pain, then they are eligible for Dignitas services. Dignitas accompanied suicides are achieved by use of a lethal, fast-acting and painless barbiturate. The process has been used with over 2,000 national and international Dignitas 'customers'. Dignitas disputes the suicide tourism category as 'derogatory' and 'misleading' (Dignitas 2014: 3; Luley 2015: 618) with regard to the motivation of the visitors.

Suicidology has typically been quantitative in orientation, focusing on an explanation of events rather than an understanding as to why they occurred (Hjelmeland and Knizek 2010). Owens and Lambert (2012) recently advanced our understanding of suicide with their ethnographic approach to the bereaved, a direct critique on the classic 'psychological autopsy method' of reconstruction. This project extends their ethnographic approach, but concentrates upon the suicide site itself as a tourist attraction. Careful and sensitive ethnographic research in and around Beachy Head (with intervention groups, tour guides, visitors and locals) will be complemented by an extensive analysis of the material culture of visits to Beachy Head (souvenirs, crosses and messages, online and offline memorials). This research will be contrasted with the five visits to Dignitas to interview members of the organisation and national critics, and to plot the local activities of recent visitors to the clinic.

***

Research questions

This is the grant that never was or, rather, the grant application that never became. The intention was to compare the two venues as supposed suicide tourism venues. This study would have enabled me to critique the new 'suicide tourism' concept being proposed. I wrote it, trying to judge and balance an important piece of new research that is needed, in my opinion. It is socially relevant, contemporary and timely, theoretical and methodological, feasible and a project that moves on from recent research at national and international levels. In my humble estimation, here was a grant application that had coherence and was potentially fundable. I wove in several evocative comments to try to give it traction in the reviewers' minds. I was enthusiastic to submit it and had solicited referees to support it from within my discipline as well as neighbouring disciplines. There was an implicit rationale for qualitative research, for ethnography and interviewing – a narrative triangulation on the subject matter – to contribute to other more quantitative studies on the contentious topic of suicide.

I had dropped the idea of accompanying suicide tourists on their way to Dignitas for fear of falling foul of Section 2 of the 1961 Suicide Act with its prohibition against '[a] person who aids, abets, counsels or procures the suicide of another', recently amended in 2009 to complicity in 'encouraging or assisting' another's suicide (HMG 2009: ch.1, sec. 59, para 2). At what point should researcher neutrality be preserved in such a research project? Could accompanying a person be considered tacit support in that the researcher is not trying to prevent the actions of another? Anthropologists Staples and Widger (2012) suggest that suicide has a sociality to it and that from emic perspectives it is diverse and not necessarily destructive. Studied from the ground up, they recognise the difficulties in studying this topic:

> Ethnography [...] is not, of course, immediately amenable to the investigation of suicide. Even in contexts in which suicide rates are very high, the likelihood of being in the presence of someone attempting suicide remains low, and taking notes in the event of such an occurrence might anyway throw-up some awkward ethical dilemmas. (Staples and Widger 2012: 199)

The typical recourse is to interview survivors of suicide attempts and the relatives of victims. This, however, they also note, is different from interviewing someone who is to be successful in their act of suicide. Owens and Lambert (2012), for example, interviewed, post hoc, 100 relatives to piece together a suicide narrative. Widger, in his more extended study of suicide and its settings in Sri Lanka, spent several years triangulating about the issue of suicide behaviour by working with suicide survivors, self-harm victims, families and village elders, as well as those working in police stations and health clinics, to develop a rounded and nuanced picture. Even in this ethnography of 'suicidal practice' (Widger 2015: xviii), Widger took care not to exoticise and further alienate already vulnerable people (ibid.: xv, 12). Suffering is very real, no matter the dimensions of its representation. As with violence, as Michael Jackson (2005: 152) points out, there is a danger in intellectualising it and thereby diminishing its effects.

The Beachy Head Chaplaincy Team wanted to have me vetted and approved for any engagement with them. This felt like a necessary and appropriate part of the research, a fair negotiation of access to my forthcoming field. I was telephone interviewed by an academic they worked with. We shared common interests and concerns. Primarily, the research should not sensationalise or draw further attention to attract copycat suicides. This was one of the hazards associated with the eye-catching *Cliffs of Despair* book title. With completion of my grant application and tentative approval from colleagues, it was starting to look like this project could go ahead. It did, however, need to pass a research review internal to the university; ethical review could come subsequent to the grant being successful.

Calling in the Chaplaincy Team

There is a sequence about the photographs I took on the cliffs of Beachy Head. They start as a view with my partner peering over the edge from behind one of the safety markers. The sequence continues and in retrospect the horror is magnified. A man walks along the side of the path towards my wife. He gestures to her and starts to talk in fast Spanish. Instinctively, she follows not just his gaze, but his steps to the edge of the cliff face. He takes her hand in his, possibly out of safety and care. With the free hand he points in front and down at seven o'clock. The fog is swirling in and out and, though sometimes it clears to reveal a new view, Cristina cannot fathom what he is on about. My concern grows as my fiancée, as she was then, stands with a stranger on the edge of the cliff that I cannot bear to be near (see Figure 2.2). They withdraw and he continues on along his route.

Ten minutes later and we too are turning around to head back to the car park. We walk more inland for my peace of mind. I am becoming increasingly perturbed at the man's gesture and my wife's automatic response. "He could have been anybody", runs through my mind. What if he had decided to jump with her, or to push her? It had been a reckless moment viewed through a viewfinder. In front of us there is a group of tourists talking animatedly to a man in a red sweatshirt. On its back is the clear lettering 'Chaplain'. He must be one of the patrols from the Beachy Head Chaplaincy Team. I have been emailing them and so decide to go over and make our acquaintance. I

Figure 2.2 Hands together at the cliff face
Source: J. Skinner, August 2015

overhear the tourists talking animatedly. They are concerned for a man they had seen some 20 minutes earlier who had been standing by himself, and pacing back and forth. He had taken off his jacket and placed it on the ground near to him. They were worried that he was in a state of mind that he might jump off the cliff. They were trying to do something. I interject with a comment about the man who had been trying to show us something down the side of the cliff face (see Figure 2.3).

The Chaplain turns to us and immediately asks us to show him where we had been. With trepidation, nervousness and some awkward excitement, we walk him back to the spot that Cristina had been led to by the tourist. The Chaplain stands as close to the edge of the cliff face as possible. He peers over to seven o'clock. He is wearing boots is all that I can remember whilst I continue to take photographs. Dissociating myself. He takes out his walkie talkie and calls his colleagues in the Chaplaincy Team as well as the coast-guard (see Figure 2.4).

Turning back to us, he describes a body at the bottom of the cliffs. I feel nauseous, and thoughts that it could have been my wife cross my mind. We leave the Chaplain to his business. Cristina still wants to see what she had been meant to see. She crawls to the cliff edge to look over, with me shouting at her to stay back and stop being stupid. Not long later, Cristina, a trainee therapist, feels sick to her stomach at the event and what she saw – though she tells me that she couldn't really see much in the mist. She is in tears at the shock and brutality of the death, its proximity to our life. She needs to process it (see Figure 2.5). This is far from the summer vacation visit I had intended. Nor is it the best of starts to a potential research project. I don't feel ready for the place or the issues. I am not sure if I ever will be.

Figure 2.3 Beachy Head Chaplain with tourists
Source: J. Skinner, August 2015

Figure 2.4 Calling in a suicide
Source: J. Skinner, August 2015

Whilst waiting for Cristina, I flick through the images on the back of my camera. Its only when enlarging them and looking at their sequence that I see, to my horror, the figure of the man fixing on Cristina in his walk along the cliffside. Whilst she is with the dog peering over the cliff, he is watching her and walking over to her. It feels like a *Scary* movie moment, being stalked, only the deceased is not part of our script. So many alternatives could have happened in the last hour (see Figure 2.6).

Figure 2.5 Processing the events
Source: J. Skinner, August 2015

Figure 2.6 Man approaching earlier
Source: J. Skinner, August 2015

We walk back to the car and head for another cliffside, one with a beach this time so that we can get perspective and distance on what has just elapsed.

Ethical review and neoliberal commentary

All large grants go through a new mechanism of approval at the university. This is understood to raise the quality of submissions to research councils and other funding bodies. It is about external projection, important for a new modern university such as Roehampton. It is about reputation, but ultimately it boils down to money – or cabbage, as Marilyn Strathern (2006: 533) succinctly expresses it – as the funded research acts as protector of scarce research funds, and the onward increase ('mission creep' [Lederman 2006]) of the audit culture in institutions develops to protect the pathway to funds. In a powerful and eloquent special issue of *American Ethnologist*, Rena Lederman edits together articles and commentaries about the hypervigilance of institutions in their cautious approach to external dealings. Reputation management extends deep down into the institutional veins, especially through the work of Institutional Review Boards, typically a research committee considering the ethics of grants from the institution. For Lederman (ibid.: 483), these committees and their discourses and debates elucidate the 'property lines' of the intellectual neighbourhood and the problematics of the anthropologist's ethnographic approach. Such an approach is blurred and not clear cut and clinical, informal by design and nature, and hence potentially dangerous and threatening to the more experimental sciences where the investigator is in control of the research design. 'Openness and contingency' (ibid.: 485) are the hallmarks of ethnographic practice. Crucially, Lederman explores the informal in academic culture, and the concern for when and who is research and research subject. 'Can a colleague be a human subject?' she asks (ibid.: 488), a person therefore entitled to some form of federal protection. She opts for disclosure. Elsewhere other anthropologists, such as Vered Amit (2000) in a chapter in Marilyn Strathern's *Audit Cultures*, and Sharon Macdonald (2012) in the edited volume *Ethnographic Practice in the Present*, veil their colleagues.

There is a disappointment in anthropologists' engagements with committees relating to institutional governance. Amit and Macdonald served on the committees and wrote warnings as to how their input was increasingly squeezed and held against them. Don Brenneis takes a more seasoned approach to the negative space of the review boards by examining their linguistics – how the language codes serve as proxies with other meanings, and how the committees present 'evaluative synecdoches' (Brenneis 2006: 539) for the projects they examine. They are but 'partial measures' (ibid.), to play with Strathern again, and come out of a context of their own, one that influences and shapes the life history of the projects they receive. It is an anticipation game for this generation, one with little expectation for success. To opt out, however, to conduct informal fieldwork on the sly, 'underground ethnography' as Katz (2006) refers to it, or to even behave and conduct oneself differently in different professional contexts, is to be exposed to the charge of 'double standards': 'moral duplexity' as characterised by Pels (1999).

This strategic process of review at my institution was unsuccessful in this instance. This was not for the reasons that I had tried to anticipate. The grant was blocked, rejected before it could be applied, and feedback was given for different reasons, ones that surprised and concerned me. It was not conveyed to me that it was about a lack of experience moving to work from tourism to suicide and tourism. Nor was it mentioned to me that the university was fearful of negative publicity. It is unlikely that such a point would be made directly given its contentious nature. Committees operate indirectly and often decisions such as appointments or dis-appointments are veiled. Instead, the research grants committee met and feedback was delegated to one of the representatives. I was told that it was not a research project for the following reasons. Firstly, there is no-one to interview by virtue of the research subjects no longer living. Secondly, were there anyone to interview, then the interviews would be invalid because the interviewees, as suicidal, 'would be mad' and hence their words would be invalid. These reactions were backed up by experience from the reviewer who had direct experience of suicidal people. Finally, the concept 'suicide tourism' was critiqued as a misnomer.

There are a number of concerns about the feedback received. There was a different reading made of the application from that anticipated. The desire to test and critique the suicide tourism concept rebounded back on me, either accidently or deliberately. It was read that I had co-opted the term for my use. It had been my plan to critically examine the concept, and to critique it with insights from empirical research. The intention was 'to understand' the concept. I had thought that, in the application, I had distanced myself from its use with the expression 'a term that colleagues refer to as'. This was lost to a different reading of the application. Mandatory grant-writing workshops I had attended at my institution had stressed the need to channel the course of the reader. One strategy is to repeat key sentences so that, for example, each paragraph in the main text leads with a strong sentence, and that sentence is taken out and used for the abstract. The impression, then, is that the main text flows and reinforces the abstract for the busy reader. I had, in the past, thought this somewhat overkill.

Another concern with the reading of the grant can be with respect to the attitude taken towards the mental health of the potentially suicidal. The reaction was that they were insane and so their testimony could not be relied on. This attitude was substantiated by reference to the reviewer's own personal experiences. This was a topical research area that elicited strong reactions because of readers' personal positions on life-and-death issues. Adding 'suicide' to 'tourism studies', I found, changed one's reading distance from the project application. Identification and projection came factored into the evaluation of the project. Distancing, long the objective of objective research, was hard to achieve, if achievable at all as another research trope, as literary theorist Todorov (1988: 4) would posit. We all have an investment in life and death. Here, the reviewer was influenced by their own personal experiences. They subsequently projected their experiences upon a reading of the application. Without over-interpreting, there is every possibility that they could have been invoking the vestiges of some religious position on the sanctity of life, such as a condemnation of suicide as murder along the lines of St Augustine (cf. Paperno 1997: 49). Moreover, they might have been aware of suicide's historical status in the UK as a crime often associated with the 'unsound mind' diagnosis (Peay 2011), perhaps dwelling overly on this designation for diminished responsibility. These mad people have nothing credible to say – if even they could – so there is no project here to research. This associates all suicides with insanity. This stance bears all the hallmarks of a Durkheimian position: 'all suicides of the insane are either devoid of any motive or determined by purely imaginary motives' (Durkheim 1979[1897]: 66). What other explanation could there be for an act of self-destruction? And yet, as social historian John Weaver (2014) has shown in coroners' records, alcohol and other addiction, ideas of sacrifice, states of mental illness, and cultures of social panic all factor into a person's deeply individual and personal suicide. It could be, then, that the reviewer was resisting the possibility that voluntary death could have rationality attached to it, thereby denying their agency or the credibility of their testimony such as in a suicide note (Perreault et al. 2016), or suicide survivors' interviews. After interviewing survivors of suicide, predominantly kin and close friends, Rita Robinson (2001: 19) doubts, though, that the pre-suicide note is clear or cogent enough to be able to pinpoint the ensuing cause of death: '[t]he victim's thinking process is too distorted by then'. But distortion is different from a nonsensical ramble. Distortion is what we live amidst, Rapport (2015) suggests, as words and actions continually mutate, alive with meaning.

Recovery

We returned home from our traumatic walk along the cliffside and following walk on the beach. On the way home we were back-tracking, driving back along the road next to the Beachy Head cliffs that we had walked along earlier. It was about three hours later after meeting with the Chaplain. There were groups of people looking over the edge. Three or four police, coastguard and chaplaincy cars were parked near to each other. We could make out the high-visibility jackets from the road. One car was longer than the rest, presumably for the body. And there were several people holding long objects. At one point I thought I could see a triangle that I presumed was to help belay a recovery team's attempt to collect what remained of the person who had died by suicide (see Figure 2.7).

When we got home, I googled for any information about the death at Beachy Head. I could only find news that the chaplaincy and the coastguard had been called out on 10 August 2015. I downloaded the images from my camera and was struck by the sequence. It still gives me the chills. Cristina let me know that she had seen what looked like a coat lower down the cliff face when she looked, after the chaplaincy team member had confirmed our fears. There was a sense of irony about the fatality: our one day out at the end of the summer and it turns into a case study for a not-quite research project. I let the Beachy Head Chaplaincy team know that I had met them on the cliffs and alerted them to the suicide jump. They welcomed the photo for future publicity.

Figure 2.7 Recovery
Source: J. Skinner, August 2015

Several weeks later, still with scarce information about the cliff suicide, colleagues encourage me to develop the research project. I talk through the events and tell them about the jumper. It is unusual to be at the place and time of a suicide, the more so if that is what you are intending to study. My colleagues don't see this as the closing down of the research project, but as motivation and experience to engage with the subject more and with increased sensitivity. At a conference presentation, one delegate makes the comment that should she 'become gaga' she wants to be driven to the same cliff and pushed off the top. She is half flippant in her comment, but she has given some thought to her mortality and what she would try to do, or have done, should her health deteriorate severely. In a powerful article – 'Jumpers' – in *The New Yorker*, Tad Friend (2003) reports on the fatal grandeur of the iconic Golden Gate Bridge of San Francisco. There, the bridge stands as a stark dividing line between life and certain death. It is a threshold location like Beachy Head. One is footsteps away from death. Friend notes that these suicide spots are frequently aesthetically pleasing places for the romanticisation of mortal thoughts. The suicide jump is idealised as a clean transformation from living to dead, body intact. The reality is quite the opposite: '[t]hose who jump imagine, wrongly, a peaceful transition to some less painful place, rather than a seventy-five-mile-an-hour impact that will burst their organs like a bomb' (Friend 2003). A jump from the Golden Gate Bridge or Beachy Head, I remind my colleague, does not necessitate immediate death. Some survive their suicide attempt with severe debilitating injuries. Those who do die have to have their remains recovered, endangering the lives of the coast-guard and cliff rescue teams (see Figure 2.7). My colleague had not thought of the trail of devastation and danger in the wake of a suicide.

The following year, I revised the above grant application. I had the support of my immediate peers in the university. They saw it as worthy work, important and full of impact. To take it forward, I was advised by a good colleague who had worked in the area of the topic to re-couch the grant as a study with the potential to assist with suicide prevention. I did not want to compromise notions of researcher neutrality, to be overly on the preventative side in any work and thus potentially alienate myself from some subjects, or to be an 'action researcher' like Ana Lopes (2015), who ended up leading the sex workers' rights movement in the UK that she had been studying. This revised version of the application was to interview a proportion of the 1,000 members of Dignitas in the UK who were registered members but had not taken up their opportunity for assisted suicide. This, for me, was an 'easier' social science version of the grant, developing interview narratives in a study of what held people back from committing suicide. It kept me away from the vertiginous cliffs of Beachy Head, and kept me out of ethical complications from the university's perspective. It was more distant for me, and it had the approval of the related right-to-life organisations Dignitas in Switzerland and My Death My Decision in the UK. This application was approved to go forward in the university research grant review; the ethics committee would follow the funding award. Ultimately, however, it was not funded by the funding body. There was no feedback this time.

Note

1   As per the England and Wales Suicide Act (HMG 1961), suicide is not illegal, but it is illegal to assist or attempt to assist or encourage another person to take their life. Northern Ireland adopted this position in the 1966 Criminal Justice Act (Northern Ireland). There is no comparable law in Scotland given the moot point as to whether or not Scottish law deems suicide or attempted suicide illegal. Scottish law on assisting or encouraging suicide falls under criminal homicide.

References

Amit, V. (2000) The university as panopticon: moral claims and attacks on academic freedom. In: M. Strathern (ed.) *Audit Cultures: Anthropological Studies in Accountability, Ethics and the Academy.* London: Routledge, pp. 215–235.

Bammer, A. (1994) Introduction. In: A. Bammer (ed.) *Displacements: Cultural Identities in Question*, Bloomington: Indiana University Press, pp. xi–xx.

Brenneis, D. (2006) Partial measures. *American Ethnologist*, 33(4): 538–540.

Burkart, A. and Medlik, S. (1981) *Tourism – Past, Present and Future.* London: Heinemann.

Dignitas (2014) Comments on the BJME paper "Suicide tourism: a pilot study on the Swiss phenomenon". Available at: http://www.dignitas.ch/images/stories/pdf/diginp ublic/nfp67/comments-bjmepaper-suicidetourism.pdf [Accessed 9 October 2015].

Dignitas (2015) Menschenwürdig leben – Menschenwürdig sterben – Forch-Zürich. Available at: http://www.dignitas.ch/images/stories/pdf/statistik-ftb-jahr-wohnsitz-1998-2014.pdf [Accessed 23 November 2014].

Durkheim, E. (1979[1897]) *Suicide: A Study in Sociology*. New York: The Free Press.

Friend, T. (2003) Jumpers: the fatal grandeur of the Golden Gate Bridge. Letter from California. *The New Yorker*, 13 October. http://www.newyorker.com/magazine/2003/10/13/jumpers [Accessed 3 July 2016].

Gauthier, S., Mausbach, J., Reisch, T. and Bartsch, C. (2015) Suicide tourism: a pilot study on the Swiss phenomenon. *Journal of Medical Ethics*, 41: 611–617.

Gross, C., Piper, T., Bucciarelli, A., Tardiff, K., Vlahov, D. and Galea, S. (2007) Suicide tourism in Manhattan, New York City, 1990–2004. *Journal of Urban Health: Bulletin of the New York Academy of Medicine*, 4(6): 755–765.

Hjelmeland, H. and Knizek, B. (2010) Why we need qualitative research in suicidology. *Suicide and Life-Threatening Behavior*, 40(1): 74–80.

HMG (1961) *Suicide Act 1961*. http://www.legislation.gov.uk/ukpga/Eliz2/9-10/60/section/2 [Accessed 26 April 2017].

HMG (2009) *Coroners and Justice Act 2009*. https://www.legislation.gov.uk/ukpga/2009/25/part/2/chapter/1/crossheading/suicide [Accessed 21 September 2018].

HMG (2012) Suicide prevention strategy for England. Available at: https://www.gov.uk/government/publications/suicide-prevention-strategy-for-england [Accessed 24 April 2017].

Hunt, T. (2000) Cliffs of despair. *Gettysburg Review*, Winter: 593–652. http://www.gettysburgreview.com/selections/detail.dot?inode=cb09d7af-d0ae-4101-ac74-82fdcd7a973b [Accessed 24 April 2017].

Hunt, T. (2006) *Cliffs of Despair: A Journey to the Edge*. New York: Random House.

Jackson, M. (2005) *Existential Anthropology: Events, Exigencies, and Effect*. Oxford: Berghahn Books.

Katz, J. (2006) Ethical escape routes for underground ethnographers. *American Ethnologist*, 33(4): 499–506.

Kaul, A. (2018) That awful margin: tourism, risk, and death at the Cliffs of Moher. In: A. Kaul and J. Skinner (eds) *Leisure and Death: An Anthropological Tour of Risk, Death, and Dying*. Boulder: University Press of Colorado, pp. 121–138.

Lederman, R. (2006) The perils of working at home: IRB "mission creep" as context and content for an ethnography of disciplinary knowledges. *American Ethnologist*, 33(4): 482–491.

Lopes, A. (2015) Talking and acting for our rights: the interview in an action-research setting. In: K. Smith, J. Staples and N. Rapport (eds) *Extraordinary Encounters: Authenticity and the Interview*. Oxford: Berghahn Books, pp. 157–174.

Luley, S. (2015) Suicide tourism: creating misleading 'scientific' news. *Journal of Medical Ethics*, 41(8): 618–619.

Macdonald, S. (2012[2010]) Making ethics. In: M. Melhuus, J. Mitchell, and H. Wulff (eds) *Ethnographic Practice in the Present*. Oxford: Berghahn Books, pp. 80–94.

O'Toole, F. (2007) "Taming the Cliffs of Moher. *The Irish Times*, 6 February. Available at: http://www.irishtimes.com/opinion/taming-the-cliffs-of-moher-1.1193784 [Accessed 24 April 2017].

Owens, C. and LambertH. (2012) Mad, bad or heroic? Gender, identity and accountability in lay portrayals of suicide in late twentieth-century England. *Culture, Medicine and Psychiatry*, 36(2): 348–371.

Paperno, I. (1997) *Suicide as a Cultural Institution in Dostoevsky's Russia*. London: Cornell University Press.

Peay, J. (2011) *Mental Health and Crime*. London: Routledge.

Pels, P. (1999) Professions of duplexity: a prehistory of ethical codes in anthropology. *Current Anthropology*, 40(2): 101–136.

Perreault, I., Corriveau, P. and Cauchie, J.-F. (2016) While of unsound mind?: narratives of responsibility in suicide notes from the twentieth century. *Histoire sociale/ Social history*, 49(98): 155–170.

Rapport, N. (2002) "Best of British!": An introduction to the anthropology of Britain. In: N. Rapport (ed.) *British Subjects: An Anthropology of Britain,.* Oxford: Berg, pp. 3–23.

Rapport, N. (2015) *Distortion and Love: An Anthropological Reading of the Art and Life of Stanley Spencer.* London: Routledge.

Robinson, R. (2001) *Survivors of Suicide.* Franklin Lakes, NJ: New Page Books.

Rojek, C. (1993) *Ways of Escape: Modern Transformations in Leisure and Travel.* London: Macmillan.

Skinner, J. (ed.) (2012) *Writing the Dark Side of Travel.* Oxford: Berghahn Books.

Srinivas, R. (2009) Exploring the Potential for American death tourism. *MSU Journal of Medicine and Law*, 91: 91–122.

Staples, J. and Widger, T. (2012) Situating suicide as an anthropological problem: ethnographic approaches to understanding self-harm and self-inflicted death. *Culture, Medicine and Psychiatry*, 36(2): 183–203.

Strathern, M. (2006) Don't eat unwashed lettuce. *American Ethnologist*, 33(4): 532–534.

Todorov, T. (1988) Knowledge in social anthropology: distancing and universality. *Anthropology Today*, 4(2): 2–5.

Weaver, J. (2014) *Sorrows of a Century: Interpreting Suicide in New Zealand: 1900–2000.* Montreal: McGill-Queens University Press.

Widger, T. (2015) *Suicide in Sri Lanka: The Anthropology of an Epidemic.* London: Routledge.

3 Ethics of the ethnographic self in nightlife tourism arenas

Danielle Kelly

Introduction

> Today was hard, I met up with some girls to chat in a bar, the sun is too hot
> and everyone is off their faces on something, it's quite scary, I feel like I stand
> out, like I'm the boring sensible parent and I should be joining in. I feel like
> they think I'm judging them, but I'm not.

This excerpt from field notes was written whilst studying the risk behaviours
of young British casual workers in the nightlife resort of San Antonio, Ibiza
in June 2012. More importantly, this is one of few confessions of my actual
feelings at that time, a level of emotional reflectivity that I chose not to
express in the final write up of my findings. I had entered the field with a keen
personal interest in dance music tourism, having spent my late teenage years
travelling to youth package holiday resorts around Spain. I arrived feeling
'prepared', having trawled through academic literature on youth tourism,
reading magazines and newspapers, and having consulted with tourists on
online Ibiza forums. Thus, I felt that I possessed some kind of 'insider
knowledge' on this specific area of study as my academic and personal interests overlapped (Bennett 2000; Moore and Measham 2006; Bhardwa 2013).
For that reason, I had not anticipated a feeling of 'culture shock' and
estrangement, and was unprepared for what was to come (Hammersley and
Atkinson 1995; Coffey 1999). Andrews (2005, 2009) found that it is possible
to be a 'British' person researching 'British' tourists, but fundamentally be
'derived from a different habitus' from the individuals you may encounter
(Andrews 2005: 250). I had once been a young tourist, dancing in nightclubs
until dawn, and downing shots of cheap blue-coloured vodka; now I was an
adult researcher in an environment to which I could no longer relate.

The aim of my research was to explore the substance use of youth nightlife
tourists in Ibiza. During my fieldwork there were two main areas of concern:
the fact that the levels of alcohol and drug consumption were above and
beyond what had been expected for this type of nightlife resort; and my
growing self-awareness, anxiety and inability to relax into the research as a
lone female researcher in a foreign country. Immediately, I was faced with a

multitude of questions: would I ever be able to fully understand this tourist culture as a simple observer on the periphery? Should I join in with their partying? Was it OK to converse with the intoxicated? Was I in any danger? Each day brought new surprises: watching a young male 'drop his first pill' in a nightclub in front of his friends; or holding back a female's hair as she vomited into the gutter. Many of these encounters were omitted from field notes for fear of losing academic credibility or being judged by my university peers as unprofessional for interacting to this level with intoxicated tourists (Coffey 1999; Blackman 2007). As Blackman states, 'there is a disciplinary requirement, and an ethical demand, that the storyteller and the narrative should be clean' (2007: 700). However, with scant literature outlining key ethical dilemmas of conducting ethnographic research in nightlife tourism destinations, it is important to explore these areas that may remain 'hidden' or uncounted for in this field (ibid.).

The term 'nightlife tourism' is used to describe holiday destinations characterised by bars and nightclubs, and tourist activities related mainly to drinking alcohol, but also to drug use (Calafat et al. 2011; Tutenges 2012). Nightlife holidays are commonly defined by ideals of 'sun, sea, sex, and sangria', with excessive and uninhibited partying and hedonistic behaviour encouraged and promoted by peers, holiday companies and the nightlife industry (Diken and Laustsen 2004; Rogstad 2004). The spatial and structural elements of these destinations are often 'risk-enabling', characterised by drinking strips and large super clubs (Briggs et al. 2011; Sonmez et al. 2013). San Antonio, Ibiza is no exception, described as a 'temporary wild zone' with a unique atmosphere characterised by dance music and experimentation with narcotics (Briggs et al. 2011; Briggs 2013). When discussing such drinking and drug cultures, we are concerned not only with populations who consume alcohol or illicit substances on holiday in moderation, but also with where intoxication forms an integral expression of a cultural identity and is normative to the tourist environment (Douglas 1987; Wilson 2005). Types of nightlife tourism include youth package holidays, stag and hen tourism, and Spring Break holidays. There are a large number of studies on nightlife tourism in Spain (Bellis 2003; Andrews 2005; Hughes et al. 2008; Briggs 2011, 2013; Kelly 2014); Bulgaria (Hesse et al. 2008; Tutenges 2009, 2012); and Florida and Mexico (Apostolopoulos et al. 2002; Sonmez et al. 2006). Young people, in particular, are attracted to package holidays offering cheap flights and accommodation (Calafat et al. 2011).

The majority of existing studies into nightlife tourism have used quantitative methods; however, ethnography is proving to be an invaluable tool for studying tourist behaviours as they occur in their natural settings (Andrews 2005, 2009; Briggs et al. 2011; Briggs 2013; Thurnell-Read 2012; Tutenges 2013). Yet the very nature of nightlife tourism means that the application of ethnographic enquiry to this field can be fraught with ethical dilemmas around the inclusion and study of intoxicated participants. In particular, issues of informed consent and the positionality and safety of the researcher must be addressed before entering the field.

Ethics and intoxication

Social research is increasingly ethically governed in a way that encourages stricter 'risk assessment' procedures (Israel 2004; Israel and Hay 2006). It has been argued that this can be both morally coercive and restrictive to the practice of proper social science (Murphy and Dingwall 2007; Spicker 2007; Dingwall 2008), and in particular the naturalistic practice of ethnography (Thorne 1980; Winlow et al. 2001). Such ethical structure can inhibit the extent to which ethnographers can participate in alcohol or drug use whilst in the field, as the risks to the safety and protection of the researcher and participants are simply too high. Thus drug and alcohol activity is often under-researched in qualitative fields because the process of study is viewed to be too ethically complicated (Bourgois 1998; Power 2001; Sin 2005). Briggs et al. (2015) argue that this is the reason why few ethnographic studies to date have been undertaken within nightlife tourism arenas in general.

The complexities and 'messiness' of ethnographic fieldwork that occur as a result of being responsive to people, behaviours and emotions cannot always be planned for, so objectivity often falls by the wayside (Bhardwa 2013; Briggs 2015). There is no 'one-size-fits-all' approach to negotiating morally complex and unique situations where actions cannot be predetermined (Buchanan et al. 2002). In Ibiza, the population I was studying were unpredictable, did not abide by timeframes, and were often preoccupied:

> In the middle of our conversation she whipped out a bag of white powder (drugs) from her purse and started dipping her finger in it then licking it off. I wasn't sure what to do? She was pretty distracted by this and stopped answering my questions. Two of her male friends appeared and she just got up and casually walked off with them without even registering that we were in the middle of something important, not even a 'bye'.

There are no 'universal guidelines' showing ethnographic researchers how to behave when studying tourist groups that are engaged in heavy alcohol or drug consumption (Buchanan et al. 2002; Briggs et al. 2015). Nonetheless, encountering tourists under the influence of alcohol or drugs in nightlife arenas is often unavoidable. Briggs found that the level of intoxication of tourists in Ibiza was so high that the use of data from only sober participants would provide an unsubstantiated and skewed view of tourists' actual behaviours (Briggs et al. 2011; Briggs 2013). Therefore to 'advance current knowledge' in this field to include intoxicated participants in the study to fully understand such behaviours was without question (Briggs et al. 2011: 19).

With this in mind, this chapter will discuss the three main ethical dilemmas apparent in the inclusion of intoxicated participants in ethnographic studies of nightlife tourism: informed consent; the degree which the researcher should participate; and the safety of the researcher and participants in such contexts. These challenges are not exclusive to tourism ethnography; however, intoxication in this context is an understudied area, currently sitting on what could be described as an 'ethical fence'.

Informed consent

Obtaining consent from participants who are under the influence of alcohol or drugs can be either a challenge or an obstacle to data collection. Intoxicated participants are vulnerable to our research actions as substances may impair their ability to make informed decisions about participation (McCrady and Bux 1999; Fisher 2004; Aldridge and Charles 2008). For that reason, uninformed consent can be the equivalent of having no consent at all (Thorne 1980). Therefore, when dealing with intoxicated individuals, we must ensure that they have an adequate level of understanding of the research topic before, during and after their involvement in a study. However, this is not a straightforward task.

> I had finished interviewing the girls in their apartment that morning and was getting ready to leave when their flatmate came bounding in clearly pretty drunk after continuing to party from the night before. She demanded that I interview her too and proceeded to tell me some 'juicy stories' about drugs and sex on the island. She was pretty intimidating so I continued to listen, but I kept thinking what a shame it was that I couldn't use it as she was too drunk to consent.

There is evidence that intoxication can lead to cases of over-compliance, with participants under the influence of alcohol being more likely to show willing to take part in studies (Measham et al. 2001). Briggs et al. (2011) found that male tourists in particular were keen to share their experiences and stories of alcohol use and sexual prowess, often exaggerating their stories. Similarly, for many drug users, the opportunity to speak frankly about their illegal activities without consequence can be incentive enough to take part in studies (Sandberg and Copes 2013). Although I had chosen not to include the drunken female in my study, this may not be the decision I would make today as my understanding of these issues has grown. It may be easier to exclude intoxicated participants, or 'skim off' the most inebriated; but instead we must spend time unpacking issues around alcohol and drug use and consent (Aldridge and Charles 2008).

Intoxication is a complex issue in itself. Intoxication 'is not a straightforwardly identifiable state that occurs in an easily measurable way' as situational factors and individual tolerance to substances must be considered (Aldridge and Charles 2008:192). Natural science disciplines may use equipment to detect blood alcohol levels of patrons in nightlife arenas, identifying clear cut-off points for study inclusion (Hughes et al. 2009). Yet regulatory procedures are lacking in qualitative research, and researchers must make subjective judgements on levels of intoxication based on individuals' appearances and their ability to converse (McCrady and Bux 1999). But how can we tell how drunk or high someone is? Factors such as slurred speech, bloodshot eyes and the ability to walk in a straight line might give this away, or a confession that a person is intoxicated (Palmer and Thompson 2010). But every individual is different. In Ibiza, it was often easier to detect alcohol intoxication than illicit drug use as the side effects were clearer. Substances like ecstasy and cocaine were harder to detect, as they simply made tourists appear alert and chatty. It is easy to see how such willing and communicative participants could be viewed as the perfect inter-viewees; that is, if you did not know that they were under the influence of illegal drugs. To further complicate the process of identification, the effects of substances may not be immediately obvious, or subjects may be hiding their drug or alcohol consumption as fully functioning users (Brick and Carpenter 2001). Similarly, sober participants may appear drunk due to tiredness or the effects of a hangover (Bennett 2000). For these reasons, we can never be truly sure if tourists we encounter have consumed any type of substance that may affect their ability to consent, so it is best to always exercise caution.

It can be particularly beneficial to the researcher to remain covert when studying areas where consent may be difficult to obtain, or where illegal activity is taking place (Israel and Hay 2006; Ward 2008), for example in environments where illegal substances may be consumed or criminal transac-tions are taking place. Remaining overt about my researcher status had felt like the 'right thing' to do at that time, for a number of reasons. Firstly, I did not feel comfortable dressing or behaving like an Ibiza tourist; secondly, I felt more secure and professional identifying as a researcher; and thirdly, because university peers had viewed covert research as something too complicated to be explained to the university ethics board. There is an argument amongst ethnographers that the collection of covert observational information in a public domain does not always require consent (Douglas 1976; Murphy and Dingwall 2007). However, in situations where intoxicated individuals are in a public area, such as the beach, this can be seen as exploitative of subjects who are unaware that they are being observed and may not have the capacity to object (Palmer and Thompson 2010). When Andrews studied British tourists in Majorca, she exercised a degree of role play in enacting the part of a lone female tourist, taking part in activities such as 'island tours, various forms of night-time entertainment including nightclubs, dancing and bar crawls' (2005: 250). In many cases, taking on the role of 'tourist' can be advantageous to data collection as it allows for easier and more naturalistic access to bars, nightclubs and hotels, and acceptance from other tourists. But this can depend on the type of environment and ability to blend in to the surroundings.

Yet this type of deliberate deception could be viewed as the polar opposite of informed consent as the researcher is dishonest about their intentions, thus violating the trust of participants (Erikson 1967). Moreover, intoxicated tourists can be more vulnerable to such deception as substances alter their capability to judge the intentions of individuals they encounter (i.e. researchers).

Nonetheless, the bottom line is that without covert research, drug and alcohol users may remain understudied. In that case, potential harm to participants must be weighed against the value of the knowledge gained (Denzin 1968; Israel and Hay 2006). Most importantly, as ethnographers we cannot simply shy away from making complex decisions in this field around positionality if it is at the expense of expanding knowledge. I will now discuss techniques that can be used to overcome difficulties and mitigate cases where consent may not be fully informed.

Individuals and groups can be consulted *pre*-data collection at a time when they are sober. Thurnell-Read (2012), in his research of male stag tourism in Krakow, Poland, met with groups prior to data collection to discuss the nature of the study and issues of confidentiality and anonymity. This allowed groups to make a decision about their participation in a controlled environment, and to negotiate when the researcher could accompany them to bars and nightclubs. Nevertheless, this method may not accommodate unpredictable or confounding factors that may compromise consensual agreement, such as tourists unintentionally disclosing information when drunk. This brings us to another option: of providing research participants with access to data given when intoxicated, to provide an opportunity *post*-data collection to read field notes or transcripts when sober (Palmer and Thompson 2010; Briggs 2011; Joseph and Donnelly 2012; Donnelly 2014). This allows the researcher to seek permission for the inclusion of stories that may have been divulged or behaviours witnessed when the participant was inebriated (Joseph and Donnelly 2012). However, it is questionable whether individuals would recall if they had disclosed information that required 'checking'; and a researcher may be available in the tourist destination for only a limited period during which they can offer face-to-face reassurances. Furthermore, observations are based on our own subjective interpretations of events and dialogues, so may be understood differently or contested by research participants, especially if the informant was intoxicated and cannot fully remember the encounter. A final method is the renewal of consent over the duration of fieldwork, which is particularly suitable in such shifting and evolving fieldwork contexts, or when the relationship between observer and observed has changed (Cohen 1976; Thorne 1980). The ethnographer may reassert their role in situations where boundaries are blurred between tourist and academic researcher, reminding participants of the nature and intention of the study. However, this method can be criticised for disrupting the naturalistic element of data collection and break down established relationships and rapport between researcher and participants (Driessen and Jansen 2013). In Ibiza, this was not without difficulty as the priority of the participants was to take part in touristic exploits like sunbathing or relaxing by the pool, rather than be pestered by a researcher who wanted to talk about their understanding of the project.

Whether using covert or overt methods, it is clear that each process is not without criticism or flaw around the issue of informed consent; but this should not discourage their use. No one individual or context is the same, and many methods can be used simultaneously depending on the time and place. Most importantly, informed consent must be continually revisited and revised throughout a research project as a reflexive and iterative process, not a one-off task. Caution must be exercised and guidance sought, where possible, in situations where consent may not be informed and inclusion of a participant is questionable. Ethnographers must rely on discretion, and have the confidence and the ability to negotiate unpredictable contexts, whilst also being able to provide a rationale for their choices. Fundamentally, the outcomes of such decisions must not compromise the safety of the participant or the researcher, or exploit a situation where individuals may be incapacitated, no matter how tempting the data may be.

The role and positionality of the researcher

As discussed, ethnographers benefit from being able to adopt an 'insider' or 'outsider' role, and to flexibly negotiate participant and non-participant observation (Spradley 1980; Gold 1958; Bernard 1994; Ritchie et al. 2014). Ethnographers can also 'surrender' themselves to the culture under study to the point where the daily life of participants becomes their own lived experience (Wolf 1964; Estroff 1981). This can be advantageous when studying tourism, as it gives the ability to place oneself directly into a field of action as an actual 'tourist' (Andrews 2009). I had felt like a fraud trying to pretend to be a tourist in Ibiza because I had assumed that the population I was studying was one homogenous group:

> The girls seem to all wear these denim 'hot pant' shorts that cut right across their bums, and cropped tops to flash their stomachs. They all seem to be really slim and tanned [...] A group of males walked past me all wearing T-shirts that look like the sleeves have been cut off with scissors, and they are all covered in tattoos. It seems to be like a uniform here, to flash the flesh. I don't think I could pull off that look.

I had spent so much time focusing on how visually different these particular tourists were from myself that I had automatically discounted the idea of trying to 'fit in'. Yet the 'tourist', particularly in a foreign environment, is not 'native' nor always part of a cultural entity with any solid parameters, as behaviours are socially constructed and contexts changeable (Urry 2002). Moreover, it is likely that individuals may have never visited a particular nightlife destination before. This brings into question the extent to which a researcher can become an 'insider' in such environments.

The behaviour of nightlife tourists can be viewed as temporal, characterised by levels of drug and alcohol use very different from their typical consumption levels at home (Bloor et al. 1998; Wickens and Sonmez 2007; Andrews and Roberts 2015). This can be particularly true in holiday environments designed to promote and encourage excessive consumption, such as binge drinking or dance music-related substance use (e.g. Ibiza, Briggs 2013; Krakow, Thurnell Read 2012). In nightlife tourism settings, the researcher's ability to take part in touristic activities may be limited due to their deviant or illegal nature. During my trip I had witnessed two male tourists paying for sexual acts from prostitutes; had been present when a female received a delivery of ecstasy pills from a local drug dealer to her apartment; and had watched a group of teenage tourists snort cocaine from the side of a toilet. Yet I had not taken part in any of these activities. Adler and Adler (1994) emphasise that the ethnographic researcher can only learn by experiencing first-hand what people see and do, and witnessing the factors that influence their behaviours. Thus many ethnographers have chosen to participate actively in the consumption of drugs and alcohol where they have felt this to be contextually appropriate (Thornton 2005; Blackman 2007; Palmer and Thompson 2010; Briggs 2013). For example, Palmer and Thompson (2010) drank beers with football fans at a stadium whilst studying the use of alcohol in Australian Rules football; and Thornton (2005) shared capsules of the club drug MDMA (3,4-methylenedioxymethamphetamine) with informants when studying British club culture. The need to drink alcohol or take drugs with populations can be fully dependent on the focus, and whether or not such activities are peripheral to the aims and research questions of a study. I wanted to study the levels of drug and alcohol use in Ibiza, spending time with tourists and asking them why they were using particular substances, like cocaine. They may have answered 'to keep me awake so I can party'; but I chose to take their word for it rather than testing out this theory for myself. Yet if we are already participating in the lives of our informants (forming friendships, attending parties, eating together), we need to define and rationalise what exactly it is that stops us from taking that extra step into alcohol and drug use. For me, it was to preserve my self-identity as both a researcher and someone who would not normally behave like this at home. I was not willing to fully surrender myself and risk blurring the boundaries of the relationships I had built with participants. There was a fear of unknown substances, being out of control, making a fool of myself, and perhaps jeopardising my whole project.

Few academics have shared their experiences of consuming alcohol or drugs with participants, often for fear of being prosecuted or expelled from academia (Adler 1985; Thornton 2005; Blackman 2007). On a basic level the practice of adults drinking alcohol is not illegal; but one can be prosecuted for consuming illicit substances. Nevertheless, alcohol use 'in the field' is generally not something that is encouraged or promoted amongst academic institutions, or condoned by ethical bodies, despite consumption falling within the realms of 'participant observation' (Blackman 2007). This is particularly true of areas where alcohol is consumed in a way that is not 'socially acceptable' or extreme, such as binge drinking (Donnelly 2014). Therefore the big question for researchers can often be 'what are the limits?' Much like drinking alcohol, ethnographers have questioned whether they can have sexual relationships with informants:

We do almost everything else with our informants; share their lives, eat with them, attend their rituals, become part of their families [...] Could a sexual relationship be any more intimate, committing or exploitative than our normal relations with the 'natives'?

(Dubisch 2003: 31)

Again, this is not something that is illegal, but it is deemed socially unacceptable within research fields, and can have much the same positive and negative impacts as intoxication, such as building or destroying researcher/informant relationships. It could be said that we are still in unchartered territory (Briggs et al. 2011), with no ethnographic textbooks offering guidance for alcohol or drug use in the tourism field. Nevertheless, we do have accounts of anthropologists facing similar dilemmas in different contexts that we can build on.

Joseph and Donnelly believe that drinking alcohol with informants has a significant influence on the three pillars of ethnography: 'building rapport, data collection and representation' (2012: 358). Yet concerns can arise when boundaries become blurred between the roles of researcher and willing participant when placing oneself in morally and socially ambiguous situations (Sherif 2001). Alcohol can be a symbolic tool for building and cementing research relationships as it is a social practice that can bring a sense of 'homogeneity' and exclusivity to groups (Wilson 2005; Briggs et al. 2011; Donnelly 2014). Donnelly (2014), in her ethnographic study of a women's roller derby league, found that drinking alcohol with the team earned her a level of respect and helped her to 'fit in' amongst the players. As I had always disclosed my researcher status, participants didn't seem to expect me to consume alcohol, and on the few times it was offered I always politely refused; but I was left questioning whether this might have affected the level to which I could build rapport with them. In nightlife contexts, being a non-drinker can be an anomaly and can lead to exclusion or the downgrading of one's status within a group (Briggs 2013). In the same way, refusing a drink can be viewed by some groups as an insult to them or rejection of their culture, which can jeopardise established relationships between the researcher and participants (Blackman 2007). Wilson (2005) decided to take a break from drinking alcohol in pubs with informants during his doctoral fieldwork, yet this led to 'deteriorating social relationships [...] A few key informants, who had become accustomed to sharing information with me in pubs, simply wondered why I had gone off the drink, and were suspicious of my motives' (ibid.: 6). Therefore researchers must be sensitive and acknowledge the cultural norms around drinking alcohol that are important to tourist practices before making a decision as to whether it is appropriate to join in.

Alcohol and drug use can heighten the emotions of individuals, whilst also lowering inhibitions (Thompson et al. 2005; Briggs et al. 2011). When building rapport with informants, researchers may be witness or subject to events or conversations that push the boundaries of acceptable behaviour, such as 'banter' that is racist, homophobic or sexualised (Palmer and Thompson 2007, 2010; Joseph and Donnelly 2012). This can place the researcher in a morally uncomfortable position, but in claiming full immersion or participation in drinking or drug cultures, researchers may be expected to 'grin and beae it' (Palmer and Thompson 2010: 433);

> I sat with the male tourists in a café while they drank beers and waited on their burgers. I chatted to them about their plans for the evening [...] They started heckling the girls passing by, shouting sexual comments at them and trying to grab their bums. I asked them politely to stop it, which made them laugh even more.

Female ethnographic researchers have highlighted that studying male drinking cultures had also exposed them to sexual advances and misinterpretation of their intentions (Andrews 2005; Palmer and Thompson 2010; Joseph and Donnelly 2012; Bhardwa 2013). Joseph and Donnelly (2012) found that 'sexual banter' was a key aspect of Caribbean men's cultural communication, and the researchers were subject to sexual innuendos and jokes as their friendly and inquisitive behaviour was misconstrued as sexual interest. Bhardwa (2013), when conducting research in nightclubs, found a level of hostility towards her from female patrons who felt threatened that she was approaching their male partners. Nonetheless, it is important to understand that although as a researcher you may be placed in difficult situations, you still have the right to exercise your own boundaries when made to feel uncomfortable. Yet again, this takes a level of confidence and ability to negotiate such situations, and an awareness of the moral and emotional limits of getting 'good' data.

Using participant observation to study alcohol and drug use can allow access to important cultural drinking practices, such as buying rounds or playing drinking games (Palmer and Thompson 2010). Nevertheless, before taking part in such activities, the researcher's intake of substances must be considered as alcohol can impair the ability to remember encounters or make meaningful conversations, thus affecting the accuracy of field notes (Joseph and Donnelly 2012; Donnelly 2014). To counteract this, Palmer and Thompson (2010), in their research with Australian football fans, worked in a pair and cross-checked each other's notes for consistency after periods of alcohol consumption. However, researchers are not always able to work in pairs, and there can be a reliance on one researcher remaining sober. On a basic level, researchers must exercise the capacity to judge how much alcohol or drugs it is appropriate to consume in the first place. This can be difficult in nightlife tourism environments where the strength and potency of substances are unknown, and where alcohol is often free-poured in bars and nightclubs. In San Antonio bars, a small vodka and coke would typically come in a double or treble measure (50–75 ml), using cheap imported spirits, and followed by a free shot of tequila. Ethnographers may feel under pressure to match individuals they are studying 'drink for drink', or to accept drinks that are bought for them, but strategies have been identified in previous studies of drinking cultures that enable the researcher to stay in control of their consumption. Such strategies include nursing a drink for a longer time, drinking low-alcohol beer or missing a round of drinks (Palmer and Thompson 2010; Donnelly 2014), but this can depend on factors such as the types of alcohol available or the level to which you are affected by peer pressure from participants. Joseph and Donnelly (2012) adopted tactics for alcohol avoidance such as spending more time with those who did not drink as much, or making excuses such as having to drive or get up early the next day. Yet these methods of avoidance may have prevented them from spending time with the heavy-drinking participants they intended to study. Tactics can be dependent on the specific context and the ability of the researcher to take control in situations where alcohol and drugs are present. It might be that you drink alcohol with some informants and not others. Nonetheless, this can relate back to issues around the refusal of alcohol from participants and the rejection of their culture.

Another concern is the transactional nature of drinking alcohol or taking drugs with participants, as substances may be used as currency or a bargaining tool for data. In nightlife tourism settings, research may commonly take place in designated drinking strips where alcohol is for sale, so there may be an obligation to take part in drinking rounds (Blackman 2007; Briggs 2013). Financial incentives may be offered to individuals to take part in a study that can indirectly fund the purchase of illicit substances. This can add a transactional element to research practice: firstly, if the researcher is paying for substances to facilitate the formation of friendships for the sake of academic career building (Duncombe and Jessop 2002; Blackman 2007); and secondly, if participants are encouraged to consume substances to draw out information from them that may not have been heard when sober (Briggs et al. 2015). These practices may be beneficial to the researcher in terms of data collection, but are a manipulation of both the informant and the scenario (Fisher 2004). Moreover, the formation of such 'fake friendships' and the gifting of alcohol or money for drugs may leave the participant feeling indebted to the researcher (Duncombe and Jessop 2002). Individuals may therefore feel an inability to withdraw from a study or remove themselves from a situation (Ward 2008). Researchers may unwittingly be purchasing alcohol for participants in quantities that they might not normally consume (McCrady and Bux 1999; Buchanan et al. 2002; Blackman 2007). As the strength of alcohol in foreign nightlife tourism arenas can differ from home country standards, this may lead to unpredictable levels of intoxication for the consumer (Bellis and Hale 2000; Hughes et al. 2011). Therefore the researcher may be placing an individual in direct harm. Taking all of this into consideration, the implications of 'lubricating social encounters' cannot be overlooked when engaging with groups, and researchers must exercise responsibility for others (Joseph and Donnelly 2012). Communication may be the key to counteracting these issues by discussing the limits of participation with informants before taking part in drinking activities. This may be in the form of ground rules such as purchasing your own drinks, contributing an equal amount of money to everyone else into a round, and being clear from the outset that there will be no financial benefit to their participation in the study. As shown, there can be a very fine line to cross into taking advantage of intoxicated study participants, but to have an awareness of this line and to set clear limits can be a good start.

Safety of the researcher and participants

Within the ethnographic literature there is much attention paid to the ethical issues around interacting with vulnerable or criminal groups, but there is little consideration of the risks involved in nightlife tourism settings. Within these environments, risks are commonly related to the excessive alcohol and drug use of tourists, particularly youth. Excessive alcohol in youth nightlife destinations has been linked to increased levels of violence (Bellis et al. 2003; Hughes et al. 2008); whilst the use of illicit substances has been linked to paranoia and aggression amongst users (Wright and Klee 2001; Sommers and Baskin 2006; Hughes et al. 2009; Calafat et al. 2013). There is also the risk of overdose and death as people experiment with unknown substances in foreign location (Bellis et al. 2003; Public Health England 2016).

Conducting ethnographic research may entail visiting bars, nightclubs or parties, so there can be a natural level of trepidation when entering arenas full of intoxicated tourists. Strategies must be introduced to ensure the safety and protection of researchers from danger, especially when conducting data collection alone. When studying tourists in San Antonio, Ibiza, I made the decision not to go out after dark alone unless accompanied by informants. Palmer and Thompson (2010) adopted this method, ensuring that when researching drinking cultures at night they worked in a pair, and kept each other informed of their whereabout. However, I could not always guarantee that I would be escorted back to my hostel after dark, and would often have to get taxis alone. Furthermore, working unsociable hours in a foreign country meant that it was not always possible to reach my university contacts back in the UK to report my whereabouts. Careful planning is essential before entering the field to ensure that there are always safe options available.

As well as risks to the safety of the researcher, there are concerns regarding the health and welfare of participants. Academic researchers may bring a clinically informed awareness of health issues around the consumption of excessive amounts of alcohol or drugs, and consequently feel a responsibility to warn people of the dangers of their behaviour. Tourists may assume that because we are studying their substance-use behaviours we are experts in illicit substances, and in not warning of them of the dangers we may be condoning and encouraging their behaviour by providing a false sense of security. When I had witnessed tourists taking substances, I felt that it was not my place to stop them, and in some ways they may have been doing this to shock me. In being present we may actually encourage higher levels of drug and alcohol use, as individuals wish to 'show off' their drinking and drug-taking skills (Briggs 2013). Consequently, researchers may become witness to the deterioration of an informant's health as they are susceptible to both long- and short-term substance use-related illness and injury (Ward 2008);

> I was interviewing a female tourist this afternoon; she had been on the island for 3 weeks and was planning on staying longer. She had bad insomnia and hadn't slept in 4 days; she thought this was because of the drugs she had used since she arrived. She told me she had started taking cocaine regularly to stop her feeling tired, rather than trying to sleep, to delay the hangover.

Ethnographers may recognise a level of responsibility over groups under study; however, it can be argued that in public spaces we are no more responsible for intoxicated individuals than any other patron on the premises (Palmer and Thompson 2010). Researchers can be also ill-prepared for circumstances out of their control, for example, if a tourist overdoses on drugs, or a fight breaks out amongst participants. It is useful to educate oneself on local health infrastructure and be able to provide signposts for information and advice around drug and alcohol use.

A number of ethical dilemmas are presented when studying drug-using populations in holiday settings, as many substances are illegal (Buchanan et al. 2002). Ethnographic methods have the potential to invade privacy and increase the anxiety of participants, who may feel vulnerable to social or legal harms as a result of their participation in such illegal activity (Fisher 2004; Fry et al. 2005), so researchers must respect the confidentiality of respondents and handle sensitive information responsibly. Just because a tourist may talk openly about drugs or use them in front of you, does not mean that they would do the same in front of others. Research relationships can be formed predicated on the trust that the researcher will protect the anonymity of informants, and not expose them to the risk of prosecution (Israel 2004). Interacting with drug users can also attract unwanted attention from other drug users, or even the police (Williams et al. 1992; Librett and Perrone 2010). Ward (2008), in her study of drug dealing in London nightclubs, frequented bars, nightclubs and after-parties, therefore unwittingly accompanying people to drug sales. Had police drug raids taken place, she also would have been at risk of arrest. For that reason, we must always remember that although *we* know that we are researcher professionals, to an outsider's eye we are no different from the tourists we are sitting with.

Discussion and conclusion

This chapter has discussed ethical issues inherent to ethnographic research with drug and alcohol users in nightlife tourism settings. Such discussions allow us to consider the intrinsic ambiguities that are present in 'real-world' research, and to explore areas of ethnographic research that may remain 'hidden' or unaccounted for in literature (Gilbert 2001; Blackman 2007). Studying intoxicated informants in tourism settings should not be seen as problematic, but as something that is both accommodated and normative in research methods. Without such accounts of tourism nightlife activity, it is harder to develop understandings of this type of touristic practice, or set contextually appropriate ethical boundaries. Furthermore, lessons that are learnt from studying tourists in drug and alcohol-related settings can be used to inform fields where intoxication forms part of other cultural identities.

It is clear that encounters with intoxicated individuals can be unpredictable, meaning that researchers cannot always anticipate and prepare for potentially risky or challenging situations. Dealing with intoxicated participants can be an ethical minefield, but we must take time to reflect, observe and digest situations of uncertainty whilst taking time to evaluate our aims and research questions. There are options for managing this type of research, but they require researcher confidence, an awareness of harm-reduction measures, and tactics for minimising the intoxication of the researcher. This can be a fluid and iterative process that evolves throughout a research project as the researcher takes time to reflect on encounters. Similarly, we can prepare by setting ourselves boundaries, whether loose or solid, before entering the field, and ensure that we have regular contact with research advisories for support.

Moving forward, ethical bodies have the potential to be adaptive and innovative in overcoming ethical challenges involved with the study of intoxicated groups if approached openly (Iphofen 2011). At present, ethnographic research does not have answers to many questions that arise in this field. The more we converse and are open about researching drinking and drug cultures in tourism settings, the more we learn from honest and realistic accounts. This can allow ethics boards to consider pragmatic measures for ethnographers conducting participant observation with tourist groups, that may involve drinking alcohol with participants or including intoxicated accounts where appropriate. The criminal aspect of drug use may serve as a limit to participation in such activities, but this should not discourage researchers from exploring such cultures in other ways within holiday destinations.

Researchers may view the ethics process as a traditional 'tick-box' exercise that ends before even entering a research arena (Katz and Fox 2004; Iphofen 2011). This chapter has emphasised that 'doing ethics' is a continual reflective process, and researchers have an obligation to apply appropriate contextual ethical measures in the field. No individual encounter will be the same as another. Methods for informed consent or participant observation do not come with a 'one-size-fits-all' manual, so research actions must be tailored for each individual setting. Within nightlife tourism arenas, a researcher could be studying a group of beer-drinking males in Spain or a single female taking ecstasy pills in a nightclub in Iceland – the settings are widely varied.

Ultimately, research practices must be relational, and must consider both the needs of the participants and the ability of the researchers.

References

Adler, P. and Adler, P. A. (1994) Observational techniques. In: N. K. Denzin and S. Y. Lincoln (eds) *Handbook of Qualitative Research*, 1st edn.. Thousand Oaks: Sage, pp. 377–392.

Adler, P. A. (1985) Wheeling and dealing: an ethnography of an upper-level drug dealing and smuggling community . *Journal of Sociology and Social Welfare*, 21(4): 180–192.

Aldridge, J. and Charles, V. (2008) Researching the intoxicated: informed consent implications for alcohol and drug research. *Drug and Alcohol Dependence*, 93(3): 191–196.

Andrews, H. (2005) Feeling at home: embodying Britishness in a Spanish charter tourist resort. *Tourist Studies*, 5(3): 247–266.

Andrews, H. (2009) 'Tits out for the boys and no back chat': gendered space on holiday. *Space and Culture*, 12(2): 166–182.

Andrews, H. and Roberts, L. (2015) Liminality. In: J. D. Wright (eds) *International Encyclopaedia of the Social and Behavioural Sciences*, 2nd edn. London: Elsevier, pp. 131–137.

Apostolopoulos, Y., Sonmez, S. and Yu, C. H. (2002) HIV-risk behaviours of American spring break vacationers: a case of situational disinhibition? *International Journal of STD and AIDS*, 13(4): 733–743.

Bellis, M. A. and Hale, G. (2000) Ibiza uncovered: changes in substance use and sexual behaviour amongst young people visiting an international nightlife resort. *Sexually Transmitted Infections*, 80(1): 43–47.

Bellis, M. A., Hughes, K., Bennett, A. and Thomson, R. (2003) The role of an international nightlife resort in the proliferation of recreational drugs. *Addiction*, 98(12): 1713–1721.

Bennett, A. (2000) *Popular Music and Youth Culture: Music, Identity and Place.* London: Macmillan.

Bernard, R. H. (1994) *Research Methods in Anthropology: Qualitative and Quantitative Approaches.* London: Sage.

Bhardwa, B. (2013) Alone, Asian and female: the unspoken challenges of conducting fieldwork in dance settings. *Dancecult: Journal of Electronic Dance Music Culture*, 5(1): 39–60.

Blackman, S. (2007) Hidden ethnography: crossing emotional borders in qualitative accounts of young people's lives. *Sociology*, 41(4): 699–716.

Bloor, M., Thomas, M., Hood, K., Abeni, D., Goujon, C., Hausser, D., Hubert, M., Kleiber, D. and Nieto, J. A. (1998). Differences in sexual risk taking between young men and women travelling abroad from the UK. *The Lancet*, 352(9141): 1664–1668.

Bourgois, P. (1998) The moral economies of homeless heroin addicts: confronting ethnography, HIV risk, and everyday violence in San Francisco shooting encampments. *Substance Use and Misuse*, 33(11): 2323–2351.

Brick, J. and Carpenter, J. A. (2001) The identification of alcohol intoxication by police. *Alcoholism: Clinical and Experimental Research*, 25(6): 850–855.

Briggs, D. (2013) *Deviance and Risk on Holiday: An Ethnography of British Tourists in Ibiza*. London: Palgrave Macmillan.

Briggs, D., Tutenges, S., Armitage, R. and Panchev, D. (2011) Sexy substances and the substance of sex: findings from an ethnographic study in Ibiza, Spain. *Drugs and Alcohol Today*, 11(4): 173–187.

Briggs, D., Gololobov, I. and Ventsel, A. (2015) Ethnographic research among drinking youth cultures: reflections from observing participants. *Folklore: Electronic Journal of Folklore*, 61: 157–176.

Buchanan, D., Khoshnood, K., Stopka, T., Shaw, S., Santelices, C. and Singer, M. (2002) Ethical dilemmas created by the criminalization of status behaviors: case examples from ethnographic field research with injection drug users. *Health Education and Behavior*, 29(1): 30–42.

Calafat, A., Mantecon, A., Juan, M. and Adrover-Roig, D. (2011) Violent behaviour, drunkenness, drug use and social capital in nightlife contexts. *Psychological Intervention*, 20(1): 45–51.

Calafat, A., Bellis, M. A., Fernandez del Rio, E., Juan, M., Hughes, K., Morleo, M., Becona, E., Duch, M., Stamos, A. and Mendes, F. (2013) Nightlife, verbal and physical violence among young European holidaymakers: what are the triggers? *Public Health*, 127(10): 908–915.

Coffey, A. (1999) *The Ethnographic Self: Fieldwork and the Representation of Identity*. London: Sage.

Cohen, F. G. (1976) The American Indian movement and the anthropologist: issues and implications of consent. In M. A. Rynkiewich and J. P. Spradley (eds) *Ethics and Anthropology: Dilemmas in Fieldwork*. London: John Wiley and Sons, pp. 81–94.

Denzin, N. K. (1968). On the ethics of disguised observation. *Social Problems*, 15(4): 502–504.

Diken, B. and Laustsen, C. B. (2004) Sea, sun, sex and the discontents of pleasure. *Tourist Studies*, 4(2): 99–114.

Dingwall, R. (2008) The ethical case against ethical regulation in humanities and social science research. *Twenty-First Century Society*, 3(1): 1–12.

Donnelly, M. K. (2014) Drinking with the derby girls: exploring the hidden ethnography in research of women's flat track roller derby. *International Review for the Sociology of Sport*, 49(3/4): 346–366.

Douglas, J. D. (1976) *Investigative Social Research: Individual and Team Field Research*. Beverly Hills: Sage.

Douglas, M. (1987) *Constructive Drinking: Perspectives on Drink from Anthropology* (Vol. 10). London: Psychology Press.

Driessen, H. and Jansen, W. (2013) The hard work of small talk in ethnographic fieldwork. *Journal of Anthropological Research*, 69(2): 249–263.

Dubisch, J. (2003) Lovers in the field: sex, dominance, and the female anthropologist. In: D. Kulick and M. Wilson (eds) *Taboo: Sex, Identity and Erotic Subjectivity in Anthropological Fieldwork*. London: Routledge, pp. 29–50.

Duncombe, J. and Jessop, J. (2002*) 'Doing Rapport' and the Ethics of 'Faking Friendship'*. London: Sage.

Erikson, K. T. (1967) A comment on disguised observation in sociology. *Social Problems*, 14(4): 366–373.

Estroff, S. E. (1981) *Making it Crazy: An Ethnography of Psychiatric Clients in an American Community*. Berkley: University of California Press.

Fisher, C. B. (2004) Ethics in drug abuse and related HIV risk research. *Applied Developmental Science*, 8(2): 91–103.

Fry, C. L., Treloar, C. and Maher, L. (2005) Ethical challenges and responses in harm reduction research: promoting applied communitarian ethics. *Drug and Alcohol Review*, 24(5): 449–459.

Gilbert, K. (2001) *The Emotional Nature of Qualitative Research*. Boca Raton: CRC Press.

Gold, R. (1958) Roles in sociological field observation. *Social Forces*, 36(3): 217–223

Hammersley, M. and Atkinson, P. (1995) *Ethnography Principles in Practice*. London: Routledge.

Hesse, M., Tutenges, S., Schliewe, S. and Reinholdt, T. (2008) Party package travel: alcohol use and related problems in a holiday resort: a mixed methods study. *BMC Public Health*, 8(351): 1–8.

Hughes, K., Bellis, M. A., Calafat, A., Juan, M., Schnitzer, S. and Anderson, Z. (2008) Predictors of violence in young tourists: a comparative study of British, German and Spanish holidaymakers. *European Journal of Public Health*, 18(6): 569–574.

Hughes, K., Quigg, Z., Bellis, M. A., Morleo, M., Jarman, I. and Lisboa, P. (2009) *Blood Alcohol Levels and Drunkenness amongst People Visiting Nightlife in the North West*. Liverpool: Centre for Public Health, Liverpool John Moores University.

Hughes, K., Bellis, M. A., Calafat, A., Blay, N., Kokkevi, A., Boyiadji, G., Do Rosario Mendes, M. and Bajcarova, L. (2011) Substance use, violence, and unintentional injury in young holidaymakers visiting Mediterranean destinations. *Journal of Travel Medicine*, 18(2): 80–89.

Iphofen, R. (2011) Ethical decision making in qualitative research. *Qualitative Research*, 11(4): 443–446.

Israel, M. (2004) Strictly confidential? Integrity and the disclosure of criminological and socio–legal research. *British Journal of Criminology*, 44(5): 715–740.

Israel, M. and Hay, I. (2006) *Research Ethics for Social Scientists*. London: Sage.

Joseph, J. and Donnelly, M. K. (2012) Reflections on ethnography, ethics and inebriation. *Leisure*, 36(3–4): 357–372.

Katz, A. and Fox, K. (2004) *The Process of Informed Consent: What's At Stake*. Boston: Children's Hospital Boston and Department of Social Medicine, Harvard Medical School.

Kelly, D., Hughes, K. and Bellis, M. A. (2014) Work hard, party harder; drug use and sexual behaviour in young British casual workers in Ibiza, Spain. *International Journal of Environmental Research and Public Health*, 11(10): 10051–10061.

Librett, M. and Perrone, D. (2010) Apples and oranges: ethnography and the IRB. *Qualitative Research*, 10(6): 729–747.

McCrady, B. S. and Bux Jr, D. A. (1999) Ethical issues in informed consent with substance abusers. *Journal of Consulting and Clinical Psychology*, 67(2): 186–193.

Measham, F. C., Aldridge, J. and Parker, H. (2001) *Dancing on Drugs: Risk, Health and Hedonism in the British Club Scene*. London: Free Association Books.

Moore, K. and Measham, F. K. (2006) Reluctant reflexivity, implicit insider knowledge and the development of club studies. In: B. Sanders (ed.) *Drugs, Clubs and Young People*. Ashgate: Aldershot, pp. 13–26.

Murphy, E. and Dingwall, R. (2007) Informed consent, anticipatory regulation and ethnographic practice . *Social Science and Medicine*, 65(11): 2223–2234.

Palmer, C. and Thompson, K. (2007) The paradoxes of football spectatorship: on field and on-line expressions of social capital among the 'Grog Squad'. *Sociology of Sport Journal*, 24(1): 187–205.

Palmer, C. and Thompson, K. (2010) Everyday risks and professional dilemmas: fieldwork with alcohol-based (sporting) subcultures. *Qualitative Research*, 10(4): 421–440.

Power, R. (2001) Reflections on participant observation in drugs research. *Addiction Research and Theory*, 9(4): 325–337.

Public Health England (2016) *Trends in Drug Misuse Deaths in England, 1999 to 2014*. London: Public Health England.

Ritchie, J., Lewis, J., McNaughton-Nicholls, C. and Ormston, R. (2014) *Qualitative Research Practice*, 2nd edn. London: Sage.

Rogstad, K. (2004) Sex, sun, sea and STIs: sexually transmitted infections acquired on holiday. *BMJ*, 329(7459): 214–217.

Sandberg, S. and Copes, H. (2013) Speaking with ethnographers: the challenges of researching drug dealers and offenders. *Journal of Drug Issues*, 43(2): 176–197.

Sherif, B. (2001) The ambiguity of boundaries in the fieldwork experience: establishing rapport and negotiating insider/outsider status. *Qualitative Inquiry*, 7(4): 436–447.

Sin, C. H. (2005) Seeking informed consent: reflections on research practice. *Sociology*, 39(2): 277–294.

Sommers, I. and Baskin, D. (2006) Methamphetamine use and violence . *Journal of Drug Issues*, 36(1): 77–96.

Sonmez, S., Apostolopoulos, Y., Yu, C. H., Yang, S., Mattila, A. and Yu, L. C. (2006) Binge drinking and casual sex on spring break. *Annals of Tourism Research*, 33(4): 895–917.

Sonmez, S., Apostolopoulos, Y., Theocharous, A. and Massengale, K. (2013) Bar crawls, foam parties and clubbing networks: mapping the risk environment of a Mediterranean nightlife resort. *Tourism Management Perspectives*, 8(4): 49–59.

Spicker, P. (2007) The ethics of policy research. *Evidence and Policy*, 3(1): 99–118.

Spradley, J. P. (1980) *Participant Observation*. New York: Wadsworth Thomson Learning.

Thompson, J. C., Kao, T. C. and Thomas, R. J. (2005) The relationship between alcohol use and risk-taking sexual behaviours in a large behavioural study. *Preventative Medicine*, 41(1): 247–252.

Thorne, B. (1980) 'You still takin' notes?' Fieldwork and problems of informed consent. *Social Problems*, 27(3): 284–297.

Thornton, S. (2005) *Club Cultures, Music, Media and Subcultural Capital*. Cambridge: Polity Press.

Thurnell-Read, T. (2012) Tourism place and space: British stag tourism in Poland. *Annals of Tourism Research*, 39(2): 801–819.

Tutenges, S. (2009) Safety problems among heavy-drinking youth at a Bulgarian nightlife resort. *International Journal of Drug Policy*, 20(5): 444–446.

Tutenges, S. (2012) Nightlife tourism: a mixed methods study of young tourists at an international nightlife resort. *Tourist Studies*, 12(2): 131–150.

Tutenges, S. (2013) Stirring up effervescence: an ethnographic study of youth at a nightlife resort. *Leisure Studies*, 32(3): 1–6.

Urry, J. (2002) *The Tourist Gaze*, 2nd edn. London: Sage.

Ward, J. (2008) Researching drug sellers: an 'experiential' account from 'the field'. *Sociological Research Online*, 13(1): 14.

Wickens, E. and Sonmez, S. (2007) Casual sex in the sun makes the holiday: young tourists' perspectives. In: Y. Apostolopoulos and S. Sonmez (eds) *Population Mobility and Infectious Disease.* New York: Springer, pp. 199–214.

Williams, T., Dunlap, E., Johnson, B. D. and Hamid, A. (1992) Personal safety in dangerous places. *Journal of Contemporary Ethnography,* 21(3): 343–374.

Wilson, T. M. (2005) Drinking cultures: sites and practices in the production and expression of identity. In: T. Wilson (ed.) *Drinking Cultures: Alcohol and Identity.* New York: Berg, pp. 8–22.

Winlow, S., Hobbs, D., Lister, S. and Hadfield, P. (2001) 'Get ready to duck': bouncers and the realities of ethnographic research on violent groups. *British Journal of Criminology,* 41(3): 536–548.

Wolf, E. (1964) *Anthropology.* New York: Norton.

Wright, S. and Klee, H. (2001) Violent crime, aggression and amphetamine: what are the implications for drug treatment services? *Drugs: Education, Prevention and Policy,* 8(1): 73–90.

4 Autoethnography and power in a tourism researcher position

A self-reflexive exploration of unawareness, memories and paternalism among Namibian Bushmen[1]

Stasja Koot

Introduction

It must have been around 2004. I lived at the Tsintsabis resettlement farm,[2] Namibia, and worked on a community-based tourism project called Tree-sleeper Camp, an eco-oriented camp site with various activities focused on the local indigenous culture of the Hai//om[3] Bushmen.[4] The traditional authority of Tsintsabis came to my door and asked me why he could not get another family member into the project. A few months earlier, we had signed a contract in which we limited the number of family employees to a maximum of two, and his family had already reached that maximum. I reminded him of the contract, even showing him all the trustees' signatures, including his own. He responded by reading out the date, saying: 'That was long ago, I feel different now. This is now.'

This type of incident is not unusual for ethnographers, but in this case I was working in the field of tourism, to become an ethnographer later. As Edward Bruner noted, working in tourism enables an ethnographer 'to study tourism from the inside [...] participating, observing, talking, traveling, eating and sightseeing with the tourists' (2005: 1). Of course, the above example about a contract does not highlight an interaction with a 'guest', a tourist, but with one of the 'hosts', a local Bushman leader. Nevertheless, this chapter also shows the importance of working in tourism: it is an analysis of my personal relation with the Bushmen as hosts in particular. The example about the contract shows the difference in perception about the importance of the legislation that the community and myself had created for the Treesleeper Camp tourism project. Based on rules and agreements originating in ideas of tourism as a development strategy, I often rationalised that my aim at the farm was solely to build up Treesleeper Camp. Therefore, I considered many suggestions by the local Bushmen that were not in line with this aim – such as ignoring contract agreements – to be a distraction from my main reason for being there.

In these early days, the name *baas* – which literally means 'boss' and is further explained in the following discussion – was given to me for fun for a while by three Dutch interns who went on to help out at Treesleeper. As a group of young and idealistic fieldworkers, we were often surprised to experience the Bushmen's humbleness (shown to us and, especially, to local white farmers). We believed they did not need to behave in such an inferior way as they often did. However, we were unaware then of the deep sense of paternalism in the region and our own relatively strong positions of power.

While I acted as a community member or 'insider' in various ways, I was simultaneously disconnected – functioning as an 'outsider' – in other ways. More than anything, my position of power created personal struggles when working for Treesleeper Camp. Therefore this chapter is also a methodological and epistemological exploration that analyses the knowledge I gained from holding different positions (insider/outsider/researcher/tourism development fieldworker), and examines how this knowledge was built up and changed over the years. I use autoethnography as a methodology – a type of ethnography that involves self-observation and reflexive investigation by the researcher; personal and cultural issues become blurred and are experienced as continually interconnected (Ellis and Bochner 2000: 739; Maréchal 2010).

Autoethnography enables academics to tell their personal research stories to professionals and other, non-expert people, including, for example, Bushmen communities (Tomaselli 2012a: 6–7). Using autoethnography in relation to a group of Bushmen, the chapter builds on earlier work by Tomaselli (2007, 2012b) and Tomaselli et al (2013). In these works, the researchers' relation(s) with the 'other(s)', or the researched, in particular the South Kalahari Bushmen (≠Khomani) of South Africa, is also problematised, mostly in tourism settings. It is important to note that in tourism there are many other relevant relations in which researcher positionality needs to be critically and self-reflexively analysed, such as the connections that can exist between the researcher and the private tourism sector, in which relations of power and paternalism play a crucial role (e.g. Koot 2016, 2017a, 2017b; Tomaselli 2017). Moreover, critical self-reflection and analyses of paternalist relations are important in the relationship with the 'other' and can also be applicable beyond community-based tourism.

Paternalism is a subject *par excellence* for such an autoethnographic analysis because 'authors use their own experiences in the culture reflexively to bend back on self and look more deeply at self-other interactions' (Ellis and Bochner 2000: 740). Consequently, the chapter adds three under-analysed but essential and interconnected elements of autoethnography: power, unawareness and memory. I argue that, despite the absence of any awareness of doing research, my experience as a development fieldworker nevertheless created important and useful knowledge. However, this unawareness also implies an autoethnography that is retrospective. Memories are crucial to it. As ethnographers tend to have 'rather poor memories', I heed Hunt and Ruiz Junco's call for an 'ongoing consideration of memory among ethnographers' (2006: 371). This leads me to conclude that what I dub an 'open retrospective analytic autoethnographic experience' contains important epistemological value, but also to acknowledge that memories are problematic because they are subject to change and decay. Memories, in my view, need serious consideration in autoethnography. By using my own memories in this tourism project, it becomes clear that I perpetuate my earlier acquired power as a development fieldworker in my 'new' role as an ethnographer.

First, I describe how I built up a body of knowledge during my different stays in Tsintsabis. The first stay was in 1999, when the idea for starting tourism was initiated. Next, I provide memories from the years 2004–2007 when I lived in Tsintsabis working for Treesleeper Camp. Specifically, I investigate events that relate to development and power among this marginalised indigenous group. In the methodological analysis that follows, I reflect on the value of such a retrospective autoethnography, how this adds to analytic autoethnography, and the value of the fact that I was unaware that I was 'doing research', which, I conclude, created an 'open' research experience but simultaneously perpetuates power relations.

Living in Tsintsabis

Care, books and becoming baas

I have been connected with the Hai//om of Tsintsabis since 1999, when I conducted fieldwork there for six months as an MA student. In those days most inhabitants were Hai//om, but today the population has become more hybrid. Then I often strolled through the dusty gardens, doing interviews and exploring the farm and its many socio-economic and cultural happenings. I learned about its different churches, the school, the history of Tsintsabis, the Hai//om's historical connection with the famous Namibian tourist attraction Etosha National Park, and lots more. I also participated in many joyful moments with community members, attended soccer matches and nightly healing sessions, and regularly drank a few beers in the local *shebeens*. In that way, I participated, observed and learned. I also started to care for the people with whom I was living and after the fieldwork, I began to develop a proposal to start community-based tourism in Tsintsabis (Koot 2013: 309–311), which in the 1990s flourished – often as one of the main pillars of larger community-based natural resource management programmes – in southern Africa. This type of small-scale tourism aims to empower marginalised communities, taking their needs and wishes as the starting point. Moreover, community members themselves should control, plan, own, manage and initiate the project (Giampiccoli and Nauright 2010: 52–53).

Many evenings were spent reading books by candlelight. Two books in particular influenced my ideas in those days. First, I was struck by the philosophical novel *Lila*, in which the anthropologist Dussenberry says of his relationship with native Americans that '[t]he only way to find out about Indians is to *care* for them and win their love and respect' (cited in Pirsig 1991: 43). Reading *Lila* made me realise that I had to let go of my quest for

Autoethnography and power   55

objectivity; it was fine – even inevitable – to develop feelings of care for the people one studied. Second, this growing empathy was stimulated by a feeling for the 'victimisation' the Bushmen had experienced, as I realised from reading Gordon's *Picturing Bushmen* (1997). This book made me 'realise more and more how important the views of other people have been, concerning the contemporary situation of the Bushmen' (Koot 2002).

Today, approximately 20 years later, my ideas have become more nuanced, but my concern for the Bushmen has never left me. This raises its own questions. Exactly which Bushmen do I care for? Does caring not imply a certain level of patronisation? Although I do not have all the answers, I feel that my concern for the people was the start of my becoming a *baas*, a word often used in Afrikaans-speaking areas, especially on farms, for the white authority. A *baas* is usually white and male (cf. Sylvain 2001). Since Tsintsabis has been surrounded by commercial farms for many years, people are deeply rooted in the social construct of *baasskap* (see also Plotkin 2002: 5–7). In this southern African patron–client relationship, beliefs about white superiority play a crucial role. This does not necessarily mean that it is only a top-down structure; in a relationship of interdependency between the patron and his clients, there is often also support for beliefs and assumptions 'from below' (Van Beek 2011: 40–41). The underlying assumptions of *baasskap* date back to the start of Western colonisation. The phenomenon is based on a family ideology: the patron is the father (*baas*) of his 'immature' children, who are seen to be in need of development. Edification, care and protection are essential elements that also provide important benefits to the clients in return for their labour, such as transport, medical assistance, basic education and a place to live (Gibbon et al. 2014; cf. Rutherford 2001). Early signs of my authority were visible already in 1999, when the first ideas for Treesleeper Camp began to develop. Tourism was then seen as a panacea for development. The local development committee had had plans for tourism to stimulate the area's economy since 1993. The request for a tourism project originated from within the community, but under my influence this changed from an idea to build a luxurious lodge to plans for a community-based campsite. I had lived among the people for a few months already and simply could not see them running a lodge or any other type of upper-class tourism enterprise. So, as an MA student, I began to influence the plans and ideas of the community according to what I myself deemed good for them. I was a young *baas* in the making.

I went back to Namibia in 2002/03 for another six months to explore the possibilities for the project. This was the start of what would become Treesleeper Camp (Hüncke 2010; Hüncke and Koot 2012; Koot 2012, 2013, 2017a; Troost 2007). From January 2004 until June 2007 I lived in Namibia, mostly in Tsintsabis itself, initially with a friend of mine, Ferry Bounin (January 2004 until November 2005). Our job was to support the founding of Treesleeper physically and institutionally, and to manage the project for the first few years.

In 2008, when I had been back in the Netherlands for more than a year, I started writing a book chapter about Treesleeper (Koot 2012). This initiated the idea for the PhD that I worked on between 2009 and 2013, including half a year of fieldwork in southern Africa and return visits to Tsintsabis in 2010. In this research, my stay in Tsintsabis and working for Treesleeper provided crucial sources of knowledge. Since 2007 I have stayed in contact with various people living in Tsintsabis, via email or Facebook.

The meaning of living in Tsintsabis for fieldwork

My long-term stay as a development fieldworker in a community-based tourism project can be compared with Karine Rousset's (2003: 18) stay of three years in West Caprivi, northeast Namibia, as an NGO facilitator. As she explains:

> [This] has given me the opportunity to familiarise myself with conservation and development issues from a practical, on-the-ground perspective. I am fully cognisant that my immersion in a development-focussed NGO world may also cloud my understanding and interpretation of events. But I believe this is balanced by the advantage of an extended period of time in West Caprivi that has allowed for a more in-depth understanding of attitudes and local politics than would have been possible had I only spent six weeks there.

Similarly, Thekla Hohmann stayed in Tsumkwe West, east Namibia, for 16 months, combining scientific and developmental work. This gave her 'the privilege to engage in participatory observation and to follow the discussion about community-based natural resource management in the field from different angles' (Hohmann 2003: 209). I experienced similar advantages from my years in Tsintsabis. In relation to my PhD fieldwork, I could draw on my 'general knowledge' of and 'feel' for the people. I learned to speak Afrikaans, which turned out to be crucial for my PhD fieldwork. Although the Treesleeper staff usually spoke English, I spoke Afrikaans to elderly people in the community and to white farmers. This not only improved my ability to communicate, it also infused my authority with the colonial legacy associated with Afrikaans.

For example, for my PhD I have strolled through the South African Kgalagadi Transfrontier Park with the local Bushman tour guide Toppies Kruiper, who would draw things in the sand to illustrate his stories. The Hai//om of Tsintsabis also often illustrated stories in the sand, usually not having any pen and paper available. But there was an additional element to the practice. A South African local respondent, Belinda Kruiper (cited in Dyll 2009: 55) asserts that 'NGOs should let the Bushmen draw in the sand to explain how they feel and what they want'. Lauren Dyll observes that '[b]y encouraging Western methods of communication *only*, [...] development workers are in fact denying the validity of local methods and knowledge, and in so doing gain only a superficial understanding of people's development needs and requirements' (2007: 122). Bushmen, I learned, often communicate by means of the things at hand. They also refer to elements such as the wind, the sun, the rain or a stone in order to explain things. When I asked what day of the week an event happened, I might be told that it was on the day when the wind blew hard. When I asked for directions, I might be advised that 'at that round stone you go that way' or 'where the trees become higher' or 'where the bushes were eaten by a kudu'. Today communication has become hybrid and people also use Western reference points (e.g., Tuesday 21 September) and equipment (e.g., pens, pencils, mobile phones and computers), but that does not mean that this 'other, more traditional' communication has disappeared.

Memories of development and paternalism at Treesleeper

Being baas

Bounin and I established the Tsintsabis Trust in 2004, which became the local (community-based) legal owner of the Treesleeper tourism project. Since registration of this body needed to be done in the capital, Windhoek, it was almost impossible for local people to do this, as they lacked the transport and means. This gave Bounin and myself the power to decide what would be in the deed of trust. Local trustees (some of whom were illiterate) only needed to sign before we returned the documents to the Master of the High Court in Windhoek. It took time for the older generation, especially, to accept and understand the structure and vision of Treesleeper. As some schoolboys explained:

> They [parents and grandparents] were afraid that the white people [Bounin and I] were going to claim their land, like white people did during colonisation and the apartheid regime. [...] After several meetings with Stasja and the [Tsintsabis] trust, they started to understand that the camp site was meant to help develop them.
>
> (Troost 2007: 66)

People did not necessarily distinguish us – young white male Europeans – from local white Namibians. Although most people remembered me from my MA fieldwork in 1999 and we arrived with a story about 'development' based on the principle of community participation in tourism, most of the elders also associated our being there with land theft, colonialism and apartheid. Moreover, the tourism industry in southern Africa is heavily white-dominated, meaning that ownership of tourism businesses (and their economic benefits) as well as decision-making processes were mainly done by whites.

Bounin and I started as trustees of the Tsintsabis Trust for pragmatic reasons. For example, we were in a position to open a bank account. While local people made up the majority of the trust, Bounin and I exerted a great deal of influence. An ex-employee and trustee said about me in 2006, a few months before I was to leave Tsintsabis, that she did 'not think it is a community project, but it is Stasja's [...] project. [...] he takes most of the decisions and he can lay his opinion on the members of the trust and the personnel of Treesleeper' (cited in Troost 2007: 58). Organisationally, Bounin and I acted from a position of power. We controlled the funds in the beginning. Although it was a *community-based* tourism project, I was the de facto *baas*. It was not only that people regarded me as a *baas* based on colonial associations and skin colour, it was practically true as well. Despite the bottom-up principles of community-based organisations, external NGOs such as ours often inadvertently create top-down structures because they take many of the decisions relating to the projects they run (cf. Hüncke 2010: 100).

Although there were similarities with *baasskap*, my position at Treesleeper also exhibited essential differences from it. For example, when I spoke to white businesspeople in the area, they tended to be amazed (and occasionally even disgusted) when I said that I lived in Tsintsabis. The boundaries between white farmers and their black workers on the commercial farms were rigid. When I visited a farm in the area – on which another Bushman tourism project (not community-based) was set up – in 2003 with a young Hai//om man, I was not allowed by the white farmer to stay overnight with the Hai//om man's family. The farmer insisted that I sleep in the farmhouse. Later, when I lived on the Tsintsabis resettlement farm 'with the people' this was often regarded as strange. Although I was not engaged in research as such, I consider those years a crucial and meaningful ethnographic experience for my later writings. The experience went far beyond acclimatisation: I became acquainted with a multitude of social and power relations and cultural practices, and learned a language, Afrikaans. Because of this lengthy stay, I experienced the daily realities of the people I lived with, which helped me later when I began 'real' research fieldwork for my PhD.

I lived in the Treesleeper office. I often chatted to the cleaner, a young woman, about Treesleeper and the local dynamics of Tsintsabis. In this way, I easily found out about issues on the farm. These included different perceptions about a failed bakery project, family intrigues, controversial leadership questions and, last, but not least, different opinions in Tsintsabis about Treesleeper. People who visited the young woman while she cleaned added their own stories and perceptions – they might be family members who would help with the cleaning, or neighbouring villagers who just came over for a chat. Treesleeper employees would also visit regularly, and I held many conversations with them. I discussed national politics, local politics, Bushman traditions and strategies for Treesleeper with the camp manager, Moses //Khumûb. Some employees would come over in the evenings to watch soccer on my television. On trips along the dirt road to Tsumeb (about 60 kilometres away), I had lengthy conversations with the villagers to whom I gave lifts. There would be friendly talks, requests for assistance or even malicious gossip. In addition to contacts with local people, I was also connected to the many outsiders that Treesleeper would bring in, such as NGOs, donors, some tourists, volunteers and student researchers.

It was not always easy. An important element of the learning process involved the harsh realities of marginalisation in rural Africa. I was shocked when I heard that a young man had hung himself one night. He was found by my neighbour, who also worked for Treesleeper. I witnessed hunger, unemployment, rape, drunken fights, the beating of women (including a Treesleeper tour-guide student who had to leave the project as a result), illness (I sometimes drove sick people to the clinic), and the spread of HIV/AIDS.

Another difficulty arose from the fact that a Dutch NGO, Kune Zuva, became interested in supporting 'spin-off' projects, often related to Treesleeper. I began to be seen as a cash cow who could be approached for funding for many different projects. I was also asked for managerial and organisational support to start these projects, as the local Bushmen did not consider themselves able to start them. Much of this could be attributed to their inexperience, but it also betrayed a belief in 'white superiority'. Some people even stated directly that it was impossible to start anything without a white man. I had become a key figure on the Tsintsabis resettlement farm, not unlike the *baas* on a commercial farm. When outsiders came to Treesleeper, whether Europeans or local farmers, they usually approached me first. One black farmer from the area even asked if I could send over a few of 'my boys' to his farm so that they could build a beautiful tourist campsite for him as well.

More NGO paternalism

After June 2007, when I left Tsintsabis, the NGO Voluntary Services Overseas supported the project for almost two more years by sending a volunteer. The position of project manager was handed over to the local camp manager //Khumûb. The volunteer's job was to assist him. Although //Khumûb valued what the volunteer brought to the project, he found working with a white (European) man in his fifties challenging. In the rural areas of a country where apartheid's traces are still highly visible, an older white man in a Bushman community is almost automatically considered an authority. Most local people listen to white people more than they do to others. This undermines local leaders. //Khumûb observed to me in 2010 that 'there is lots of involvement of different organisations, and not at the positions that they just advise but they are also directly sometimes involved in management to say things must be done this way and this way'. He believed not enough attention was being given to the communities' feelings and ideas, which fostered top-down development and paternalism. Similarly, in the early and mid-1990s in the Nyae Nyae Conservancy where the Ju/'hoansi Bushmen live, Elizabeth Garland noticed strong paternalist behaviour by many of the white expatriates working for the Nyae Nyae Development Foundation of Namibia. This NGO – also with a strong focus on tourism as an important element of community-based natural resource management – was regarded as 'indigenous' but was 'white-driven' in practice, and some of the expatriates' assumptions were influenced by notions of white superiority. The Bushmen were regarded as not altogether ready for modern life. Agriculture and democracy were considered crucial tools for their economic and political development (Garland 1999: 83–85).

This sort of paternalism was also exhibited in Tsintsabis by the Connected to Namibia Foundation (CTNF), a small Dutch initiative that supported Treesleeper with a financial donation of about €3,000 in 2005. A CTNF member from the Netherlands planned to visit Tsintsabis at a time when I would be absent. //Khumûb and I decided it would be appropriate to take her to the Etosha National Park in the project's car. //Khumûb would be in charge of the trip, but members of camp management would join her on the visit. Upon my return I learned that the woman and the camp management had visited several other tourist places in northern Namibia. //Khumûb explained that the woman had wanted to visit these destinations and said he had not felt comfortable restricting her to visiting Etosha. She was an older, white woman, after all, and a potential donor as well. More members of this same foundation visited Treesleeper in 2011. Although they had had no prior involvement in the project, they reported as follows:

> Our foundation has been *heavily involved* in setting up Treesleeper. Today Treesleeper has become a well-run community campsite and *the foundation can withdraw*. During our short visit last Sunday the future plans of Treesleeper turned out to be highly ambitious. There are big and luxurious lodges and a swimming pool being built at this stage. [...] *The current staff will, regardless of their good intentions, simply not be ready to handle this.* [...] *These people have good intentions, but they do not have what is necessary for this.*
>
> (CTNF 2011, my italics and translation)

This not only demonstrates how organisations can boast about a project in which they have only played a minor role, but it also exhibits a Eurocentric, derogatory and paternalistic attitude towards the project's staff. These people never even spent a night in Tsintsabis. Their attitude, however, is comparable in some ways to my own behaviour as an MA student when I dismissed the idea of building a tourist lodge and argued for a community-based campsite instead. At least, by that time, I had stayed in Tsintsabis and Namibia for a few months.

In general, Bushmen in Tsintsabis show dependency on others (often NGOs) to help them obtain a better future. In their self-perception, they are subordinate to people who position themselves as superior to them (such as white farmers), and they ascribe to whites the ability to solve problems and fulfil their needs (Hüncke 2010: 102–105, cf. Koot 2015). These attitudes are transferred to NGO workers, including myself when I lived in Tsintsabis. The NGO workers unduly influence decisions because of their 'higher education' and 'greater knowledge' of the 'outside world'. Of course, not all NGO fieldworkers are white, and throughout history Bushmen have maintained patron–client relationships with various black groups as well (cf. Wilmsen 1989).

Methodological analysis: open, retrospective, analytic autoethnography in tourism

The question that I wish to raise here concerns the value of my experiences in the field from an autoethnographic point of view. Autoethnography has been heavily dominated by so-called 'evocative or emotional autoethnography' that is distanced from analytic and realist ethnographic traditions. Anderson (2006), though, developed the idea of an 'analytic autoethnography' which rests on three main pillars: the researcher must be a full member of the group or setting that is being studied; s/he should be present in her/his publications; and s/he should work within an analytic research agenda in order to improve theoretical understandings of wider social phenomena (ibid.: 373–375). Whereas the first two pillars do not necessarily distinguish analytic auto-ethnography from the evocative tradition, the third does. While Ellis and Bochner stress that an autoethnographer needs to gaze 'outward on social and cultural aspects of their personal experience' (2000: 739), thereby emphasising the importance of the connection between the researcher's per-sonal experience and a wider, socio-cultural analysis, Anderson claims that evocative autoethnography 'seeks narrative fidelity *only* to the researcher's subjective experience, [while] analytic autoethnography is grounded in self-experience but reaches beyond it as well' (2006: 386, emphasis added). It might, for example, use in-depth interviews and other kinds of data. Ander-son can be understood as emphasising the possibilities of a mature auto-ethnographic methodology, one which can provide for realist ethnographies that take social settings and problems into account. Evocative ethnographers, on the other hand, continue to emphasise 'writing from the heart' since 'we enact the worlds we study' (Denzin 2006: 422–423). I researched and analysed paternalism and tourism as a development strategy in my PhD and later research, although the ideas I developed were strongly influenced by my prior working experience in community-based tourism at Treesleeper. My research was analytic insofar as it embedded paternalism in a wider historical and political economic context. I gathered new data as well, along with an MA student (Hüncke 2010), and conducted three more in-depth interviews during my fieldwork in 2010. However, the core findings that formed the basis of the PhD were derived from a retrospective analysis rather than from an 'analytic agenda' (Anderson 2006: 386–388). I had no research agenda when I worked as a development fieldworker in tourism. In that sense, these experiences were completely 'open'.

Memories, unawareness and power

The fact that my research was based on prior experience of working as a development fieldworker (functioning as a community member in some ways while remaining an outsider in others) gave it three important characteristics. First, my writing was based on memory. A PhD student, Sylvia Smith, once wondered when embarking on an autoethnography: 'I haven't been keeping notes or anything. [...] Where would I start?' (cited in Ellis and Bochner 2000: 750). This question acknowledges the complexities of a retrospective approach. It is perhaps inevitable, therefore, that my current perspectives have influenced my memory. Thoughts and feelings appear, disappear and reappear, and not necessarily in a chronological or linear way (Ellis and Bochner 2000: 751–752). Arguably, the analytic process that went into my PhD retrospectively changed my experience of working in tourism in Tsintsabis. When I started my PhD I was still working at a Dutch NGO, which changed my views about development and paternalism, not least because of the visibility of the power relations that prevailed between myself and my colleagues on the one hand, and the people among whom we worked on the other. Retrospective autoethnography is inevitably clouded. The least one can do is acknowledge this – something I neglected to do in my PhD dissertation (see Koot 2013: 309–311; cf. Hunt and Ruiz Junco 2006: 371). The past, it is worth emphasising, is 'a social construct that only emerges referentially and selectively, inevitably formed and transformed by means of re-experience and interpretation' (Argenti and Röschenthaler 2006: 33), in which 'memory allows us to structure the past in relation to the present' (ibid.).

Second, the fact that I was unaware that I was 'doing research' while living in Tsintsabis proved epistemologically valuable and ethically problematic. In relation to the latter, my unawareness automatically creates an unawareness on the part of the research subjects as well. Therefore there has been no possibility to build up informed consent (cf. Tolich 2010). Epistemologically, the knowledge generated through the manifold experiences of everyday life is very different from that gained from a specific research perspective. Working in the community meant that I held an important social position, one that was very different from that of researcher. My experiences of the community were very broad. I was 'open' to reality as I encountered it, working on a tourism project together with the people. Although in autoethnographic contexts social scientists are usually members of the group being studied, they also identify as researchers. These multiple foci set them apart from their subjects (Anderson 2006: 380). I stood outside the group in Tsintsabis in some ways, but not because I was *a researcher*. I was oblivious of the danger Anderson (2006: 389, italics added) warns researchers against:

> [T]he researcher must exercise extreme caution not to let his or her research focus fade out of *awareness* in the face of other pressing and enticing engagements in the field. Furthermore, the autoethnographer must not allow herself or himself to be drawn into participating heavily in activities in the field at the expense of writing field notes.

In this line, Maréchal insists that the researcher should retain 'a distinct and highly visible identity as *a self-aware scholar* and social actor' (2010: 44, italics added). Such warnings did not apply to my situation. I was able to turn my experience into an interesting ethnographic analysis based on 'openness' and 'broad knowledge', rather than on awareness and field notes. I disagree, therefore, that an ethnographer should not 'participate heavily' in the life of the community and prioritise field notes instead – it is the participation itself that forms the core of the creation of knowledge in the first place. Despite their importance, field notes are secondary; they are a result *of* participation. And, in my case, memories proved more meaningful than field notes. The knowledge I acquired was broader than it would have been if I had followed an analytic agenda. Furthermore, this knowledge proved to be 'fluid in time'; it was influenced and changed by my later experiences. This leads me to the third and final point: power.

Because of the autoethnographer's central position – in the end *her/his* memories are decisive – a situation arises in which the relation between the autoethnographer and the 'other' is always asymmetrical. In my case, I moved from one such asymmetrical, negotiated power relation (development fieldworker in tourism) to another (tourism researcher) (cf. Tomaselli et al. 2013). If I had followed an autoethnographic approach from the outset, with a focus on my own experiences and memories, I might easily have neglected the voices of the Bushmen with whom I lived (cf. Koot 2017b). Nevertheless, using the retrospective autoethnographic approach that I relied on led to different forms of exclusion. The voices of the Bushmen in Tsintsabis who were not part of the Treesleeper tourism project were arguably less 'visible' in my research than those of my former Treesleeper colleagues. Using my experiences as a development fieldworker as the basis of my tourism research has afforded me insights into *baasskap* from an emic point of view – something that is very rare. Despite the limitations of my approach, it has produced important knowledge about social situations that could not have been arrived at in a different way. Such knowledge of people who have worked in (sustainable) tourism can be crucial to bridge the gap that, according to Noel Salazar (2017), so often exists between (critical) tourism studies on the one hand, in which tourism itself is analysed, and the practitioners' side on the other, in which tourism management strategies are being developed to make tourism work. In addition, I argue that such knowledge is equally crucial to bridge the gap between ethnographers and development workers.

Conclusion

While engaging in development work in community-based tourism among the Hai//om in Tsintsabis, Namibia, I learned that paternalism is a widespread phenomenon among them, resulting from (often unconscious) assumptions about white superiority. There is a tendency among outside experts (young or old, male or female) to disregard local knowledge and systems, and assume a position of authority. The process is also supported 'from below': many Bushmen allow whites to do this.

This analysis of NGO paternalism towards Bushmen would not have been possible without my working experience as a development fieldworker, which gave me an 'overwhelming advantage of allowing me to be the closest I could come to studying tourism from an ethnographic perspective' (Bruner 2005: 2). I experienced working in community-based tourism both as a community member and as an outsider. I was in a position of power in the community. Even after I had become a 'real' self-aware researcher, using autoethnography, I acted from a position of power. Memory, unawareness and power are important issues in autoethnography, and various scholars (e.g., Anderson 2006; Maréchal 2010) argue that one should stay aware of one's position as a researcher in autoethnography, but this raises the question of what to do when this is impossible. In this chapter, I have shown that the value of experiences of power based on memories lies in the fact that they can create ethnographically enriching insights. Hopefully, many more retrospective analytic autoethnographies will appear in the future.

Notes

1 An earlier version of this chapter appeared in 2016 as 'Perpetuating power through autoethnography: my research unawareness and memories of paternalism among the indigenous Hai//om in Namibia', in *Critical Arts* 30(6): 840–854. See: http://www.tandfonline.com/loi/rcrc20.
2 Resettlement farms have been set up by the Namibian Government after independence (1990) with the aim of redistributing white-owned commercial farms to the benefit of the larger black population as a base to start various development initiatives, mostly agricultural production and social welfare (Gargallo 2010).
3 The various Bushmen groups in southern Africa use 'click sounds' in their different languages. These are written as '//', '/', '!' and '≠'.
4 The term 'Bushmen' is understood by some to be derogatory and/or racist. It was dropped in favour of the term 'San', which itself has a derogatory meaning. People in Tsintsabis themselves mostly prefer 'Bushman'. The continued use of 'San' by some academics seems to further mystify the people who in Namibia are called, by most people, 'Bushmen'. There is no reason to pretend that the change of a term would reduce the invidiousness and racism that exists in the various relationships with other cultures, which is where the terms derive their emotive content (Gordon and Sholto Douglas 2000).

Acknowledgements

I thank Lisa Koot-Gootjes and two anonymous reviewers for their useful comments on an earlier draft of this chapter.

References

Anderson, L. (2006) Analytic autoethnography. *Journal of Contemporary Ethnography*, 35(4): 373–395.
Argenti, N. and Röschenthaler, U. (2006) Introduction – Between Cameroon and Cuba: youth, slave trades and translocal memoryscapes. *Social Anthropology*, 14(1): 33–47.
Bruner, E. (2005) *Culture on Tour: Ethnographies of Travel*. Chicago: University of Chicago Press.

CTNF (2011) Een rustige ochtend, Treesleeper, weer naar de garage, het hostel en Ida. Connected to Namibia Foundation. Available at: http://connected-to-namibia.reism ee.nl/reisverhaal/153413/een-rustige-ochtend-treesleeper-weer-naar-de-garage-he t-hostel-en-ida/ [Accessed 21 January 2014].

Denzin, N. K. (2006) Analytic autoethnography, or déjà vu all over again. *Journal of Contemporary Ethnography*, 35(4): 419–428.

Dyll, L. (2007) In the sun with Silikat. In: K. G. Tomaselli (ed.) *Writing in the San/d: Autoethnography among Indigenous Southern Africans*. Plymouth: AltaMira Press, pp. 117–130.

Dyll, L. (2009) Community development strategies in the Kalahari: an expression of modernization's monologue? In: P. Hottola (ed.) *Tourism Strategies and Local Responses in Southern Africa*. Wallingford: CAB International, pp. 41–60.

Ellis, C. S. and Bochner, A. (2000) Autoethnography, personal narrative, reflexivity: researcher as subject. In N. Denzin and Y. Lincoln (eds) *Handbook of Qualitative Research*, 2nd edn London: Sage, pp. 733–768.

Gargallo, E. (2010) Serving production, welfare or neither? An analysis of the group resettlement projects in the Namibian land reform. *Journal of Namibian Studies*, 7: 29–54.

Garland, E. (1999) Developing Bushmen: building civil(ized) society in the Kalahari and beyond. In: J. L. Comaroff and J. Comaroff (eds) *Civil Society and the Political Imagination in Africa: Critical Perspectives*. Chicago: University of Chicago Press, pp. 72–103.

Giampiccoli, A. and Nauright, J. (2010) Problems and prospects for community-based tourismin the new South Africa: the 2010 FIFA World Cup and beyond. *African Historical Review*, 42(1): 42–62.

Gibbon, P., Daviron, B. and Barral, S. (2014) Lineages of paternalism: an introduction. *Journal of Agrarian Change*, 14(2): 165–189.

Gordon, R. J. (1997) *Picturing Bushmen: The Denver African Expedition of 1925*. Claremont: David Philip.

Gordon, R. J. and Douglas, S. S. (2000) *The Bushman myth: the making of a Namibian underclass*. Boulder: Westview Press.

Hohmann, T. (2003) 'We are looking for life. We are looking for the conservancy.' Namibian conservancies, nature conservation and rural development: the N≠a-Jaqna Conservancy. In: T. Hohmann (ed.) *San and the state: Contesting Land, Development, Identity and Representation*. Köln: Rüdiger Köppe Verlag, pp., 205–254.

Hüncke, A. (2010) Treesleeper Camp: impacts on community perception and on image creation of Bushmen. MA thesis, African Studies Centre, Leiden.

Hüncke, A. and Koot, S. (2012) The presentation of Bushmen in cultural tourism: tourists' images of Bushmen and the tourism provider's presentation of (Hai//om) Bushmen at Treesleeper Camp, Namibia. *Critical Arts*, 26(5): 671–689.

Hunt, S. A. and Ruiz Junco, N. (2006) Introduction to two thematical issues: defective memory and analytical autoethnography. *Journal of Contemporary Ethnography*, 35 (4): 371–372.

Koot, S. (2002) Sketches of Tsintsabis. Unpublished manuscript.

Koot, S. (2012) Treesleeper Camp: a case study of a community tourism project in Tsintsabis, Namibia. In: W. E. A. van Beek and A. Schmidt (eds) *African Hosts and their Guests: Cultural Dynamics of Tourism*. Woodbridge: James Currey, pp. 153–175.

Koot, S. (2013) Dwelling in tourism: power and myth amongst Bushmen in southern Africa. PhD thesis, African Studies Centre, Leiden.

Koot, S. (2015) White Namibians in tourism and the politics of belonging through Bushmen. *Anthropology Southern Africa*, 38(1/2): 4–15.

Koot, S. (2016) Contradictions of capitalism in the South African Kalahari: Indigenous Bushmen, their brand and *baasskap* in tourism. *Journal of Sustainable Tourism*, 24(8/9): 1211–1226.

Koot, S. (2017a) Ecotourism as an indigenous modernity: Namibian Bushmen and two contradictions of capitalism. In: H. Kopnina and E. Shoreman-Ouimet (eds) *Routledge International Handbook of Environmental Anthropology*. London: Routledge.

Koot, S. (2017b) Poor picking: a response to Keyan Tomaselli and a plea for critical research in neoliberal times. *Journal of Sustainable Tourism*, 25(8): 1197–1200.

Maréchal, G. (2010) Autoethnography. In: A. J. Mills, G. Durepos and E. Wiebe (eds) *Encyclopedia of Case Study Research 2*. London: Sage, pp. 44–47.

Pirsig, R. (1991) *Lila: An Inquiry into Morals*. London: Bantam Press.

Plotkin, H. C. (2002) *The Imagined World Made Real: Towards a Natural Science of Culture*. London: Rutgers University Press.

Rousset, K. (2003) To be Khwe means to suffer: local dynamics, imbalances and contestations in the Caprivi Game Park. MA thesis, University of Cape Town.

Rutherford, B. A. (2001) *Working on the Margins: Black Workers, White Farmers in Postcolonial Zimbabwe*. London: Zed Books.

Salazar, N. (2017) The unbearable lightness of tourism … as violence: an afterword. *Journal of Sustainable Tourism*, 25(5): 703–709.

Sylvain, R. (2001) Bushmen, boers and *baasskap*: patriarchy and paternalism on Afrikaner farms in the Omaheke Region, Namibia. *Journal of Southern African Studies*, 27(4): 717–737.

Tolich, M. (2010) A critique of current practice: ten foundational guidelines for autoethnographers. *Qualitative Health Research*, 20(12): 1599–1610.

Tomaselli, K. G. (ed.) (2007) *Writing in the San/d: Autoethnography among Indigenous Southern Africans*. Plymouth: AltaMira Press.

Tomaselli, K. G. (2012a) 'Die geld is op' – storytelling, business and development strategies. In: K. G. Tomaselli (ed.) *Cultural Tourism and Identity: Rethinking Indigeneity*. Leiden: Brill, pp. 1–15

Tomaselli, K. G. (ed.) (2012b) *Cultural Tourism and Identity: Rethinking Indigeneity*. Leiden: Brill.

Tomaselli, K. G. (2017) Picking on the poor: the contradictions of theory and neoliberal critique. A response to Stasja Koot's paper on the contradictions of capitalism for indigenous tourism in the South African Kalahari. *Journal of Sustainable Tourism*, 25 (8): 1182–1196.

Tomaselli, K. G., Dyll-Myklebust, L. and Van Grootheest, S. (2013) Personal and political interventions via autoethnography: dualisms, knowledge, power and performativity in research relations. In: S. Holman Jones, T. E. Adams and C. Ellis (eds) *Handbook of Autoethnography*. Walnut Creek: Left Coast Press, pp. 576–594.

Troost, D. (2007) Community-based tourism in Tsintsabis: changing cultures in Namibia. BA thesis, Inholland University, Haarlem.

Van Beek, W. E. A. (2011) Cultural models of power in Africa. In: J. Abbink and M. de Bruijn (eds) *Land, Law and Politics in Africa: Mediating Conflict and Reshaping the State*. Leiden: Brill, pp. 25–48.

Wilmsen, E. N. 1989. *Land Filled with Flies: A Political Economy of the Kalahari*. Chicago: University of Chicago Press.

5 'Crafting an entrance'

Gender's role in gaining and maintaining access in tourism ethnography and knowledge creation

Fiona Eva Bakas

Introduction

Qualitative research in the study of tourism is rapidly gaining acceptance as a valid research method, with progressively more articles using qualitative methods being published over the past few years (Wilson and Hollinshead 2015). Consequently, there is a growing interest in the intricacies of how knowledge is produced through qualitative methods, such as ethnography. This chapter explores tourism ethnography intricacies by drawing on observations, experiences, feelings and fieldnotes collected whilst completing ethnographic fieldwork on 'The relationship between female tourism handicraft entrepreneurship and gender roles and relations in Greece'.

The current conception of gaining and maintaining access in ethnographic research is that this is the process by which researchers gather data via interpersonal relationships with participants. Gaining access to research participants is far from being an organised and neat process, with gender playing a significant role in how participants act within and contribute to tourism ethnographies. Much past literature has presented research practice as an idealised, sterile and systematised process (Harrington 2003). More recent research has expanded understandings of the process of doing social research, by exploring the complex ways in which research experiences and methodological issues inform research findings (Cunliffe and Karunanayake 2013).

Methodological approaches addressing the process of gaining access to research populations remains under-theorised and continues to be informed by a model that reduces participants to an instrument in the field, and gaining access to them as something that occurs naturally (Crowhurst 2013). Whilst developing links with participants has been explored in the context of data collection within precarious, dangerous or delicate situations, for example within prisons (Drake and Harvey 2014) or drug user communities (McNeil et al. 2015), less has been written on the complexities of approaching informants within tourism settings.

Engaging with the people who work in tourism, in ethnographic work, can be challenging since tourism labour tends to be seasonal and intensive, with many tourism businesses open 24 hours a day, seven days a week. Looking at tourism handicraft entrepreneurs in rural Greece as a case study (Bakas 2014), one of the main barriers in gaining admission to tourism entrepreneurs is related to time use, as during peak season they are constantly interacting with clients or engaged in making the handicrafts they sell, often on 12-hour shifts. During the off-season the tourism handicraft shops are closed and entrepreneurs are hard to locate.

Literature review

One of the longstanding concerns regarding ethnography is researchers' anxiety associated with gaining and maintaining access to participants. Another concern is the apparent dissonance between tourism ethnography research and the state of the art of current anthropological progress. For example, there seems to be a failure within tourism research to mirror the move towards interpretive/critical anthropology approaches and depart from methodologies that 'seem to celebrate myopic and introverted impressionist ethnographies' (O'Gorman et al. 2014: 55). Analysing the ways in which gender influences tourism ethnography is a means of progressing tourism ethnography knowledge using a critical approach.

Tourism ethnography and gaining access

Arguably, access into social settings is one of the most difficult and important stages of ethnography (Bryman 2004). Bearing in mind that access is an emergent process dependent on the characteristics of the researcher, the participants and the research context, a definition of gaining access will be attempted (Carey et al. 2001). Past studies have made various attempts to classify and define 'gaining access' to research participants, such as Buchanan et al. (2013), who propose a four-stage model of 'getting in, getting on, getting out and getting back'. The stages investigated in this chapter relate to the first two: getting in (gaining access) and getting on (maintaining access). Gummesson (2000) identifies three types of access: *physical* access meaning the ability to get close to the object of study; *continued* access, which refers to maintaining ongoing physical access to the object of research; and *mental* access, which means being able to understand what is going on in the investigation settings.

Hurdles related to gaining access to research participants are often neglected within the area of tourism, as most scholars do not disseminate the intricacies of how qualitative data were collected (Okumus et al. 2007). Gaining access is rarely straightforward. Researchers are de facto in weak bargaining positions when seeking access, as their main bargaining resources are appeals to progress tourism theory (Chege 2014). The complication of offering more to participants in exchange for their time has its risks. An example is an ethnographer who turned into an activist to help her participants in Guatemala and then suffered severe PTSD symptoms on her return home (Warden 2013).

Whilst there is a lack of consensus in the literature about how appropriate it is to pay incentives, offering monetary resources in exchange for participants' time is ethically debatable. Since participation should be voluntary, if people participate just for money, which they need, then it is no longer considered a voluntary act (Sieber and Tolich 2013; Webster et al. 2013).

Adding to this, the tourism industry has certain characteristics that make the task of gaining and maintaining access more complex. These characteristics include the interdependence of different sectors, the often small scale of operators, fragmentation of the market, spatial separation of origins and destinations, seasonal visitation patterns and the intensity of the working day and week (Costa et al. 2013).

Tourism work is very demanding in terms of time, hence engaging in participant observation is difficult as tourism workers may feel 'too busy' to participate. Recent research finds that the subjective experience of busyness – feeling too busy – has a significant effect on participation in research (Vercruyssen et al. 2014). The main reason for reduced participation in research is due to work–family conflict and time pressure (Vercruyssen et al. 2011). Since work–family conflict is highly gendered, with female workers experiencing this pressure to a much greater extent than male workers, it is significant to look at the ways in which gender roles influence gaining and maintaining access to ethnographic participants. This chapter focuses on the issues related to gaining and maintaining *continued* access to research participants in a tourism ethnographic setting, or what Buchanan et al. (2013) refer to as 'getting on' with conducting research.

Gender in tourism labour

'Gender' is not something that someone *is* or something that a person *has*; it is the mechanism by which notions of what constitutes masculine and feminine are produced and normalised (Hughes 2002). Gender is a form of social power, and can be considered society's 'most pervasive organizing principle' (Ahl and Nelson 2010: 7). Gender *roles* involve behaviours that are repeated over time, thus becoming internalised as a natural way of being (Beauvoir et al. 2000). Butler highlights the importance of culture in gender role construction by stressing that 'not biology, but culture becomes destiny' (1999: 8). So it can be argued that gender should be viewed as a 'result of upbringing and social interaction' (Ahl 2006: 597) rather than as a 'synonym for women' (Peterson 2005: 500). According to a recent report, travel and tourism grew by 3.3% in 2016, generating US$7.6 trillion worldwide, which is 10.2% of global GDP when the direct, indirect and induced impacts are taken into account (WTTC 2017). According to the report, the tourism industry supported a total of 292 million jobs in 2016, that is, one in ten of all jobs globally.

The role gender plays within tourism is of special interest, as women are often encouraged to enter tourism employment due to its flexibility and its 'suitability' for women to engage in these activities without challenging gender norms regarding women's roles as home-based carers. An example is engagement in the production of handicrafts to sell in the tourist-souvenir market, as in the cases of Mexican weavers (Cohen 2001) and Mayan crafts-women (Cone 1995). As these craftswomen are able to work on their crafts at home, they are perceived as being able to combine this activity with childcare and thus to adhere to feminine subjectivities connected to care.

An increasing number of academics have dealt with the significance of gender roles in tourism since Swain's (1995) and Kinnaird and Hall's (1994) research on the subject. More recently, Aitchison (2009), Pritchard (2014), Ateljevic (2009), Tucker and Boonabaana (2011) and Figueroa-Domecq (2015) are examples of academics who have critically appraised the role of gender within tourism research. One of the criticisms Swain (1995) makes about previous attempts to include gender in tourism analyses is that by failing to define gender, they have failed to show how 'interlocking dimensions of gender'(ibid.: 251) operate within tourism. The cultural context within which the gender roles are observed constitutes one of these dimensions. The following section offers a critical description of the gender roles in the case study area that is the focus of this chapter.

Gender roles that connect femininity to being constantly active

In Greece, despite a General Secretariat of Gender Equality being established in the 1980s, within academia feminism as a theory had rather negative connotations, with no funding being given for university gender and equality projects until 2000 when the European Union (EU) started supporting research proposals with a feminist focus (Vaiou 2008). Perhaps as a result of limited feminist research that uses gender as an analytical category, an EU report into gender equality policies in Greece found that gender stereotypes are seldom questioned and that gender is referred to in its social sense, implying the existence of 'a strong biological component' (Pantelidou Maloutas et al. 2008: 25).

For Greek rural women, the Orthodox Church has been a controlling element, determining the 'correct' way that a woman should act. The 'correct' way includes being subservient to her husband, being humble and modest, staying within the household boundaries and being chaste (Du Boulay 1986). Womanhood in Greece involves completing 'nurturing, cooking, cleaning' tasks; women are not supposed to have idle hours and are meant to appear constantly busy (Lazaridis 2009: 56). This also highlights how women's time is devalued, as 'sitting idle' is related to power since it is a male prerogative (Herzfeld 1991).

Ferguson reports on the increasing significance of time pressures to the female tourism workers in her study, who ask for help from 'their male partners, children and other family members in order to keep the household running' (2010: 871) as their time is limited since becoming involved in tourism work. Globally, time-use studies are used to measure the time spent doing unpaid household tasks and as an indicator of gender equality (UNRISD 2010). Time-use studies indicate both the need for a value to be put on time spent completing household tasks, and how time use is gendered, as women complete double the share of household tasks. On average in OECD countries, men complete 137 minutes of housework per day compared with women's 271 minutes per day (OECD n.d.). Indeed, women are most likely to suffer from 'time poverty', which is defined as the lack of time to rest after working (Bardasi and Wodon 2010). Both these observations illustrate how gender roles connected to femininity may influence tourism workers' perceptions of time and suggest that this could also influence the ability of female tourism workers to participate in ethnographic studies.

Methods

Feminism is particularly suited to this study as it critiques existing structures with the aim of bringing to the fore women's experiences and perspectives that have been ignored by traditional research (Alvesson and Skoldberg 2009). This study illuminates the experience of a female researcher completing research in a patriarchal context and female participants' experiences.

The epistemology behind this research is postmodern in nature, and I accept that reality is socially constructed. The research is situated within an interpretivist paradigm that entails an ontology in which social reality is regarded as the product of processes by which social actors negotiate the meanings for actions and situations (Munkvold and Bygstad 2016). Interpretivist approaches are more relevant for mapping contesting and changeable realities of mixed social and mixed cultural settings that characterise tourism encounters (Hollinshead 2006). The 'truth' was hence co-constructed with participants, at the same time accepting that there is no universal truth, but rather there are context-bound, non-generalisable truths (Tribe 2006). The methodological framework of this study was influenced by a feminist theoretical perspective (Pillow and Mayo 2004). Hence the study aims to be attentive to issues of difference, question social power, work towards social justice, and create knowledge that is ultimately, if not directly, of benefit to women. The research question that guides the present study is: 'How do gender roles influence gaining and maintaining access to tourism ethnography participants and subsequent knowledge production within the Greek context?' In order to answer this question, a particular ethnographic experience is drawn upon.

The research presented in this chapter is part of a larger study on the relationship of social reproductive gender roles and tourism handicraft entrepreneurship roles, which was conducted in Rethymno, Crete and Metsovo, Epirus in Greece as part of my PhD fieldwork in 2012. Crete is Greece's largest island and is renowned for its sea-and-sun international tourism, beautiful beaches, natural beauty and Minoan civilisation.

The study had 13 female ethnographic participants and took place during June 2012 to January 2013. Whilst I met many potential participants, only about half of the total of potential participants approached eventually participated. The present study is based on observations of the female handicraft tourism entrepreneurs who participated in the study, and of some female handicraft tourism entrepreneurs who did not choose to contribute. Four bios of women who participated are presented to give an idea of the participants' backgrounds.

Rethymno is the third-largest seaside city in Crete, and has high tourist visitation rates during May–October. Rethymno still bears the remnants of Venetian influences, such as *Fortezza*, an imposing Venetian castle, and also Turkish influences in the form of minarets. Most locally made tourist souvenirs are fabric-art, olive tree wood sculptures, pottery or stone carvings.

Bio 1 – Ioanna, migrant tourism handicraft entrepreneur, Rethymno, Crete

Ioanna is a 45-year-old immigrant from Albania, trained as a primary school teacher, who now has a shop selling embroidered fabrics and crocheted items in Rethymno's Old Town area, which is the busiest part of the town. She only opens the shop during the tourist season, which runs from May until October. Often working 12–14-hour days, six days a week (on Sundays she takes the afternoons off), Ioanna particularly looks forward to the winter season when everything returns '*to normal*', as she says, and she will be able to invite people for dinner, cook, and help her daughter with her homework. Ioanna crochets many of the items that she sells.

About 30 minutes' drive from Rethymno, in the mountains, lies a small village called Margarites, which is full of potters who make and sell their art to passing tourists.

Bio 2 – Katerina, potter in Margarites village, Crete

Katerina is 40 years old and comes from a family of potters. She has been potting since she was six years old. In 2010 she finally managed to convert the old family home into a studio and shop using EU LEADER funds. She has two teenage daughters who also help in the business, taking over from her at midday and doing household work during the summer. Katerina regularly goes to church, hence the teachings of Greek Orthodox religion are quite prominent in her life, influencing her perceptions of what is 'correct'. Consequently, she adheres to quite strict gender roles regarding household duties, and laughs when I ask if her husband helps her with these.

Metsovo is a secluded town perched in the mountains of northwest Greece, which is home to a large number of 'Vlachs', an Eastern Romance-speaking minority who are traditionally shepherds. It attracts many domestic tourists all year round because of its natural beauty, lavishly decorated monasteries and renowned rural-inspired cuisine.

Bio 3 – Annetta, weaver and tourism entrepreneur, Metsovo, Epirus

Annetta is a 60-year-old weaver who supplies her goods to the tourism market through her rooms-to-rent business and her brother's souvenir shop. She is part of a large family active in the tourism industry in Metsovo. Annetta represents a very traditional type of rural woman who is very close to the church and believes women's primary responsibility is towards the family. This was practically indicated to me as she was responsible for all household tasks, and indeed even wiped her husband's moustache after eating. Annetta was constantly busy with her hands, knitting or cooking, each time I visited her.

Bio 4 – Mrs E, elderly female crocheter, Rethymno, Crete

Mrs E is an 80-year-old woman who crochets using a traditional Cretan method called *saita* and owns a shop on a street in Rethymno where high numbers of tourists pass. An ex-home education teacher for many years, Mrs E represents the older generation of women in Greece with regards to gender roles. She believes that women work to the detriment of the family, and that certain tasks, such as embroidery, should not be carried out by men. Her insistence that I should get married, on every occasion that I visited, is indicative of her perception of what a 'correct' woman should do, and reveals how caring is connected to femininity, as marriage is seen as essential to being female.

My visits to participants were on a weekly basis and I spent 2–3 hours with them depending on the circumstances. For example, sometimes the participants invited me for lunch or social outings, in which case I spent more time with them.

Participants in this study own and operate their own businesses and make their own handicrafts as souvenirs for tourists. When selecting the ethnographic sites, one of the essential characteristics of these sites was for me to have a 'gatekeeper' there. The gatekeepers in this study consisted of one of my high-school friends who used to be a female tourism entrepreneur in Rethymno, and a friend's parents who were medical academics in Epirus. My gatekeepers, were not 'formal' gatekeepers in the sense of allowing me to access participants who I would have not been able to otherwise, as for example in the case of accessing sex offenders at a probation centre (Reeves 2010), but they were significant in helping me 'ease' into the research setting. I found that having a gatekeeper was significant in more practical terms, such as providing me with temporary housing and emotional support after landing in a relatively unknown area with few social acquaintances (Schensul and LeCompte 2012).

Whilst issues of gaining access within ethnography often use gatekeepers as their primary object of study and reference, in this study I focus more on the gendered issues associated with gaining entry into *participants'* lives and maintaining the participant–researcher relationship. More specifically, this chapter focuses on how gender roles influence *gaining* access to potential ethnographic participants; and how gender roles influence the ethnographic methods needed in order to *maintain* access within a tourism setting.

Thematic analysis of fieldnotes and interview transcripts informs this study. Analysis was conducted by re-listening to participants' interviews, partially transcribing them, translating them and typing up handwritten fieldnotes. Choosing to handwrite fieldnotes and then type them up was a conscious decision as I wanted to re-live the notes by transforming them into a written form of narrative, and thus have the nuances of experiential knowledge constructed in the field, fresh in my mind. In addition to typing up the fieldnotes, I also made notes in the margins, thus partially analysing the fieldnotes in terms of content related to the research question. Recollections of ethnographic moments enrich this study's thematic analysis.

Findings

Practicalities of gaining access to complete tourism ethnography

Gaining access to visit the participants frequently was initially difficult, not only because tourism handicraft entrepreneurs were busy and I was visiting their workplace, but also because the majority were completely unfamiliar with this type of method. This was partly because I was utilising non-conventional forms of investigation (in the eyes of participants, questionnaires were considered the most conventional method of research), such as ethnography and participant observation. An example of this is the instance when one silversmith in Epirus told me explicitly not to approach the silversmiths at the KEPAVI (Centre for Traditional Entrepreneurs in Ioannina) with the method of participant observation. He advised me to give them a questionnaire instead, as he said they '*are not very open-minded and may be suspicious of your motives*' (interview, Alexandros, male silversmith in Epirus). Despite the rise in use of experimental methods in tourism and hospitality, there is limited literature on how unfamiliarity with these methods influences participation and subsequent knowledge production (Fong et al. 2016).

To overcome the problem of gaining access, due to potential participants' unfamiliarity with the methods used, I devised an introductory ethnographic interview. Since interviews are a known and accepted method of doing research, this method allowed me to overcome the first hurdle of gaining access to participants. This initial interview also allowed respondents to relax somewhat as they realised that '*there is nothing they cannot answer*' (fieldnotes, Annetta, 18/10). The use of interviews in this manner was necessary to 'validate' participant observation as a research method and to avoid jeopardising the whole research project. It also illustrates the importance of maintaining flexibility when carrying out research projects (McCormack et al. 2013).

At the end of the first interview, participants were asked if they would like to continue meeting with me on a weekly basis. However, from the initial interviews it was apparent that many participants were uncomfortable with the idea of me just visiting and spending time with them, especially female participants. As I write in my fieldnotes: '*It is difficult to explain my participant observation role – very difficult especially when people are used to questionnaires/interviews and not long-term research*' (fieldnotes, Frosso, 24/07).

Gender's role in gaining access techniques used in tourism ethnography

The first ethnographic moment that illustrates how gender roles influence gaining access to potential participants is set in Rethymno, Crete. A young female handicraft entrepreneur, HarJew, who made delicate silver and semi-precious stone jewellery and owned a shop on a busy tourist street in Rethymno, was initially keen to participate in the study and after the first interview arranged a date for me to visit her again. However, when I went to visit, her husband was at the shop in her place and on subsequent occasions that I passed by the shop to see if she was there, she was rarely present. Once, when I came across her in her shop, she told me that she had been caring for their one-year-old son more intensively and thus was not able to come to the shop as much as she wanted. This is an example of how gender roles, which connect femininity to primary responsibility for caring, can influence tourism entrepreneurs' ability to participate in ethnography. Consequent knowledge production is also influenced, since these female tourism workers' voices are effectively absent.

Another instance when gaining access to ethnographic participants was influenced by gender roles took place in Metsovo, Epirus. Here, I was looking forward to interacting with women who work in tourism in a secluded rural area. People in Metsovo operate under gender roles that connect femininity with being subject to their husbands' jurisdiction. This, however, meant that to interview any women there, I needed to ask the permission of their husbands. As I write in my fieldnotes: '*Annetta said that we would have to ask the women's husbands "license" in order for them to participate in the survey!*' (fieldnotes, Annetta, 10/10). Participant observation requires multiple visits and I was not convinced that sitting and talking to the women under the watchful eye of their husbands would create valid knowledge. I felt that participants would be constantly monitored by their husbands, and open relationships of trust between researcher and researched would have been hard to form. Hence, I desisted from engaging in participant observation in Metsovo, apart from with Annetta who had been introduced to me by my gatekeepers and was 'allowed' to participate. Once more, gender roles influenced how access was gained and the knowledge that was created.

As well as making it impossible to gain access to some female tourism entrepreneurs, gender roles also influenced the techniques used to successfully gain access. I found that participating by learning or helping gave me an excuse to be present at female participants' workplaces as a researcher, even though my research method was not fully understood. The effectiveness of this technique for gaining access is recorded in the fieldnotes: '*She [Mrs E] is keen to teach me how to make things using a "saita". So a perfect excuse for hanging around*' (fieldnotes, Mrs E, 08/06). A *saita* is a Cretan plastic instrument for crocheting, whereon a thin thread is wound and then used, together with thumbs and fingers, to make multiple knots and hoops that form delicate lacy circles and flowers. Although gaining access in this way can be a particularly effective method to also maintain access on a long-term basis, it is not always easy to be accepted by participants as it means them investing time in training you. About this, I wrote: '*Such a good way of meeting a person – helping in the studio – but not easy to be done/accepted by the artist*' (fieldnotes, Frosso, 28/08). Indeed, since I experienced a 50% failure rate in accessing participants, gaining access was a cause for celebration, as I recorded in the fieldnotes:

> *Frosso said that I could come on Tuesdays and help – yey! It is the best thing as when I went there she was asking if I needed anymore interview questions and I could tell that it would be uncomfortable just to sit there* (fieldnotes, Frosso, 24/07).

I found that allowing participants to continue adhering to gender roles connecting femininity to 'being constantly busy' by helping them create their handicrafts offered an excellent opportunity to investigate the larger study's questions. In addition, I observed that the time spent co-creating handicrafts with female participants was when they seemed to relax and open up, making the process of co-constructing valid knowledge more efficient. As I write in my fieldnotes: '*Now I understand why the women crochet together and chat. Indeed living and experiencing something together gives you a different level of insight into their lives*' (fieldnotes, 04/07).

Getting over the initial barrier of gaining access to participants then brought on the second hurdle, that of maintaining access to participants. This was one of my greatest worries, which I express in the fieldnotes by wondering how I could maintain access after Mrs E had taught me how to crochet using the *saita*. I wrote: '*What will I do when I have learnt? What will be my excuse for passing by?*' (fieldnotes, Mrs E, 27/06).

Maintaining access in tourism ethnography and 'being constantly active' feminine gender roles

As I found out during the fieldwork, maintaining access within ethnography is not a one-off event, but a continuous push and pull, and therefore part of an ongoing process to be revisited every day over the course of the fieldwork (Reeves 2010). Maintaining access to participants cannot be negotiated on a single occasion; it requires continued negotiation and renegotiation (Siwale 2015). One of the factors influencing this process of renegotiating access is gender roles. Since tourism micro-entrepreneurship is characterised by long working days, it is particularly pertinent to analyse how gender roles influencing how female tourism entrepreneurs spend their time may affect the researcher's ability to maintain access. I found that participants worked so many hours during the tourist season that they felt exhausted, mostly because they were a one-woman business with no-one to replace them. For example, Ioanna said she was *'feeling exhausted from being at the shop for 12–13 hours flat every day'* (interview, Ioanna).

Past literature has identified the existence of gender roles linking femininity to being constantly active in Greece (Lazaridis, 2009). According to this research, being constantly busy is what a 'correct' woman should do; not doing so, for example sitting and chatting to a researcher, can be harmful to their reputation. In the field, I found that for the female tourism entrepreneur-participants, sitting and chatting with someone on a regular basis was awkward for them. This literature and my experience in the field led me to investigate how these gender roles can influence a researcher's ability to maintain access to female participants.

The existence of these 'constantly active' feminine gender roles is illustrated by various ethnographic moments. Mrs E shows that there is an element of intergenerational acculturation of gender roles connecting being constantly busy to femininity. I wrote: *'She [Mrs E] said that she has been taught to be busy all the time and this is what she is used to.'* (fieldnotes, Mrs E, 17/07). Katerina talks of how she perceives being constantly busy as an internalised 'need', even though she thinks it is a bit of a 'sickness', perhaps illustrating the juxtaposition between past and present gender roles. I wrote: *'She mentioned how she needs to be constantly busy, otherwise she feels she is wasting her time! Even when she comes home from potting and her hands hurt, she will do some crocheting or something to be occupied. She feels it as a bit of a sickness'* (fieldnotes, Katerina, 10/07). Many of the other female participants with whom I spoke also illustrated through their actions, rather than their words, that being constantly busy was important to them. An example of this is how, whenever I visited female participants, they were always busy making their handicrafts if they did not have customers. I wrote: *'When Ioanna was not selling/talking to customers she was sewing curtains'* (fieldnotes, 17/07). All these examples illustrate the link between time use and feminine gender roles.

However, tourism-induced time pressures do mean that gender roles are being negotiated amongst tourism entrepreneurs' families. For example, Mariniki, a female potter in Margarites village, Crete, negotiated for a more equal distribution of household tasks by demanding recognition from her male partner that her time was not 'infinitely elastic' (Young 2003: 113). By doing this she challenges notions of femininity being bound to concepts of a 'correct woman' being constantly busy. Frosso narrates how her family is understanding if she 'neglects' housework, and is not constantly busy, as she says: '*It will be different if I say I am tired, I can't complain, everyone understands. The demands on me are fewer – since I work so many hours, they turn a blind eye to whatever has to do with the house.*' This concept of inaction as active negotiation is significant in the Greek context, where femininity is closely connected to ideals of immaculate housekeeping (Lazaridis 2009) and 'sitting' is considered a masculine prerogative (Herzfeld 1991). This may be indicative of a change in the gender roles connecting femininity to being 'constantly busy', but further research needs to be conducted to ascertain the extent to which this is happening.

Conclusions

This chapter analyses the ways in which gender roles operate within an aspect of tourism methodology on which scarce literature exists: gaining and maintaining access in tourism ethnography. Using an ethnographic investigation on tourism handicraft entrepreneurs in Greece in 2012 as a source of empirical data, the complex role that gender plays within tourism ethnography is explored. More specifically, this chapter investigates how knowledge production within tourism ethnography is influenced by gender roles by analysing how gender roles influence: *gaining* access to potential ethnographic participants; the ethnographic methods needed to *maintain* access within a tourism setting; and, ultimately, knowledge creation within tourism ethnography.

The literature review shows that it is generally accepted that within a feminist framework, gaining and maintaining access is essential for the creation of valid knowledge (O'Reilly, 2012). However, less has been written on the practicalities of creating valid knowledge through a tourism ethnography. There are particular difficulties in engaging the people who work in tourism in ethnographic work, as tourism labour is seasonal and intensive, with many tourism businesses open 24 hours a day, seven days a week. In addition, as a researcher I was de facto in weak bargaining positions when seeking access, as my only bargaining resource was an appeal to progress tourism theory. My 50% failure rate to engage in participant observation with potential participants illustrated this. The reasons why gaining and maintaining access in the study's context was particularly problematic were participants' lack of acceptance of participant observation as a research method; tourism workers' long working hours; and gender roles connecting femininity to appearing constantly busy.

Gender roles are very context-specific, and various ethnographic instances illustrated how femininity is connected to 'being constantly busy' in the Greek context. Situating this study in a global context, time-use studies, which are used as indicators of gender equality, highlight the significance of investigating these time-related gender roles in more depth. Female tourism entrepreneurs felt that sitting and chatting with someone on a regular basis would be harmful to their reputation, as that was not what a 'correct' woman should spend her time doing. These gender roles were transmitted by intergenerational acculturation, as illustrated by Mrs E; but the younger generation seems to be questioning these gender roles, as illustrated by how Katerina calls them 'sick'.

Accepting that the 'truth' is socially constructed via co-constructing knowledge with participants, in this study I found that 'being constantly busy' gender roles influenced the knowledge co-created in a number of ways. Firstly, for some of the female tourism workers, gender roles effectively barred them from participating in the ethnographic study and hence in tourism knowledge construction. This happened in two ways: primary caring responsibilities limited female entrepreneurs' availability to talk; and having to get their husband's permission to participate in the study because of a highly patriarchal mentality made women accountable to their husbands.

The second focus, regarding how the creation of knowledge is influenced by gender roles in this study, relates to the methods used to gain and maintain access. I found that by engaging in handicraft production, I was able to conduct participant observation without disrupting established gender roles. Helping participants to make handicrafts at their workplace was an acceptable occupation for me to engage in whilst talking to the time-poor female tourism entrepreneurs. In addition, the time spent co-creating handicrafts with female participants was when they seemed to relax and open up, increasing the possibilities that the knowledge co-constructed between us was valid within the feminist framework in which I was working. Hence, it can be concluded that using a technique of gaining access that is 'gender-role appropriate' can increase the ability of a researcher to gain and maintain continued access, as well as increase the opportunities to co-construct valid knowledge with participants.

All these instances show how gender operates as a form of social power, organising social structures. Hence this study also helps to make the workings of gender within tourism more visible, contributing in this way to the global movement to increase the visibility of how gender operates within our society. Addressing a gap in the tourism research literature on tourism ethnography, this chapter aims to encourage the inclusion of the state of the art of anthropological progress within tourism research. This is accomplished by investigating the nuances of how gender roles relate to time use, influence gaining and maintaining access to ethnographic subjects, and how they influence subsequent knowledge production.

References

Ahl, H. (2006) Why research on women entrepreneurs needs new directions. *Entrepreneurship: Theory & Practice*, 30(5): 595–621.

Ahl, H. and Nelson, T. (2010) Moving forward: institutional perspectives on gender and entrepreneurship. *International Journal of Gender and Entrepreneurship*, 2: 5–9.

Aitchison, C. (2009) Gender and tourism discourses: advancing the gender project in tourism studies. In T. Jamal and M. Robinson (eds), *The Sage Handbook of Tourism Studies*. Los Angeles and London: Sage.

Alvesson, M. and Skoldberg, K. (2009) *Reflexive Methodology: New Vistas for Qualitative Research*. London: Sage.

Ateljevic, I. (2009) Women empowerment entrepreneurship nexus in tourism: processes of social innovation. In J. Ateljevic and S. J. Page (eds), *Tourism and Entrepreneurship: International Perspectives*. Burlington: Elsevier, pp. 75–90.

Bakas, F. E. (2014) *Tourism, Female Entrepreneurs and Gender: Crafting Economic Realities in Rural Greece*. Dunedin, New Zealand: University of Otago.

Bardasi, E. and Wodon, Q. (2010) Working long hours and having no choice: time poverty in Guinea. *Feminist Economics*, 16: 45–78.

Beauvoir, S. D., Parshley, H. M. and Crosland, M. (2000) *The Second Sex*. London: David Campbell.

Bryman, A. (2004) *Social Research Methods*. Oxford: Oxford University Press.

Buchanan, D., Boddy, D. and McCalman, J. (2013) Getting in, getting on, getting out, and getting back. In: Bryman, A. (ed.), *Doing Research in Organizations (RLE: Organizations)*. Abingdon, UK and New York: Routledge, pp. 63–77.

Butler, J. (1999) *Gender Trouble: Feminism and the Subversion of Identity*. New York: Routledge.

Carey, R. F., McKechnie, L. E. F. and McKenzie, P. J. (2001) Gaining access to everyday life information seeking. *Library & Information Science Research*, 23(4): 319–334.

Chege, N. (2014) 'What's in it for me?': Negotiations of asymmetries, concerns and interests between the researcher and research subjects. *Ethnography*, 16(4): 463–481.

Cohen, J. H. (2001) Textile, tourism and community development. *Annals of Tourism Research*, 28: 378–398.

Cone, C. A. (1995) Crafting selves: the lives of two Mayan women. *Annals of Tourism Research*, 22: 314–327.

Costa, C., Panyik, E. and Buhalis, D. (2013) *Trends in European Tourism Planning and Organisation*, Vol. 60. Bristol: Channel View Publications.

Crowhurst, I. (2013) The fallacy of the instrumental gate? Contextualising the process of gaining access through gatekeepers. *International Journal of Social Research Methodology*, 16(6): 463–475.

Cunliffe, A. L. and Karunanayake, G. (2013) Working within hyphen-spaces in ethnographic research. *Organizational Research Methods*, 16(3): 364–392.

Drake, D. H. and Harvey, J. (2014) Performing the role of ethnographer: processing and managing the emotional dimensions of prison research. *International Journal of Social Research Methodology*, 17(5): 489–501.

Du Boulay, J. (1986) Women – images of their nature and destiny in rural Greece. In: J. Dubisch (ed.), *Gender and Power in Rural Greece*. Princeton, NJ: Princeton University Press.

Ferguson, L. (2010) Tourism development and the restructuring of social reproduction in Central America. *Review of International Political Economy: RIPE*, 17: 860–888.

Figueroa-Domecq, C., Pritchard, A., Segovia-Pérez, M., Morgan, N. and Villacé-Molinero, T. (2015) Tourism gender research: a critical accounting. *Annals of Tourism Research*, 52: 87–103.

Fong, L. H. N., Law, R., Tang, C. M. F. and Yap, M. H. T. (2016) Experimental research in hospitality and tourism: a critical review. *International Journal of Contemporary Hospitality Management*, 28(2): 246–266.

Garthwaite, K. (2016) The perfect fit? Being both volunteer and ethnographer in a UK foodbank. *Journal of Organizational Ethnography*, 5(1): 60–71.

Gummesson, E. (2000) *Qualitative Methods in Management Research*. London: Sage.

Harrington, B. (2003) The social psychology of access in ethnographic research. *Journal of Contemporary Ethnography*, 32(5): 592–625.

Herzfeld, H. (1991) Silence, submission, subversion: toward a poetics of womanhood. In: P. Loizos and E. Papataxiarhis (eds) *Contested Identities: Gender and Kinship in Modern Greece*. Princeton, NJ: Princeton University Press.

Hollinshead, K. (2006) The shift to constructivism in social inquiry: some pointers for tourism studies. *Tourism Recreation Research*, 31(2): 43–58.

Hughes, C. (2002) *Key Concepts in Feminist Theory and Research*. London: Sage.

Kinnaird, V. and Hall, D. R. (1994) *Tourism: A Gender Analysis*. Chichester: Wiley.

Lazaridis, G. (2009) *Women's Work and Lives in Rural Greece: Appearances and Realities*. Farnham: Ashgate Publishing.

McCormack, M., Adams, A. and Andreson, E. (2013) Taking to the streets: the benefits of spontaneous methodological innovation in participant recruitment. *Qualitative Research*, 13: 228–241.

McNeil, R., Kerr, T., Lampkin, H. and Small, W. (2015) 'We need somewhere to smoke crack': an ethnographic study of an unsanctioned safer smoking room in Vancouver, Canada. *International Journal of Drug Policy*, 26(7): 645–652.

Munkvold, B. E. and Bygstad, B. (2016) The Land of Confusion – clearing up some common misunderstandings of interpretive research. Presented at NOKOBIT 2016, Bergen, 28–30 November.

O'Gorman, D., MacLaren, A. C. and Bryce, D. (2014) A call for renewal in tourism ethnographic research: the researcher as both the subject and object of knowledge. *Current Issues in Tourism*, 17(1): 46–59.

O'Reilly, K. (2012) *Ethnographic Methods*. New York: Routledge.

OECD (n.d.) Employment: Time spent in paid and unpaid work, by sex. Paris: Organisation for Economic Co-operation and Development. http://stats.oecd.org/index.aspx?queryid=54757 (accessed 17 November 2017).

Okumus, F., Altinay, L. and Roper, A. (2007) Gaining access for research: reflections from experience. *Annals of Tourism Research*, 34(1): 7–26.

Pantelidou Maloutas, M., Nikolaou, A., Kakepaki, M., Tsinganou, I., Thanopoulou, M. and Maratou Alipranti, L. (2008) *Report analysing intersectionality in gender equality policies for Greece and the EU*. Vienna: Institute for Human Sciences (IWM).

Peterson, S. V. (2005) How (the meaning of) gender matters in political economy. *New Political Economy*, 10: 499–521.

Peticca-Harris, A., deGama, N. and Elias, S. R. S. T. A. (2016) A dynamic process model for finding informants and gaining access in qualitative research. *Organizational Research Methods*, 19(3): 376–401.

Pillow, W. and Mayo, C. (2004) Toward understandings of feminist ethnography. In: S. N. Hesse-Biber and M. L. Yaiser (eds) *Feminist Perspectives on Social Research*. New York: Oxford University Press.

Pritchard, A. (2014) Gender and feminist perspectives in tourism research. In: A. Lew, C. M. Hall and A. M. Williams (eds) *The Wiley Blackwell Companion to Tourism*. Oxford: Wiley Blackwell, pp. 314–324.

Reeves, C. L. (2010) A difficult negotiation: fieldwork relations with gatekeepers. *Qualitative Research*, 10: 315–331.

Schensul, J. J. and LeCompte, M. D. (2012) *Essential Ethnographic Methods*. Walnut Creek: Altamira Press.

Sieber, J. E. and Tolich, M. B. (2013) *Planning Ethically Responsible Research*, Vol. 31. New York: Sage.

Siwale, J. (2015) Why did I not prepare for this? The politics of negotiating fieldwork access, identity, and methodology in researching microfinance institutions. *SAGE Open*, April/June. http://doi.org/10.1177/2158244015587560

Swain, M. B. (1995) Gender in tourism. *Annals of Tourism Research*, 22: 247–266.

Tribe, J. (2006) The truth about tourism. *Annals of Tourism Research*, 33(2): 360–381.

Tucker, H. and Boonabaana, B. (2011) A critical analysis of tourism, gender and poverty reduction. *Journal of Sustainable Tourism*, 20(3): 437–455.

UNRISD (2010) *Time Use Studies and Unpaid Care Work*. New York: Routledge for United Nations Institute for Social Development.

Vaiou, D. (2008) Space for feminism in Greek academe? In: P. Moss and K. F. Al-Hindi (eds) *Feminisms in Geography: Rethinking Space, Place, and Knowledges*. Lanham, MD: Rowman & Littlefield.

Vercruyssen, A., Roose, H. and Van de Putte, B. (2011) Underestimating busyness: Indications of nonresponse bias due to work–family conflict and time pressure. *Social Science Research*, 40(6): 1691–1701.

Vercruyssen, A., Roose, H., Carton, A. and Van de Putte, B. (2014) The effect of busyness on survey participation: being too busy or feeling too busy to cooperate? *International Journal of Social Research Methodology*, 17(4): 357–371.

Warden, T. (2013) Feet of clay: confronting emotional challenges in ethnographic experience. *Journal of Organizational Ethnography*, 2(2): 150–172.

Webster, S., Lewis, J. and Brown, A. (2013) Ethical considerations in qualitative research. In: J. Ritchie, J. Lewis, C. McNaughton Nicholls and R. Ormston (eds) *Qualitative Research Practice: A Guide for Social Science Students and Researchers*, 2nd edn. Los Angeles: Sage, pp. 77–110.

Wilson, E. and Hollinshead, K. (2015) Qualitative tourism research: opportunities in the emergent soft sciences. *Annals of Tourism Research*, 54: 30–47.

WTTC (2017) *Travel & Tourism Global Economic Impact & Issues 2017*. London: World Travel & Tourism Council. https://www.wttc.org/-/media/6204f042e20f4792a dc325e60ab72454.ashx

Young, B. (2003) Financial crises and social reproduction: Asia, Argentina and Brazil. In I. Bakker and S. Gill (eds) *Power, Production, and Social Reproduction: Human In/Security in the Global Political Economy*. New York: Palgrave Macmillan.

6 The permanent and the ephemeral in tourism fieldwork[1]

Filipa Fernandes and Francisco Martins Ramos†

Introduction

Having in mind that immersion and presence are archetypes for anthropological fieldwork (Amit 2000), this chapter explores the multiple relationships, journeys and difficulties of gathering data in the field of tourism in a range of different settings and from the perspectives of two anthropologists. Despite reflection on the production of knowledge through fieldwork in tourism studies, only a few researchers have approached the difficulties of collecting data and the ethical/personal issues raised by this process. This chapter explores the authors' own experiences in Portugal (the Atlantic island of Madeira, and Monsaraz in the Portuguese region of Alentejo on the border with Spain), and in Angola, on the west coast of central Africa, with particular reference to the unusual situation that working in a tourism setting presents – of interacting with visitors whose presence is ephemeral in the field. We explore ethnographic aspects of our own experiences in distinct cultural contexts, where interaction between ourselves and the hosts and guests leads us to methodological flexibility and deep reflexivity.

Doing fieldwork, a rite of passage for anthropologists, can be a life-long project involving a great level of commitment and investment in terms of time and energy from the researcher, whether this is undertaken in alien or even in familiar places. Anthropological history offers various examples of anthropologists who never did adapt, or had difficulties adapting to local circumstances: for example, Nigel Barley (1986) in the Cameroon, Julian Pitt-Rivers (1973) in Spain and Brian O'Neill (1984) in Portugal. A researcher's integration in the group, village or local community is often presented with obstacles to her/his complete adaptation to the local culture. This is one of the main reasons why it is necessary to consider the initial contacts (in terms of days, weeks or months) as fundamental to the practice of fieldwork.

For example, Nigel Barley (1986) set up home near the Dowayo community in the Cameroon to study its culture and traditions; however, he experienced hostility from locals, boredom, illness and an elusive society. More than an anthropologist, he became a driver, teacher, nurse and servant during his fieldwork. Pitt-Rivers (1973) provides another example, as he confessed that he never adapted to the small community of Spanish Andalucia where he did fieldwork, since he was considered by some local inhabitants as a CIA agent or a spy. And, in a third example, Brian O'Neill (1984) was associated with the theft of a cow when he arrived speaking Galician in the Portuguese community of Fontelas. Fontelas is based in the Trás-os-Montes Region, which borders the Galician region of Spain. The incident in which O'Neill was implicated related to the disappearance of some cows from Fontelas and when, some days later, they were returned to the community from Galicia, the episode delayed O'Neill's integration into the local community. This was because in the minds of the people of Fontelas he was somehow connected to cows' vanishing over the border. The feelings of not belonging or being treated as an outsider experienced and expressed in these examples are not unfamiliar in anthropology. Indeed, even Malinowski wrote that he never adapted to the daily life of the Trobriand islanders, saying that integration was difficult due to his human condition (by which we understand how he as a person responded to situations and events in the field) and sickness (Malinowski 1967). And yet the experiences described by Barley, O'Neill, Pitt-Rivers and Malinowski tend to be seen as exceptions that cannot be fully understood without considering the normal integration of anthropologists in their field of study.

In considering our own position we, the authors, both have an anthropological background in terms of our academic discipline. We began our anthropological journey by undertaking research in Madeira Island (Fernandes 2006) and in Monsaraz (Ramos 1992). Fernandes (2006) studied the levadas – a canal system dating from the sixteenth century for the purpose of water distribution and now the site of walks and walking tours – of Madeira Island as a space of memory and social relations centred on water. Ramos's (1992) doctoral work took a threefold perspective. Firstly, the study of a community; secondly, an analysis of the daily life of a small rural village – Monsaraz, Alentejo, in Portugal; and thirdly, to provide an identification and interpretation of the most significant mechanisms within the practice of social relations. At the same time, it focused on aspects related to social change, family, urban contact and the presence of tourism.

In the years since the fieldwork was first undertaken, the increasingly important phenomenon of tourism in Portugal became our focus of attention, with each of the authors working in different Portuguese contexts. Fernandes started to conduct research about tourism in Madeira Island, a Portuguese autonomous region, located 900 km from mainland Portugal, 600 km from the Moroccan coast and 450 km north of the Canary Islands. Her research had the goal of studying cultural heritage as a tourism resource, specifically the case of the aforementioned levadas (Fernandes 2013). Ramos conducted fieldwork both in Monsaraz village, about 180 km from Lisbon, the Portuguese capital (Ramos 1992); and in Luanda, the capital city of Angola.

There is little doubt that tourism research is a relatively recent subject of enquiry by anthropologists. It is widely acknowledged (see e.g. Crick 1994: 2) that the first anthropologist to study tourism was Theron Nuñez (1963). He was concerned with the effects of weekend tourism by Americans in a Mexican community and the processes of acculturation. Following this work, several researchers and authors decided to consider the social, economic and cultural importance of tourism activity as an important tool for development, for the contact of cultures and respective acculturation process. One important anthropological reference is the book edited by Valene Smith (1989 [1977]), *Hosts and Guests: The Anthropology of Tourism* which was a landmark for the 'freedom' of the anthropological approach to tourism. As Smith and fellow anthropologist Dennison Nash were to note some time later, 'tourism fits easily into anthropological concerns. Anthropologists are interested in everything human, whenever and wherever that occurs. The ways of life of different peoples are of special interest to them' (Nash and Smith 1991: 13). Today, there is huge interest in the study of tourism based on both the supply side and the demand side of vacationing. Local communities have become extremely important as objects of study (even if previously they had not attracted anthropological attention), thus presenting new issues to research.

There are many valuable contributions from socio-cultural anthropology to understanding tourism (e.g. Selwyn 1996; Santana 1997; Smith and Brent 2001; Graburn, 2002; Macleod 2004; Cole 2008; Leite and Graburn 2009; Salazar 2010; Fernandes 2013; Salazar and Graburn 2014; Fernandes and Pereiro 2015). First of all, the methodological contribution which distinguishes anthropology from other disciplines in the form of field work and the comparative method (Gmelch 2004; Bruner 2005b). Secondly, we have a the-oretical-conceptual contribution (Burns 1999), which emphasises cultural relativism, highlighting a holistic and qualitative approach to the study of tourism, seeking to account for the meanings that social actors give to their actions. Finally, it is important to note the contribution of multiple ethnographies that have helped to understand this phenomenon (e.g. Crick 1989; Bruner 2005a). The purpose of many ethnographies in a tourism setting lies in the interpretation of the role of tourism in an effort to help deal with its impacts better. Research undertaken by anthropologists can be seen as an extraordinary voyage: as Marcel Proust attests, 'the real voyage of discovery consists not in seeking new landscapes but in having new eyes' (1929: 160).

Conceptual questions

In many respects the anthropologist and the tourist share the same territory: both travel, they meet, often speak to each other or local people. In spite of many analogies it is hard to compare their roles, intentions or objectives. They are 'two brother enemies' as the French anthropologist Franck Michel (1998) observes. And although the anthropologist can, many times, function as a tourist, it is difficult for a tourist to be an ethnographer, in spite of good pictures, interesting descriptions, or his/her ludic behaviour and approach. In the authors' personal discussion (2017) of the role of the fieldworker compared to the tourist, Professor Ramos observed that, in general, whereas the tourist seeks superiority and difference, the anthropologist seeks inequality. These ideas resonate with arguments put forward by, for example, Lundberg (1972), Quan and Wang (2004) and Low (2011).

At this point therefore it is useful to remind ourselves of the different approach to the field by these different actors, summed up in the words of Frank Michel:

> the anthropologist differs essentially from the tourist by the fact that he/she prefers the serious to the ludic [...] work to rest, independence to dependence, profession to hobby, speech to image, and, in a way, questions to answers.
>
> (Michel 1998: 41; author's translation).

Differences emerge in that the anthropologist works and stays for a relatively long period of time (sometimes up to two or three years) in a community, where they try to become integrated into the local way of life. In contrast, the tourist passes through, staying for a brief, shorter period of time: in a word, the tourist is ephemeral. That is the main difference, although some authors (e.g. Guiart 1967; Gueunier 1986; Michel 1998) have pointed to similarities. In addition, both hosts and guests as informants are also often elusive: they lie, or give the wrong information because of poor memory, indifference, and a concern with the advocacy of their own interests or in an attempt to impress the researcher (Ramos 2015).

The reflection on the issues of anthropological research, the positioning of the anthropologist and challenges in the realm of tourism research highlight the complexity of the encounters in 'touristic border zones', a term used by Edward Bruner, which he describes as 'a point of conjuncture, a behavioural field that I think of in spatial terms usually as a distinct meeting place between the tourists who come forth from their hotels and the local performers, the "natives"' (Bruner 2005a: 17). The researcher may play very different roles – such as tourist, or member of the visited population. Michel (1998) considers that an ethnologist is first of all a visitor, a foreign tourist. Knowing this, we raised a question: when do we do anthropological fieldwork? The answer to this question, as Bruner (2005b) points out, remains challenging for many anthropologists partly because their research is located in various locations, involving various relationships and translocal activities.

Living in a mobile world, with countless interconnections and overlapping contexts, ethnographic fields are arduously constructed and 'shaped by the conceptual, professional, financial and relational opportunities and resources accessible to the ethnographer' (Amit 2000: 6). For this reason, this construction involves multiple relationships, challenges, difficulties and engagements. As noted, this can be problematic even in the 'traditional' fieldwork setting, and is perhaps even more so in the context of tourism because, as we have noted, the tourist presence tends to be comparatively ephemeral. In one of our experiences, studying tourism has not been seen as favourable, with travel for tourism research purposes somehow seen as a 'subsidized holiday' (Hall 2011: 7) or 'academic tourism' (Mowforth and Munt 1998: 194). Doing fieldwork was, for some people in the field/academy, somehow like being on a permanent holiday with limited hours of work. Indeed, as anthropologist Pierre van den Berghe states in the opening to his monograph *The Quest for the Other*, on ethnic tourism in San Cristobal, Mexico, 'judging by the smirk which the mere mention of tourism brings to the face of my colleagues, most social scientists do not take tourism seriously' (1994: 3). He attributes this attitude less to social anthropology than to other academic disciplines, but 'nonetheless, most of my colleagues strongly imply that a professed interest in tourism constitutes little more than a clever ploy to pass off one's vacations as work' (ibid.). Although the plethora of research and publications that have emerged in the anthropological study of tourism since van den Berghe's work would suggest that this attitude is diminishing, as we observe, it is not completely gone.

Another point is how to establish our credentials and trust as a researcher when tourists are at tourist destinations for a very short period of time. As noted in the preceding discussion, Pitt-Rivers experienced difficulties adapting to the life of the local community he was engaged with in Spain in part because he could not form bonds of trust based on ideas held by locals that he was a spy. Similarly, Laura Dixon describes how she was mistaken as a journalist for a UK tabloid newspaper with a mission to do an exposé about tourists' 'bad behaviour' (personal communication, 2018). Hazel Andrews explains how the purpose of her presence in the field was often misunderstood as she was thought by tourists and, on one occasion, by the local police to be a timeshare sales person (personal communication, 2018). Likewise, Fernandes (2013) was also subject to misunderstandings about what she was doing, being mistaken several times for a tourist and frequently for a tourist/mountain guide. These misconceptions added to the difficulties all researchers faced in negotiating the field and developing fieldwork relationships.

Anthropological studies of tourism also face further issues. Tourism is both affected and influenced by the complex socio-economic and cultural processes of contemporary globalisation and transnationalism. Furthermore, due to its nature as a form of temporary mobility (Hall 2005), tourism is temporary and ephemeral. These factors contradict the 'traditional' idea of anthropological fieldwork, which takes place in more easily identifiable communities and social groupings with a less transient population (Hastrup and Hervik 1994). However, it should be noted that more contemporary accounts of ethnography also acknowledge the difficulties of working in environments that are characterised by much more mobility than previously encountered (cf. Gupta and Ferguson 1997). As Amit (2000: 14–15) observes,

> episodic, occasional, partial and ephemeral social links pose particular challenges for ethnographic fieldwork. How do we observe interactions that happen sometimes but not necessarily when we are around? How do

we participate in social relations that are not continuous, that are experienced most viscerally in their absence?

So, although these issues are not as unique to the study of tourism as perhaps they once were, the fact that tourists are short-term visitors to destinations has repercussions for the planning and conduct of fieldwork. One could study them by joining a group tour; interview tourists before, during or after they travel; or use other techniques (e.g. Harrison 2003; Malone 2011). However, being within a group has its advantages, besides having the opportunity to observe, participate and engage in informal conversations and listen to stories, all pieces of precious information that will enhance our writings. Another approach, as mentioned by Bruner (2005b), is to study destinations, or more specifically villages, heritage sites and attractions, the places visited by tourists or the places described in tourist books and other written or visual materials. The next section considers the experiences of the authors in more detail.

Ethnographic experiences: insights and reflections

Having set out some background to some of the issues that make anthropological work challenging, specifically in relation to the study of tourists, the chapter now turns to the specific experiences of the authors and includes a description of the fieldwork contexts.

To start, it is necessary to note that both the authors have an anthropological background from the Technical University of Lisbon (Instituto Superior de Ciências Sociais e Políticas). They have both developed an interest in the study of tourism. Their respective fieldwork approached tourism activity, one in Madeira Island; the other in the Portuguese province of Alentejo and later in Luanda, the capital of Angola. First to be discussed is the example from Madeira, which begins with an outline of the field.

Fieldwork site 1: Madeira

Madeira, a mountainous island of 740.7 km^2, is a Portuguese autonomous region located 900 km from mainland Portugal, with a population of over 260,000. The island's economy is dominated by public administration and tourism. In 2016, 1,162,621 tourists stayed in one of the island's 156 hotels, with the tourism sector accounting for 10% of GDP (DRE, 2017). Around two-thirds of the island consists of the Parque Natural da Madeira (Natural Park of Madeira), and with its natural and cultural attributes the island is an attractive destination for tourists. Madeira has been a destination for Northern European tourists since the nineteenth century, being especially popular among the British, German and Scandinavian markets.

One of the main tourism products is the 'levadas', human-made irrigation canals with pathways that run alongside. They are used simultaneously by local people in relation to the execution of their daily tasks, canal maintenance staff, tourists and other recreationists. Since the 1940s the levadas have come to cover almost the entire area of the island, and in so doing have become a regional cultural symbol, a space of consumption and cultural attraction for tourists who go to gaze at natural and cultural heritage (Fernandes 2010, 2013, 2015). The majority of these canals are located in the Natural Park of Madeira, which also includes the Laurisilva of Madeira, designated a natural World Heritage Site by UNESCO in 1999. Since the 1990s these canals have become one of the main regional tourism products.

Since there are seasonal variations in tourist numbers throughout the year, and especially for the hiking tourists, data collection in this area was challenging, added to the fact that tourists' stays are ephemeral. Although the tourists stayed for several days in the island, there were further issues because their presence is spread around the 22 official trails (52 trails exist on the island). This meant that mobility was an important issue and flexibility was needed in order to cope with the research agenda. Furthermore, at that time several tourism companies operated on the ground, making it difficult to collect information as each one organised hiking activities throughout the week in most of the regional hiking trails.

The difficulty in collecting data occurred because of the number of trails and companies operating. At one time there were nine organized walking tours operating throughout the week, some of which offered similar experiences. The problem that arises, albeit perhaps obviously, is that it is not possible for one researcher to be in more than one place at once, and choices exercised over where to go and when will inform the production of knowledge as encounters and experiences will inevitably be missed.

Additionally, most of the island's municipalities had responsibilities regarding local development, with tourism being considered an important sector. In addition, there were multiple government agencies – approximately 13 – involved in the organization and management of the levadas as a tourism product and part of the tourism system. These civic agencies operated alongside private concerns. Each of the agencies had its own responsibilities and action plans. The number of organisations with their own interests added to the hardship of being in the field, negotiating fieldwork relationships, and ultimately the collection of data. This is because although the researcher endeavoured to interview representatives of all the organisations, some were reticent to give any information due to the researcher's university role. Some of these issues remain too sensitive to report on.

For these reasons, the best approach was to use multiple strategies regarding data collection within the regional tourism system – that is, the interdependent elements that together contribute to making a destination (Laws 1995). The anthropologist's work was challenged every day, not only due to the variability of the existing official hiking trails, but especially due to the complexity (Laws 1995; Manente and Minghetti 2006), flexibility and dynamics of the regional tourism system (Santana 1997).

The field work took place between 2009 and 2011, in intermittent periods. In order to gather data, the author used different strategies adopting a mixed methodology, using participant observation, interviews and surveys to collect a variety of information. Adding to this the researcher also took hundreds of pictures. At the destination, it was necessary first to analyse the relations between the existing actors within the regional tourism system and their responsibilities, roles and competences in the destination relating to the product 'the levadas'; and second to examine both the public structures including the regional government and municipalities and the private ones including tourism companies, accommodation and intermediaries (travel agencies), and the touristic offer related to the levadas. For this purpose ethnography was the best option as it allowed the researcher to collect and analyse dense, rich and detailed data. Semi-structured interviews were also used to collect data from the municipalities (seven municipalities were covered out of a total ten), from eight tourism companies and one travel agency. The researcher also interviewed the Regional Director of Tourism, the Marketing Coordinator of the Madeira Promotion Bureau, the Madeira Walking Festival Director, the Director of Madeira Rural (which offers countryside accommodation on the island), plus a director of regional forest management and members of three local hiking groups. In addition, the researcher joined several local hiking groups, paid to take part in several tourists' hiking programmes, and became a member of a group of consumers during hiking activity (some companies facilitated access by not requiring payment for participation in activities). Also, the researcher participated in two Madeira Walking Festivals, during which different techniques for data collection were used.

Participant observation allowed the mapping of places, landscapes, events and times of representation of the tourist spaces, namely hiking trails, capturing activities and identifying social actors. Informal conversations were useful to gather information about tourists' activities and their stories throughout the hiking activities. In addition, these conversations were helpful in order to capture the tourist guides' and companies' daily activities and operations. Surveys were used aiming to identify and examine the motivations and interests of visitors for the discovery, visit, consumption and experience of the levadas. The main difficulties faced throughout the fieldwork were collecting data, not only from multiple entities with different responsibilities, competences and roles in tourism product development, but also from tourists due to their ephemeral presence in the field and reluctance to respond to surveys due to not wanting their leisure time to be interrupted, or their lack of incomprehension regarding the work of the anthropologist. As the field diary (11 August 2009) reveals:

> We walked a little further until we reached the road where the cars were waiting for us. We stopped at a cafe on the way down to Calheta. I distributed only three questionnaires, one to a Portuguese and two in Spanish. Some of the individuals on the tour showed they did not want to pass

on information, others were so busy with the children that I did not even dare ask them for such a thing.

One of the strategies used to overcome this difficulty was contacting some hikers after their travel via email in order to request completion of the questionnaires. Most cases were successful, whilst others were only partially completed or completely unsuccessful.

Another example of collecting data in tourism settings is the work developed by Francisco Martins Ramos in Monsaraz, Alentejo province, to which the discussion now turns.

Fieldwork site 2: Monsaraz

Monsaraz is an old Alentejo medieval town located near the Portuguese–Spanish border and situated on the left bank of the Guadiana River. The town had lost its administrative and strategic influence by the mid-twentieth century. However, by the end of the 1960s the community was 'discovered' as a tourism destination, based on its monuments and the unique architecture of the houses, its small and hospitable population, its admired landscape, and as a place offering an alternative to the stresses and strains of urban living, making it attractive to artists and those seeking a more relaxed way of life.

Ramos conducted fieldwork for his doctoral degree in this village between the end of 1987 and mid-1991. Amongst other issues, the research focused on the tourism phenomenon. His research agenda comprised the use of ethnography, namely participant-observation, interviews and informal conversations. Added to this some bibliographic research was undertaken and many photos were taken. In contrast to Fernandes's work in Madeira, Ramos lived in Monsaraz, although his hometown was 30 km away. During this time he never lost the position of transient resident and outsider who chose to live there to 'write a book'.

The town's proximity to Spain had always attracted Spanish visitors, mainly for gastronomic reasons as they came to enjoy the local food. But by the 1970s the town was attracting cultural tourists motivated by the town's history, architecture and attractive environment. First, there were individual tourists, both domestic and international, who, by word of mouth to friends and family, passed on information about the town. As interest in Monsaraz grew excursion groups started to arrive, followed by tour operators bringing international tourists, and finally, visitors purportedly interested in learning about the town and its environs. As Ramos (1992) notes, 'many tourists (illiterate in history, traditions, art) gape at the "stop of time"[2] in Vila Velha and visit it as if they were a zoo of rare and/or unique species'.

In 2004 the Alqueva Dam was opened in the Alentejo region, and since then has attracted many tourists, especially daily visitors. Alqueva Dam, one of the largest artificial lakes in Western Europe, altered the rural landscape, resulted in changes to the irrigation of agriculture, and contributed to an increase in rural and nature-based tourism. Those who come for these activities are ephemeral visitors, they stay for only a few hours and do not stay overnight in the town, which makes their visit even more transitory in nature than tourists who do stay. These day visitors take some pictures and then leave the community in a rush. The longer-stay tourists tend to be the elderly and artists, who in most cases stay for up to a week. The main point in relation to fieldwork to emerge from Ramos's work is to highlight the short-term timeframe of tourists' and day trippers' visits. The week-long sojourn of tourists and the even shorter trips of the day visitors made building relationships that could inform data collection difficult. Other difficulties encountered by Ramos in his fieldwork are explored in his notes relating to the third field site.

Fieldwork site 3: Luanda

Our final example of data collection took place in Luanda, the capital of Angola. After the end of the civil war in 2002, many tourism activities developed despite the lack of infrastructure. Because of this there were new developments, including new hotels and restaurants, rebuilding of roads and construction of resorts, and political decisions were made about the planning of tourism activities. Luanda became a business tourism centre of great importance due to the economic reconstruction of the country, attracting investors, entrepreneurs and business people from around the world, most notably from Portugal, Spain, France, China and South Africa. These business tourists stay in Luanda hotels for periods of less than one week. During their stay they can visit the nearby Mussulo Island, see the Quiçama National Park, or enjoy the Luanda beaches and restaurants. However, despite these opportunities to engage in different kinds of touristic practices, their stay is transitory and brief, and many hours are occupied in meetings – their presence is ephemeral. Again, the contrast with the work of the anthropologist is evident. The researcher stayed for longer periods, and in the case of Luanda faced enormous barriers to being accepted in an elusive society that is still marked by the distrust originated by the war, and the development of a new and strong power established by the leaders of several institutions. There is strong control of all informants by their supervisors and leaders, making fieldwork very problematic and time-consuming. Compared with other forms of research, ethnographic work is already characterised by the length of time involved in collecting the data, and the situation encountered in Luanda added to the time-consuming nature of this type of practice. This brief outline of the problems that Ramos encountered during his fieldwork in Luanda highlights again that whereas the anthropologist stays, the tourist passes through.

Final comments

Compared with other areas of anthropological research, tourism is a relatively recent object of study in anthropology. The anthropological approaches to this global activity have produced several results that have materialised in thesis, articles, research reports, seminars and conferences worldwide. Anthropology is crucial for understanding human relations and the effects of contact between people of different cultures and geographical areas.

A hallmark of anthropology as an academic discipline is ethnographic fieldwork, particularly participant observation and the anthropologists' interactions with the local actors, residents or visitors involved in the tourism process. As already highlighted, the presence of these visitors varies in terms of time, location and motivation, and is usually for shorter periods of time compared with those spent by the researcher. These factors can hinder the work and inhibit the development of contact between researcher and subjects. The anthropologist works in a chosen community where she/he stays for a significant period of time, varying from a few months to several years; the tourist, by contrast, passes through for a limited period of time, during which they are often under pressure to see and do as much as possible. The tourist's presence is ephemeral when compared with the anthropologist's comparative permanence.

As outlined in the preceding discussion, the fact that tourists are short-term visitors to a destination has repercussions for the planning and conduct of fieldwork. Of the strategies that could be used, one option is to join a tour group and interview the tourists or have informal conversations during the activity. Interviewing tourists before, during or after they travel is a regular strategy. Being within a group has its advantages: besides offering the opportunity to observe, participate and engage in informal conversations and listen to stories, it affords the opportunity to gain pieces of precious information that will enhance our writing. However, it has the disadvantage of affecting the type of research undertaken because the tourists' presence is ephemeral, so they cannot be interviewed again in the setting in which their touristic practice has taken place. To interview tourists is a frustrating game of cat-and-mouse in which the anthropologist holds the attention of the tourists for some time, only to have to let it go again – some do not want to be contacted, others have already disappeared, and many are unavailable, not wishing to be disturbed during their leisure time.

Madeira, Monsaraz and Luanda are examples of tourism-related situations that pose several barriers to anthropologists in their fieldwork. In addition to the normal constraints that full fieldwork involves, the nature, profile and behaviour of tourists all present obstacles that surpass the difficulties found by researchers in many other fieldwork locations.

Notes

1 In memory of Emeritus Professor Francisco Martins Ramos. The authors would like to thank the editors for their comments on the first draft of this chapter.
2 By this it is meant that the features of the town present an atmosphere in which time appears to have stopped.

References

Amit, V. (2000) Introduction – constructing the field. In: V. Amit (ed.) *Constructing the Field. Ethnographic Fieldwork in the Contemporary World*. London: Routledge, pp. 1–18.

Barley, N. (1986) *The Innocent Anthropologist*. London: Penguin Books.

van den Berghe, P. (1994) *The Quest for the Other*. London: University of Washington Press.

Bernard, H. R. (1995) *Research Methods in Anthropology. Qualitative and Quantitative Approaches*, 2nd edn. Walnut Creek: Altamira Press.

Bogdewic, S. P. (1999) Participant observation. In B. F. Crabtree and W. L. Miller (eds) *Doing Qualitative Research*, 2nd edn. Thousand Oaks: Sage, pp. 47–70.

Burns, P. M. (1999) *An Introduction to Tourism and Anthropology*. London: Routledge.

Bruner, E. M. (2005a) *Culture on Tour. Ethnographies of Travel*. Chicago: University of Chicago Press.

Bruner, E. M. (2005b) Tourism fieldwork. *Anthropology News*, 46(5): 16–19.

Cole, S. (2008) *Tourism, Culture and Development: Hopes, Dreams and Realities in East Indonesia*. Clevedon: Channel View Publications.

Crick, M. (1989) Representations of international tourism in the social sciences: sun, sex, sights, savings and servility. *Annual Review of Anthropology*, 18: 307–344.

Crick, M. (1994) *Resplendent Sites, Discordant Voices: Sri Lankans and International Tourism*. Reading: Harwood Academic.

DRE (2017) *Estatísticas do Turismo da Região Autónoma da Madeira. Resultados Definitivos – 2016*. Funchal: Direção Regional de Estatística da Madeira.

Fernandes, F. (2006). Levadas de Heréus na Ilha da Madeira. Partilha, conflito e memória da água na Lombada da Ponta do Sol [Levadas of Heréus in Madeira island. Sharing, conflict and memory of water in Lombada da Ponta do Sol]. Master's thesis, Technical University of Lisbon.

Fernandes, F. (2010) A cultura da água: da patrimonialização das levadas da Madeira à oferta turística. *PASOS: Revista de Turismo y Patrimonio Cultural*, 8(4):529–538.

Fernandes, F. (2013) Pelos caminhos da água. As levadas e veredas da ilha da Madeira como recurso turístico [Through water courses. The 'levadas' and 'veredas' of Madeira Island as a tourism resource] PhD thesis, Universidade de Évora.

Fernandes, F. (2015) Built heritage and flash floods: hiking trails and tourism on Madeira Island. *Journal of Heritage Tourism*, 11(1): 88–95

Fernandes, F. and Pereiro, X. (2015) Antropologia e turismo: dos trilhos, atores e espaços à genealogia da turistificação da Antropologia em Portugal. *PASOS. Revista de Patrimonio y Turismo Cultural*, 13(2): 333–346.

Gmelch, S. B. (2004) Why tourism matters. In: S. B. Gmelch (ed.) *Tourists and Tourism: A Reader*. Long Grove: Waveland Press, pp. 3–21.

Graburn, N. H. H. (2002) The ethnographic tourist. In: G. M. S. Dann (ed.) *The Tourist as a Metaphor of the Social World*. Wallingford: CAB International, pp. 19–39.

Gueunier, N. (1986) Le fantôme de l'étnographie. *Sociétés*, 8: 17.

Guiart, J. (1967) L'ethnologie, qu'est-elle? *Cahiers Internationaux de Sociologie*, XI.

Gupta, A. and Ferguson, J. (1997) Culture, power, place: ethnography at the end of an era. In: A. Gupta and J. Ferguson (eds) *Culture, Power, Place: Explorations in Critical Anthropology*. Durham and London: Duke University Press, pp. 1–33.

Hall, C.M. (2005) *Tourism: Rethinking the Social Science of Mobility*. Harlow: Pearson.

Hall, C.M. (ed) (2011) *Fieldwork in Tourism. Methods, issues and reflections.* London: Routledge.

Harrison, J. (2003) *Being a Tourist. Finding Meaning in Pleasure Travel.* Vancouver: The University of British Columbia Press.

Hastrup, K. and Hervik, P. (1994) Introduction. In: K. Hastrup and P. Hervik (eds) *Social Experience and Anthropological Knowledge.* London: Routledge, pp. 1–9.

Jorgensen, D. L. (1989) *Participant Observation. A Methodology for Human Studies.* Thousand Oaks: Sage.

Laws, Eric (1995) *Tourist Destination Management. Issues, Analysis and Policies.* London: Routledge.

Leite, N. and Graburn, N. H. H. (2009) Anthropological interventions in tourism studies. In: T. Jamal and M. Robinson (eds) *The Sage Handbook of Tourism Studies.* Thousand Oaks: Sage, pp. 35–64.

Low, S. M. (2011) Claiming space for an engaged anthropology: spatial inequality and social exclusion. *American Anthropologist,* 113(3): 389–407.

Lundberg, D. E. (1972) Why tourists travel. *Cornell Hotel and Restaurant Administration Quarterly,* 12(4): 64–70.

Macleod, D. V. L. (2004) *Tourism, Globalisation and Cultural Change. An Island Community Perspective.* Clevedon: Channel View Publications.

Malinowski, B. (1967) *A Diary in the Strict Sense of the Term.* Stanford: Stanford University Press.

Malone, K. A. (2011) The coach fellas: tourism performance and expectation in Ireland. In J. Skinner and D. Theodossopoulos (eds) *Great Expectations. Imagination and Anticipation in Tourism.* Oxford: Berghahn Books, pp. 137–154.

Manente, M. and Minghetti, V. (2006) Destination management organizations and actors. In: Buhalis, D. and Costa, C. (eds) *Tourism, Business, Frontiers. Consumers, Products and Industry.* Oxford: Elsevier Butterworth-Heinemann, pp. 228–237.

Michel, F. (1998) Des manières d'être et de faire du touriste et de l'anthropologue. In: F. Michel (ed.) *Tourismes, Touristes, Sociétés.* Paris: L'Harmattan, pp. 35–44.

Mowforth, M. and Munt, I. (1998) *Tourism and Sustainability. New Tourism in the Third World.* London: Routledge.

Nash, D. and Smith, V. (1991) Anthropology and tourism. *Annals of Tourism Research,* 18: 12–25.

Nuñez, T. A. (1963) Tourism, tradition and acculturation: *weekendismo* in a Mexican village. *Ethnology,* 2(3): 347–352

O'Neill, B. (1984) *Proprietários, Lavradores e Jornaleiras.* Lisboa: Dom Quixote.

Pereiro, X. (2010) Ethnographic research on cultural tourism: an anthropological view. In: G. Richards and W. Munsters (eds) *Cultural Tourism Research Methods.* Wallingford: CABI Publishing, pp. 173–187.

Pitt-Rivers, J. (1973) *Tres ensayos de antropología estructural.* Barcelona: Anagrama.

Proust, M. (1929) *The Captive, the Fugitive. In Search of Lost Time.* Available at: http://gutenberg.net.au/ [accessed 22 February 2018]

Quan, S. and Wang, N. (2004) Towards a structural model of the tourist experience: An illustration from food experiences in tourism. *Tourism Management,* 25(3): 297–305.

Ramos, F. M. (1992) Os proprietários da sombra – Vila Velha revisitada. PhD thesis, Universidade de Évora.

Ramos, F. M. (2015) *Antropologia do Turismo, aulas na Universidade Metodista de Angola.* [*Anthropology of Tourism, Lectures from Methodist University of Angola.*]

Salazar, N. B. (2010) *Envisioning Eden. Mobilizing Imaginaries in Tourism and Beyond.* New York: Berghahn Books.

Salazar, N. B. and Graburn, N. H. H. (eds) (2014) *Tourism Imaginaries. Anthropological approaches.* New York: Berghahn Books.

Santana, A. (1997) *Antropología y Turismo. Nuevas hordas, viejas culturas?*Barcelona: Editorial Ariel.

Selwyn, T. (ed). (1996) *The Tourist Image: Myths and Myth Making in Tourism.* Chichester: John Wiley.

Smith, V. L. (ed.) (1989[1977]) *Hosts and Guests: The Anthropology of Tourism*, 2nd edn. Philadelphia: University of Pennsylvania Press.

Smith, V. L. and Brent, M. A. (eds) (2001) *Hosts and Guests Revisited: Tourism Issues of the 21st century.* New York: Cognizant Communication Corporation.

7 Being in the field in Bali

A reflection on fieldwork challenges in community-based tourism research

Claudia Dolezal

Introduction

In this chapter I reflect on my fieldwork experiences researching power relations in community-based tourism in Bali. I discuss the difficulties of negotiating and being in a 'foreign field' as early career researcher, notably under time and money constraints. Conducting fieldwork abroad in foreign and exotic environments has been a well established practice for anthropologists since Malinowski's ground-breaking notion of participatory observation. Some argue that fieldwork constitutes the core characteristic that distinguishes anthropology from other disciplines in the social sciences (Gupta and Ferguson 2007). Anthropologists have been returning from the field with a wide range of data, including notes, field diaries, photographs, films, tapes and digital recordings. This also applies when studying the phenomenon of tourism. Tourism, involving the movement of people and interactions between often culturally diverse societies, has long been subject to anthropological inquiry. Early researchers such as Nash (1996), Bruner (2005) and Picard (1992) have emphasised the importance of adopting an anthropological lens to understanding the touristic subject, often by means of extensive fieldwork periods in the developing world. It is this lens that I also adopted for my research in Bali – as part of a shorter fieldwork period, though, than was initially propounded by Malinowski.

Independent of duration, these phases of ethnographic fieldwork pose a range of challenges to the researcher, some of which are well documented in the anthropological literature. These include changes in research focus and direction (Cerwonka and Malkki 2007), and the researcher's entanglement in complex power relations (Simpson 2006). In addition to these often demanding situations, as anthropologists in the twenty-first century we increasingly deal with a range of new political and structural challenges (Rivoal and Salazar 2013). More than ever before, we face an obligation to deliver 'impact' in the places where we conduct our fieldwork, given the academic pressures imposed by the institutions we often find ourselves in. The limited time and funding available, with a need to optimise output, often leads to the application of notions of participatory and action research, all to make our research more valuable for the contexts we investigate (Kesby et al. 2007). Those we were once 'studying', turn into 'informants', 'participants' and 'co-researchers', all terms that create a utopic idea of equality and local benefit, as well as an illusion of power sharing (Cornwall 2010; Leal 2010).

Despite the obvious time and money challenges we face as anthropologists and researchers, we celebrate our successes, turning our analysed data and knowledge into publications and thereby writing the 'other'.

Rarely, though, do we discuss the challenges we face while conducting research under difficult circumstances: what may not go according to plan, the precarious situations we find ourselves in, and the fieldwork encounters that we would have rather avoided. There are some exceptions who do discuss this, such as Andrews (2012) reflecting on the practice of participant observations as part of ethnographic fieldwork; however, these are still rare in ethnographies of tourism. Pillow (2003) holds that there is a well established belief that discussing these challenges could violate our authoritative voice as researchers and hence reduce the validity of our knowledge claims. I argue that this is particularly the case for doctoral and early career researchers, who have few, if any publications, and hence have not had a chance to establish their authority in academia. One obvious reason for this is that they tend to have less fieldwork experience than their well established counterparts, as Simpson (2006) openly discusses in sharing his fieldwork experience for his doctoral research in Sri Lanka. At the same time, despite this lack of authority, I argue that the status of the early career researcher allows a greater justification for speaking openly about one's failures and conflicts in the field, which I attempt to do here by drawing on my own doctoral fieldwork experiences in Bali.

Undertaking interpretive research, which acknowledges the values and background of the situated researcher in the narrative, means that the researcher experiences increased acceptance of admitting those 'failures' (Denzin 2001). Interpretive research is characterised by an influx of emotionality and reflexivity, a practice that assists in critically questioning the researcher's experiences and how these impact on relationships with research participants and the data (Behar 2003; Guillemin and Gillam 2004). Failures in the field are part of the ethnographic research process, which is largely characterised by uncertainty and ever-changing relationships with the people one encounters (Cerwonka and Malkki 2007). Rivoal and Salazar (2013) even argue that uncertainty and serendipity are the very *essence* of ethnographic fieldwork and hence need to be part of the analysis. After all, as Simpson learned in the field, 'you don't do fieldwork, fieldwork does you' (2006: 125). However, to date only a limited number of researchers openly share the confusions that are part of their ethnographic experiences.

My research approach here therefore rejects the notion of the disembodied and detached researcher. In this chapter, I offer a personal account of fieldwork I conducted in Bali, Indonesia for my doctoral research, which was aimed at generating a critical understanding of empowerment in community-based tourism on the island. Community-based tourism is regarded as alternative form of tourism, with characteristics such as the active participation of communities in planning, implementing and managing tourism, and close contact between tourists and residents (Goodwin and Santilli 2009; Boonratana 2010). It is usually regarded as a bottom-up and sustainable form of tourism, given that it is driven by community members, who should, ideally, all participate in and benefit equally from tourism activities (Telfer and Sharpley 2008). The research I discuss here was carried out over one visit to the island for three and a half months, during which time I lived in three villages that regarded themselves as engaging in community-based tourism. In this chapter I reflect on some of the challenges and disillusionments upon entering and being in the field and the community-based tourism setting, and the methodological struggles of researching under pressure of limited time and money. It is the moments of difference, confusion and conflict to which I turn, regarding them as opportunities to truly understand the topics we study and the people we work with.

Part of the confusion is the different roles I adopted while being in the field, as researcher, a white, 'rich' European, but also a tourist. I was therefore, as an anthropologist researching tourism and tourists, firmly a part of the touristic spaces that I was meant to be studying. This meant that I actively participated in the tourism encounter that was the focus of my analysis, inherently shaping the setting that I initially set out to understand from the position of an outsider. A similar situation was experienced by Bruner, who researched tourists in Indonesia while also being their tour guide, finding himself 'between a touristic and ethnographic discourse' (2005: 230). At the same time, paradoxically, I had a romanticised imagination of the communities that I would stay with, hoping to be accepted as a friend or researcher – but realised that local realities were much less 'innocent' as I became entangled in the complex power structures of tourism in the villages. Being regarded as a tourist essentially helped me understand the role of the foreigner in the village, with money being an important factor shaping resident–tourist interactions.

Caught amidst the different positions we take on as anthropologists in the field, this chapter thus pleads for a greater use of reflexive practices to deal with some of the confusions and inner conflicts we face. Part of my analysis here is a discussion of the perception of the notion of the 'field' and how this changes as fieldwork progresses. This is because I am convinced that only in reflecting on the time of fieldwork and the challenges we face can we better understand fieldwork, the methods we use and the pressures we face as researchers.

The Balinese village: a 'field' of complexity and difference

> But what of 'the field' itself, the place where the distinctive work of 'fieldwork' may be done, that taken-for-granted space in which an 'Other' culture or society lies waiting to be observed and written? This mysterious space – not the

'what' of anthropology but the 'where' – has been left to common sense, beyond and below the threshold of reflexivity

(Gupta and Ferguson 2007: 2).

The notion of the 'field' is indeed a mysterious one, with a variety of attempts in the anthropological literature to define it (Marcus 1995; Amit 2000; Gupta and Ferguson 2007). In a postmodern sense, the field is essentially perceived as intertwined with home and the values and background of the anthropologist (Mosse 2005). It is difficult to be ascribed to a defined group of people, as we are less spatially bound than ever before in a globalised world of ever-increasing mobility (Appadurai 1991). Nevertheless, as fluid as this postmodern field may be, it is as much defined by geographical boundaries as it is abstract in nature. After all, it is in places that we find ourselves living and researching during fieldwork. This does not mean, however, that these sites are studied in isolation from the wider world system; but as Marcus (1995: 102) argues, in defining the notion of 'multi-sited ethnography', it puts

> questions to an emergent object of study whose contours, sites and relationships are not known beforehand, but are themselves a contribution of making an account that has different, complexly connected real-world sites of investigation.

In the research I discuss here, prior to departing for fieldwork, I perceived the field mainly as those real-world sites defined by geographical boundaries. For me, the field comprised three rural villages, a clearly established area which three communities inhabited – or, at least, what I thought at the time could be regarded as communities. However, the Balinese village, which I only got to know better by living and *being* there, was a complex one to understand.

I started my empirical research in April 2013 at the age of 24 to investigate community-based tourism on the island. While I had experience researching community-based tourism in Thailand and had previously lived in Southeast Asia for my studies and research, the island of Bali was different from any other place I had visited or lived in. As the only Hindu island (i.e. Balinese Hinduism, a unique form of the religion found only in Bali) in a majorly Muslim country, Bali presents a unique socio-cultural setting, characterised also by strong migration flows by Muslim nationals from other parts of the country. Bali is influenced largely by the caste system and the complex structure of the Balinese village (Eiseman 1990). Geertz (1959) argues that although there is no uniform social structure in Balinese villages, its components are similar to a range of layers of social organisation, including, amongst others, shared obligation to worship at a given temple, common residence, kinship ties and membership in voluntary organisations. The *desa* (Balinese village) is also a religious organisation, with sub-communities being formed dependent on caste status. The Balinese caste system (*kasta*) is made up of four groups (in descending order of privilege): *Brahmana* (high priests), *Satria*,

Wésia and *Sudra* (peasants) (Howe 2005). While the majority of Balinese are part of the lowest caste, the villages discussed in this chapter presented highly diverse communities. For example, it is notable that it is usually members of the higher-caste groups who are most involved in tourism and who possess tourism-specific skills in the villages in which my fieldwork was based. It is these complex power relations rooted in the socio-cultural context of Bali that I began to understand and become entangled in only as the fieldwork progressed, and which also became the very core of what I now call my 'findings'.

I was particularly interested in understanding the notion of empowerment and the interactions between residents and tourists in three villages that called themselves community-based tourism villages (*desa wisata*). I felt I had clearly defined my subject of study as well as the field that was subject to my anthropological inquiry. I was prepared to investigate and question whether community-based tourism's empowerment ethos, pleading for greater local agency than mainstream tourism, applies in the case of Bali. Even though I put clear boundaries around the places and the topic that I studied, as the research progressed, the notion of the geographically and thematically defined field extended beyond the three villages. As the weeks passed by, I studied not only the microcosm of community-based tourism in the villages, but also the wider tourism landscape in Bali and the power relations in the national tourism system. I realised that my study of community-based tourism, as small-scale and well defined as it seemed, could not be isolated from the broader picture, and that it was essentially a window into larger tourism power structures. By learning more about tourism in Bali and talking to the tourism ministry and tourism board, I began to realise that the macro-structures of tourism politics on the island had a great impact on the localities under study. The villages were not isolated entities, even if one may think of community-based tourism as an alternative form of tourism located outside the mainstream tourism spaces. Indeed, as the research has shown, the villages are well connected to mass tourism, relying on similar kinds of interactions and assistance in the form of funding, foreign investment and training.

As the fieldwork progressed, the geographically well defined boundaries of the field therefore became increasingly blurred. More importantly, the field to me was an area of difference, which I perceived as a place to study and learn about. My gatekeeper was a local NGO, the Bali Community-Based Tourism Association, which helped villages to become *desa wisata*. I first got in touch with them when I went to Southeast Asia for a conference the year before my fieldwork. While I had previously conducted research on community-based tourism in Southeast Asia, specifically Thailand (Dolezal 2011, 2015), I found myself in a novel socio-cultural and religious context in Bali. I had no opportunity to live on the island before my research started, and hence tried to ease my entry into the field by means of regular liaison with the NGO. By sharing my plans of the kind of research I wanted to conduct (i.e. ethnographic research with some participatory mapping techniques), I intended to clarify expectations and hence reduce potential fieldwork issues.

Regarding Bali, and the villages where I lived, as geographically distanced from home as well as places of cultural difference gave me insights into how I perceived the fieldwork. Indeed, in my first week upon arrival, I kept emphasising the aspect of 'work' in my diary. An analysis of my notes revealed that I regarded fieldwork as a mission to complete, despite challenges of loneliness, lack of purpose and feelings of isolation. As Crapanzano argues, 'the anthropologist's sense of time, marked as it is by a beginning and an ending – an arrival and a departure – is telic. It has a goal, in fact a moving goal' (2012: 550). Despite identifying myself as an anthropologist rather than a tourist, fieldwork was a journey for me, a destination away from home that I would go to and depart from again (Amit 2000). This clear division between home and away is a characteristic of tourism that early academics have noted, where the holiday is compared to a sacred journey away from home (Graburn 1977). While a move away from one's usual environment also characterises anthropological work in other settings, studying the subject of tourism and thus being part of the touristic spaces in Bali placed me somewhat naturally into the role of the tourist in residents' eyes – in addition to other roles I performed during fieldwork. While I do not deny that I occasionally took on the role of the tourist, which I will elaborate on later in this chapter, I was primarily setting foot on the island with the intention to do my 'work', that is, to learn about community-based tourism in Bali and collect 'data'. Most importantly, though, being part of a *community*-based tourism setting led me to think – somewhat naively – that I was going to become part of a sharing and caring community while conducting my research.

Entry into the field and its anthropological challenges

Despite intense preparation prior to fieldwork, my arrival in Bali was not easy, characterised by a disillusioning awareness of the socio-cultural differences and challenges that I was going to face during my time on the island. In my diary I reflected on the disappointments and frustrations of feeling that I would never be able to fully grasp Bali's culture, rich in religious and cultural symbols and practices that meant very little to me. Even though I prepared through extensive reading before I left home, I found myself in a field that was characterised by difference, more foreign to me than any other place I had lived before. With its unique religion and culture, Bali was a novel environment to me, in addition to being geographically far removed from my place of residence (the UK and Europe).

Upon arrival in Bali, I spent a few days in the tourist centre of Sanur, in the south of the island, where I experienced my first struggles in grasping the socio-cultural context. I had gained a good theoretical understanding of some of the cultural practices of the Balinese from my reading, but still was overwhelmed by a sense of cultural distance and loneliness. Religious offerings that I found on the ground and the symbols I came across in temples and on the streets meant nothing to me, even if I understood their meaning on paper.

After all, these symbols and practices were not part of my culture and daily life and, even though I may have understood their meaning for the Balinese, they had little significance to me as a person. In the devastating state of loneliness that I found myself in upon entering the field, these differences impacted on my emotional state and made me feel yet more isolated.

Upon arrival in the villages, each of which I lived in for around one month, my host 'fathers' introduced me to other residents and local cultural practices. They were the ones who could speak English (in addition to interpreters, given that my Indonesian language skills were limited) and who offered me accommodation in their house complex. By participating in the daily life and religious practices of the families, I began to learn more about the socio-cultural context and life of my informants. Nevertheless, the world I was researching remained immensely foreign to me for a long time. Although I had previously lived in a number of countries that were culturally different from my home country, I experienced what would usually be referred to as culture shock, occurring 'when one is placed into an environment with different symbols and with different notions of types of and acceptable levels of risk than what is 'normal' in one's own culture' (Irwin 2007:4). Although anthropologists regularly suffer from culture shock and negative emotions, the idea exists that being trained as an anthropologist should help to avoid this (ibid.). I increasingly came to recognise though that, as Coffey states, 'fieldwork is personal, emotional and identity work' (1999: 1). Emotion is not something that contaminates the field and consequently has to be 'managed' or 'dealt with' to produce more valid research; rather, it shapes the self, its identity and, in turn, relationship with others. During my fieldwork, this emotional confusion appeared in the form of loneliness and culture shock, which caused what Irwin (2007) describes as loss of identity, isolation and depression, which will become obvious later in this chapter.

Indeed, in the first days and weeks of my research I had a feeling that I could not make sense of the world around me, failing in my role as an anthropologist and researcher. Was I not supposed to be the one who was creating new knowledge as I was working my way up to doctoral level? I had strong doubts about this, as I knew that my informants were the true experts in the field, knowing best what was happening in their villages. I came to terms with the fact that I was essentially an outsider and that I would not be able to 'produce meaning until [I understood] how to comport [myself] in a socially acceptable way' (Irwin 2007: 3) in the context that I studied.

Given that I saw the field as a geographical location that was separate, and very different from my usual place of residence, I was desperately seeking to become part of the field as much as I could, somehow I was even expecting it. Part of the reason for this expectation was, on the one hand, my notion that the anthropologist would always be speaking from 'inside' the society under study, taking on an emic perspective (Geertz 1973) to present a more accurate view of reality. On the other hand, I realised that I had a very romantic idea of the 'communities' I was to be researching, constituting a net of social relationships that I should ideally be part of as anthropologist. After all, these communities were presented to tourists and the outside as harmonious places of togetherness through the promotion by the NGO. Although I was aware of the heterogeneous nature of villages in Southeast Asia and the ambiguous notion of 'community', at the same time the notion felt to me like what Bauman (2001: 1) describes as 'a "warm" place, a cosy and comfortable place, [...] a roof under which we shelter in heavy rain, like a fireplace at which we warm our hands on a frosty day'. A reason for this perception may be my own personal background and life back in the UK, where, at the time, I did not feel a sense of belonging, finding myself in a country away from my family and friends in Austria. I was somehow, as an isolated doctoral researcher, searching for a sense of community in a community-based tourism context.

Even though I did encounter a friendly welcome by my host families, most of the time I felt I did not belong anywhere, neither to the villages, nor to the tourist groups. While the idea persisted in my mind that being part of the families would give me a more 'real' account of the social world under study, I realised that I would never be a true part of the families, no matter how long I stayed. I slowly came to terms with the fact that being geographically close to my informants did not automatically translate into being socio-culturally or emotionally close and understanding their world in the same way as them. The realisation of the boundaries of social science and inter-pretive research that I faced led to further disillusionment and doubts about the value of my fieldwork. I became aware that I could never fully present reality as it was experienced by my informants, and that all I could ever secure were limited perspectives of social spheres. Eventually, I accepted this as given and stopped 'suppressing subjectivity' while accepting that, even though I drew on other people's stories, 'it [was] my narrative that [became] the meta-narrative' (Mosse 2005: 14) and the final story of my written work.

As the paragraphs above show, the notion of difference became an impor-tant one for me and I realised, upon analysing my fieldwork diary, that my field notes in the first few weeks of fieldwork were infused 'with difference, since indeed [...] [I was] quite different from all or a class of those under study' (Warren 2000: 193). I put myself into the position of the *stranger* (Simmel 1950), being unable to identify myself with the field, a construct that I had created myself, consisting of the local context, its culture and the people. I felt a 'unity of nearness and remoteness' (Simmel 1950: 402) – close because I shared certain attributes with the group, such as being human and holding certain basic human values (e.g. helping others, respect for the elderly); but simultaneously remote because I realised that these attributes did not stem from an interaction or relationship with the people I encountered.

In order to overcome these inner conflicts, and as a consequence of my position as a non-native anthropologist, I desperately tried to learn more about the local context and people's lives by engaging in in-depth conversa-tions with residents, my informants. I was what anthropological inquiry refers to as in the process of making the foreign familiar (Marcus and Fischer

1986). I sought 'to learn more in order to overcome distance' (Hammoudi and Borneman 2009: 271), and started 'fishing for facts' (Crapanzano 2012: 551) by scheduling interviews and asking the families questions about Bali and their lives. However, much more than familiarising myself with the environment in order to ease my daily life, I was trying to create social relationships, maybe even friendships, given that I felt lonely and isolated, spending much time by myself when my host families were at work. At the same time, though, the families were also aware that I would leave again soon and that I would be moving to the next village to continue my work, which made it difficult to establish long-lasting relationships.

Besides engaging in conversations with people to relieve the daunting feeling of loneliness that dominated my fieldwork, I was also trying to collect 'data' in order to complete my field 'work'. I found myself under immense time pressure, paying a daily rate for my accommodation and food in the villages. All of a sudden, time became a major factor that influenced my thinking – and I became somewhat obsessed with it. I tried to make myself be occupied and schedule interviews, which, at the same time, helped me to think less about how lonely I felt. Scheduling those interviews with informants was a challenge in itself. Upon arrival in the villages, I faced great difficulties in reaching my research participants. I began to realise that the community welcoming me with open arms to conduct interviews and organise village meetings was a mere illusion. This was due firstly to my host families, who often kept me from talking to other residents to avoid revealing inequalities (which, anyway, I witnessed later on); secondly to a misleading idea that my gatekeeper, the NGO, gave me; and thirdly to self-delusion. The readings on fieldwork methods I had done before going to the villages gave me the naïve idea that residents would happily contribute to research projects and share ideas and information.

My reading did not include the challenges of fieldwork and of trying to reach villagers who are busy leading their daily lives and pursuing hard work in the fields, making it difficult to ask them to compromise their time for my research. I was largely ignored by people and felt that they cared very little about me and my research. Anyway, why would villagers care about my research, when they could not even see an immediate benefit from it? I began to struggle with ethical conflicts – after all, I did not want to exploit people for information without them gaining a benefit from it. I wanted to return the favour in some way; however, I realised that my idea of 'giving back', organising a capacity-building workshop on community-based tourism, did not resonate with the villagers' needs. What they asked for was help in promoting tourism to boost tourist numbers and generate more income. I felt that I could not assist with this task as I was not a tour operator or travel agent. Further, as an anthropologist researching tourism, I was too aware of the negative impacts of tourism in rural areas. It therefore seemed to me that villagers misunderstood my true identity in the field and tried to make sense of my presence by allocating certain roles to me. This led me into a fieldwork limbo – a situation of confusion about my own identity in the field.

The fieldwork limbo: identity and the role of money in tourism fieldwork

As the fieldwork progressed, I kept collecting data in the form of interviews, diary entries and informal conversations. I adapted to the lifestyle as much as I could, and learned about cultural practices and what role tourism played. Familiarity with the once foreign suddenly did not seem so far out of reach any more – I was developing a daily routine and started adapting to local etiquette and customs. Despite all the efforts I made, and the fact that I accepted the messy nature of fieldwork, I still found myself in a state of limbo, in the position of a stranger caught between distance and closeness.

At times, the process of data collection and familiarisation with the field seemed like a paradox – I was getting closer to my informants' world, while at the same time I felt even more distanced once I better understood their world. I came to realise that in many aspects we were entirely different and so was our idea of community-based tourism, the very topic that I was so passionate about. The more I observed and learned about the tourism practices in the villages, the more disappointed I was about what I discovered. Two of the villages did not pursue tourism that was community-based in any way, and instead of community participation and widespread benefit, I observed elite domination, power inequalities between castes, and foreign investment – in simple terms, similar dynamics as can usually be observed in mainstream so-called mass tourism. I felt that I had chosen a 'wrong' field, a field that did not qualify for my study on empowerment. How could I ever possibly discover and understand the meaning of empowerment in community-based tourism, if what I witnessed did not even qualify as community-based tourism (according to the literature)? My supervisors kept telling me to 'stick in there' – they must have already known that what I was experiencing was the beginnings of a worthwhile study on the realities of the practice of community-based tourism.

Overall, I got a strong impression that community-based tourism was about money – it was a business, just like any other tourism venture. Even though this is, on the whole, the nature of tourism, tourists expressed their concerns about a lack of 'real' social relationships. Although tourism is largely an economic transaction, community-based tourism should evoke more romantic feelings of 'real' interactions and relationships with residents (Salazar 2012). In this case, it seemed that my values of community and togetherness were under threat from what I saw in practice, even though I was well aware of the profit-oriented nature of many tourism ventures in the developing world. As a result, I felt more like an outsider, similarly to Kleinman's admission about his experience of fieldwork: '[i]f you are not "on their side" then you cannot fully understand why they do what they do. I did not mind experiencing negative feelings; the problem was that these feelings were directed against the group' [under study] (1991: 192). How can we ever – being as open and non-judgmental as we wish to be – feel empathy for a group of people who act quite differently from our own personal values?

Clearly, this could 'violat[e] our valued self' (Kleinman 1991: 192) and cause great inner ethical conflict, one of anthropology's notable challenges.

Equally, I increasingly began to regard social relationships between myself and my host families as being dominated by money. Essentially, I was regarded as a tourist, someone who contributed money to the family income by paying for accommodation and food. In conversations, the importance of money became obvious in that hosting tourists increases not only one's status, but also the family income. While I understood this importance and happily made my contribution, I also witnessed the unequal distribution of benefits in the village, with my host families keeping most tourists in their own house complex. In addition, this monetary relationship qualified me 'only' as a tourist, while I was trying to be who I really was (in my eyes): a researcher. When strolling through the village, I was observed by residents, whose gaze, while usually greeting me with a friendly 'hello', put me into the category of tourist. I could not hide the fact that I was a white and female foreigner, who was very different from anyone else in the village.

In addition, my status as a wealthy white foreigner somehow qualified me as a potential investor. Some of the villagers invited me to invest in their businesses or to buy rice fields, which made our fieldwork encounters yet more precarious. I was shocked by the offers, but started to perform the role of a potential investor, given that I did not want to break the relationships with my key informants. While I did not agree with their way of doing business, I did not express a contrary position in order to avoid trouble. Nevertheless, I felt great inner conflicts. After all, I did not want to invest in a business that I did not support or believe in. My values were under threat again as I realised that my informants wanted something from me, and vice versa, and so one may say that our encounter was never innocent or totally truthful. Even though there was no reason for me to be treated differently from other tourists, deep inside I had felt that as a researcher and anthropologist I would – at least to some extent – be treated like a family member. Money contributed to the creation of a 'business relationship' between us, rather than an innocent social relationship – at least, this is what it was for me.

One may think that performing the role of the tourist would enable a smooth pathway through fieldwork; after all, I regularly interacted with tourists who came to visit the villages. This could potentially have enabled identification with other 'foreigners', which was, in fact, what I hoped for. Paradoxically, however, I could not even identify with tourists, who arrived in the villages equipped with their cameras to quickly capture the geographical and cultural beauties. For me, they were ignorant and rude, not trying in any way to adapt to the local context or understand residents' way of living – how could they, given the short period of time they spent there? It suddenly seemed that the time that I was in the villages was not so short, after all. Even though I had hoped that being among other Europeans would give me a sense of belonging and remind me of 'home', I was yet more caught up in the limbo of the stranger, fighting my battles of loneliness while trying to get closer to the people I was studying. I was also fighting the objectification of people, both of my own under the locals' gaze, and of the locals under the tourist gaze, a group who I to which I did not want to belong. In fact, I realised I was myself fighting the very processes of objectification that I came to study in Bali as part of the tourism encounter.

It was only through encounters with other tourists that I noticed that I was much closer to the villagers I lived with than to anyone else during fieldwork. As time passed by, I increasingly understood their realities, their values and their ways of doing tourism, and slowly they 'began to humanize in mind' (Friedman 1991: 114). In retrospect, I now understand that the dilemmas I was facing must have been the dilemmas of the anthropologist in the fieldwork limbo, who, while often perceived as tourist, fights her/his battles of being accepted for who s/he really is.

Conclusion

By drawing and reflecting on some of my fieldwork experiences in Bali, in this chapter I have discussed the difficulties of negotiating the field, as well as the challenges of conducting fieldwork under time and money constraints. These are pressures that increasingly more anthropologists face, even though it is the duration and the depth of empirical evidence of anthropological fieldwork that largely distinguishes it from other disciplines. As Gupta and Ferguson suggest, 'the single most significant factor determining whether a piece of research will be accepted as (that magical word) "anthropological" is the extent to which it depends on experience "in the field"' (2007: 1). While I agree that long periods of fieldwork can indeed enable thick description in a Geertzian way, this is not always possible due to the money and time pressures that both doctoral students and established academics alike experience. We must therefore find ways of conducting research that are both worthwhile to residents and the academic community, and at the same time feasible in the various political economies of research in which we operate. Reflecting on our experiences and sharing these with fellow researchers, as I have endeavoured to do in this chapter, is a starting point.

The experiences I draw on here bring to the fore some of the problems that we face as anthropologists (or social science researchers more broadly) when entering a 'field' that is unknown and strange to us. The point I make in this chapter is that, no matter how much we prepare beforehand, nothing prepares us for the realities of fieldwork. These realities are challenging precisely because we cannot prepare for them and because they are inherently personal. By means of an open reflection on these personal challenges and disillusionments while doing fieldwork, I problematise the idea that the anthropologist will necessarily speak from 'inside' the society under study, which is an idea that often seems to be transmitted to students embarking on fieldwork. I agree with Simpson (2006) that we need to face our research and fieldwork with humility if ethnography is to remain our primary tool of data collection.

There is a need to recognise the limits and limitations of our research and to accept our position as outsiders when conducting research away from home. As I have shown in this chapter, short fieldwork periods in foreign fields can make deep relationships difficult to forge. On the one hand, this is due to a lack of time to allow for relationships of trust to emerge with participants; on the other hand, the pressure of completing one's research time-efficiently puts strains on social relationships in the field. This does not mean, however, that our research will be any less valid. In fact, I did, in the end, gain valuable insights into community-based tourism in Bali and the broader power relations in the tourism landscape. The difference from an extended stay in the field was, though, that my fieldwork was uneasy and my positionality in the field was unclear, which led to a range of conflicts that I needed to analyse before dedicating myself to dealing with my core findings.

In this chapter I have demonstrated that a closer analysis of field notes, including changing perceptions of the field and field encounters, informs the knowledge-creation process in anthropology. A more open account of the travails of doing fieldwork enables us to understand the challenges and social interactions that underlie our written findings as they are communicated to the reader. In the case presented here, analysing the social interactions I was part of also enabled me to better understand the subject I was studying. I set out as a researcher to understand the phenomenon of community-based tourism from villagers' and tourists' points of view, but at the same time found myself being part of these touristic spaces and being given the role of the tourist at the same time. Paradoxically, I became entangled in the tourism encounter, which I had initially planned to observe as an outsider. These confusions are a regular part of anthropological research into tourism in areas where it is still used as new livelihood strategy. In those contexts, residents perceive tourism as a business in need of the tourist dollar, with the anthropologist being given the role of the tourist who can offer financial support. Entering touristic spaces and processes as a white anthropologist can therefore signify taking on shifting roles, one of them being the tourist who, for residents, constitutes a window into the Western world. This situation I ended up facing therefore stood in stark contrast to the romanticised idea I had in mind when initially entering the different *community*-based tourism settings in Bali.

It is those vested interests, and the precarious fieldwork encounters in the empirical world, to which our analyses need to turn. This chapter has traced anthropology's epistemological claims by evidencing the early career anthropologists' navigation through fieldwork characterised by money and time pressures. It emphasises that it is not only worthwhile but necessary to make field encounters, and our perception of the notion of the 'field' itself, our primary points of analysis in order to fulfil our attempts to make anthropology a yet more reflexive and rigorous endeavour. Tourism is by no means an exception, and is a study context that – maybe more than others – demands a thorough reflection on the anthropologist's role as foreigner in foreign fields.

References

Amit, V. (2000) Introduction. Constructing the field. In: V. Amit (ed.) *Constructing the Field. Ethnographic Fieldwork in the Contemporary World*. London: Routledge, pp. 1–18.

Andrews, H. (2012) Mapping my way: map-making and analysis in participant observation. In: L. Roberts (ed.) *Mapping Cultures. Place, Practice, Performance*. Basingstoke: Palgrave, pp. 216–236.

Appadurai, A. (1991) Global ethnoscapes. Notes and queries for a transnational anthropology. In: R. Fox (ed.) *Recapturing anthropology*. Santa Fe: School of American Research Press, pp. 191–210.

Bauman, Z. (2001) *Community. Seeking Safety in an Insecure World*. Cambridge: Polity Press.

Behar, R. (2003) Ethnography and the book that was lost. *Ethnography*, 4(1): 15–39.

Boonratana, R. (2010) Community-based tourism in Thailand. The need and justification for an operational definition. *Kasetsart Journal, Social Sciences*, 31: 280–289.

Bruner, E. (2005) *Culture on Tour. Ethnographies of Travel*. London: University of Chicago Press.

Cerwonka, A. and Malkki, L. H. (2007) *Improvising Theory. Process and Temporality in Ethnographic Fieldwork*. Chicago: University of Chicago press.

Coffey, A. (1999) *The Ethnographic Self. Fieldwork and the Representation of Identity*. London: Sage.

Cornwall, A. (2010) Introductory overview – buzzwords and fuzzwords. Deconstructing development discourse. In: A. Cornwall and D. Eade (eds) *Deconstructing Development Discourse. Buzzwords and Fuzzwords*. Bourton-on-Dunsmore: Practical Action Publishing and Oxfam, pp. 1–18.

Crapanzano, V. (2012) 'At the heart of the discipline'. Critical reflections on fieldwork. In: A. C. G. M. Robben and J. A. Sluka (eds) *Ethnographic Fieldwork. An Anthropological Reader*, 2nd edn. Oxford: John Wiley and Sons, pp. 547–562.

Denzin, N.K. (2001) *Interpretive Interactionism*, 2nd edn. London: Sage.

Dolezal, C. (2011) Community-based tourism in Thailand. (Dis)illusions of authenticity and the necessity for dynamic concepts of culture and power. *Austrian Journal of South-East Asian Studies*, 4(1): 129–138.

Dolezal, C. (2015) The tourism encounter in community-based tourism in Northern Thailand. Empty meeting ground or space for change? *ASEAS – Austrian Journal of South-East Asian Studies*, 8(2): 165–186.

Eiseman, F. B. (1990) *Bali: Sekala & Niskala. Essays on Religion, Ritual, and Art*. North Clarendon: Tuttle Publishing.

Friedman, D. (1991). Feeling. In: M. Ely, T. Anzul, D. Friedman, A. Garner and A. McCormack Steinmetz (eds) *Doing Qualitative Research: Circles Within Circles*. Abingdon: RoutledgeFalmer, pp. 107–137.

Geertz, C. (1959) Form and variation in Balinese village structure. *American Anthropologist*, 61(6): 991–1012.

Geertz, C. (1973) *The Interpretation of Cultures*. New York: Basic Books.

Goodwin, H. and Santilli, R. (2009) *Community-based Tourism. A Success?* ICRT occasional paper 11. Bonn: GTZ.

Graburn, N. (1977) Tourism: the sacred journey. In: V. Smith (ed.) *Hosts and Guests: The Anthropology of Tourism*. Philadelphia: University of Pennsylvania Press, pp. 17–32.

Guillemin, M. and Gillam, L. (2004) Ethics, reflexivity, and 'ethically important moments' in research. *Qualitative Inquiry*, 10(2): 261–280.

Gupta, A. and Ferguson, J. (2007) Discipline and practice: 'The field' as site, method and location in anthropology. In: A. Gupta and J. Ferguson (eds) *Anthropological Locations. Boundaries and Grounds of a Field Science.* Berkeley: University of California Press, pp. 1–46.

Hammoudi, A. and Borneman, J. (2009) Afterthoughts. The experience and agony of fieldwork. In: J. Borneman (ed.) *Being There: The Fieldwork Encounter and the Making of Truth.* Berkeley: University of California Press, pp. 259–272.

Howe, L. (2005) *The Changing World of Bali: Religion, Society and Tourism.* Abingdon: Routledge.

Irwin, R. (2007) Culture shock. Negotiating feelings in the field. *Anthropology Matters Journal*, 9(1): 1–11.

Kesby, M., Kindon, S. and Pain, R. (2007) Participation as a form of power. Retheorising empowerment and spatialising participatory action research. In: S. Kindon, R. Pain and M. Kesby (eds) *Participatory Action Research Approaches and Methods: Connecting People, Participation and Place.* Abingdon: Routledge, pp. 19–25.

Kleinman, S. (1991) Field-workers' feelings: what we feel, who we are, how we analyze. In: W. B. Shaffir and R. A. Stebbins (eds) *Experiencing Fieldwork: An Inside View of Qualitative Research.* London: Sage, pp. 184–195.

Leal, P.A. (2010) Participation. The ascendancy of a buzzword in the neo-liberal era. In: A. Cornwall and D. Eade (eds) *Deconstructing Development Discourse. Buzzwords and Fuzzwords.* Bourton-on-Dunsmore: Practical Action Publishing and Oxfam, pp. 89–100.

Marcus, G. E. (1995) Ethnography in/of the world system. The emergence of multi-sited ethnography. *Annual Review of Anthropology*, 24: 95–117.

Marcus, G. E. and Fischer, M. M. J. (1986) *Anthropology as Cultural Critique. An Experimental Moment in the Human Sciences.* Chicago: University of Chicago Press.

Mosse, D. (2005) *Cultivating Development. An Ethnography of Aid Policy and Practice.* London: Pluto Press.

Nash, D. (1996) *Anthropology of Tourism.* Oxford: Pergamon.

Picard, M. (1992) *Bali. Tourisme culturel et culture touristique* [*Bali. Cultural Tourism and Touristic Culture*]. Paris: l'Harmattan.

Pillow, W. S. (2003) Confession, catharsis, or cure? Rethinking the uses of reflexivity as methodological power in qualitative research. *Qualitative Studies in Education*, 16(2): 175–196.

Rivoal, I. and Salazar, N. B. (2013) Introduction. Contemporary ethnographic practice and the value of serendipity. *Social Anthropology*, 21(2): 178–185.

Salazar, N. B. (2012) Community-based cultural tourism: issues, threats and opportunities. *Journal of Sustainable Tourism*, 20(1): 9–22.

Simmel, G. (1950) *The Sociology of Georg Simmel.* New York: The Free Press.

Simpson, B. (2006) 'You don't do fieldwork, fieldwork does you.' Between subjectivation and objectivation in anthropological fieldwork. In: D. Hobbs and R. Wright (eds) *The Sage Handbook of Fieldwork.* London: Sage, pp. 125–138.

Telfer, D. and Sharpley, R. (2008) *Tourism and Development in the Developing World.* London: Routledge.

Warren, C. A. B. (2000) Writing the other, inscribing the self. *Qualitative Sociology*, 23(2): 183–199.

8 Pilgrimage tourism and cultural route team ethnographies in the Iberian Peninsula

A collaborative study

Xerardo Pereiro and Martín Gómez-Ullate

Introduction

The shift from individual ethnography to team ethnography poses a significant challenge for tourism anthropology. This chapter discusses the advantages and disadvantages of two ethnography projects carried out by multidisciplinary teams with different views of tourism and tourism research. This fieldwork experience revealed a new joint encounter with the Other, permanent negotiations regarding anthropological skills, and different epistemologies of tourism.

The methodology integrated different qualitative techniques comprising anthropological fieldwork research from September 2015, interviews with local tourist agents and tourists, document analysis and discussion groups with researchers and social agents (Phillimore and Goodson 2004; Gutiérrez Brito 2006; Ateljevitch and Munsters 2010). With this multi-method triangular approach, it was possible to produce a qualitative exploratory understanding of the regeneration of pilgrimage routes to Santiago de Compostela – the Portuguese Inland Way (Caminho Português Interior de Santiago, CPIS) and the Spanish Vía de la Plata (Silver Way), with which the CPIS converges. Beginning in September 2015, the authors walked the Portuguese Inland Route to Santiago de Compostela from Farminhão (Viseu, Portugal) to Verín (Galicia, Spain), a distance of approximately 230 kilometres. During the walks, the route was recorded visually, taking photographs every few metres and filming, and the formal and informal signs of the routes were analysed. The authors spoke with workers in restaurants and bars, hotels and hostels, entrepreneurs, guides, tour operators, pilgrims and the local population. Thanks to this fieldwork experience, it was possible to obtain a detailed understanding of the CPIS. In addition, in-depth team interviews were undertaken with key stakeholders, including one of the promoters behind the regeneration of the route, Ana Rita Dias (Vila Pouca de Aguiar Tourism councillor), and the president of the Vila Real Association of Hikers (Associação de Caminheiros de Vila Real) behind the creation of the route, Hernâni Carvalho. Finally, a set of 32 in-depth interviews with Portuguese pilgrims following the route was analysed.

This chapter is structured as follows: firstly, tourism ethnography as a method and its evolution from individual to team research is discussed; secondly, a case study based on the experience of team research regarding tourism and pilgrimage in the Iberian Peninsula is presented; and finally, some conclusions and questions for the future are posed.

Anthropologists researching tourism: a global need

Anthropology has made four types of contribution to the research and study of tourism: epistemological-theoretical-conceptual; methodological; accumulated anthropological knowledge from tourism and the influence of anthropology on tourism studies and research; and ethical and deontological contributions.

Taking the first contribution, according to the perspective of cultural relativism, anthropology favours a holistic and integral approach to tourism, trying to understand the meanings that social agents attribute to their actions and critically questioning the international geopolitics of tourism (Pereiro 2009; Macleod and Carrier 2010). This anthropological view has humanised tourism and its practitioners, rethinking the activity itself and its social and cultural effects (Burns 1999; Chambers 2000; Bruner 2005). The methodological approach, based on long-term participant observation, is precisely what distinguishes anthropology from other disciplines: ethnography, fieldwork in long-term continuous stages, and the comparative method (Atkinson and Hammersley 1994; Gmelch 2004). By using the methodological tools of participant observation and intensive coexistence with the people studied, tourism anthropology has drawn attention to the development of tourism and its problems around the planet by giving voice to its agents and actors.

The third type of contribution is the reflexive anthropological knowledge accumulated from field investigations, which can be analysed in the relevant tourism ethnographies, providing a more multifaceted perspective. The purpose of these ethnographies is to interpret the role of tourism in contemporary societies, helping to deal with the effects of tourism by maximising benefits and minimising harm (Santana 1997; Simonicca 2004; Gmelch 2004; Pereiro et al. 2012). These tourism ethnographies are useful and have had a significant impact in several ways, for example through the creation and construction of responsible tourism and better and more sensitive travellers (Chambers 2005); the development of enriching intercultural contacts that diminish ethnocentrism and racism, and are useful for raising awareness of cultural diversity and symmetrical interchange and mixing as positive human traits; guiding tourism practices towards respecting cultural identities, learning about and understanding them according to the principles of cultural relativism; and understanding change and the socio-cultural effects of tourism as a social process (Carvajal 1992: 40–41). The latter contribution concerns ethics and deontology, that is, anthropology provides ethical support for more sustainable and responsible tourism development policies and practices to minimise negative effects and maximise benefits (Pereiro and De León 2007;

Pinto and Pereiro 2010). In this respect, the ethical role of anthropology is applied, interventive, committed and involved in the development of tourism with a human face.

Diversities in tourism anthropology and diverse tourism

When anthropology focuses on tourism, it does not interpret it from a single point of view, but rather presents a diversity and plurality of views and theoretical approaches that have been evolving and becoming more complex over time. Some authors have attempted to summarise and organise this diversity of axes and approaches. Tom Selwyn (2001), for instance, identifies tourism anthropology as a subfield of anthropology framed within other travel categories (migrants, refugees, exiles, etc.) and identities in diaspora and displacement contexts. For him there are three major themes in tourism anthropology: the semiology of tourism; problems with the political economy of tourism; and the relationship between tourism and development. The semiology of tourism concerns images and the symbolic paraphernalia of tourism (postcards, brochures, guides, souvenirs). It also includes the anthropological study of museums (history, memory, identity) and the relationship between cultural heritage and tourism. Selwyn conceptualises cultural heritage as part of the language of tourism and underscores how important this topic is to understand the nature of contemporary consumption, the construction of the Other, and the interdisciplinarity of tourism anthropology (e.g. the study of landscape symbolism).

Selwyn's second theme focuses on tourism business networks and international tourism (cf. Crick 1994) as a political economy of tourism (cf. Selwyn 2007), analysing how localities integrate into national, regional and political economic structures through tourism. The relationship between tourism and globalisation is central here (Nogués Pedregal 2005). The Spanish eastern and southern coasts provide a notable case of the impact of tourism on the landscape, and environmental degradation and social deterioration due to expanding corruption and the mafia, which involves a significant percentage of politicians and public officials. The third theme concerns the relationship between tourism and development, a long-standing focus of interest in tourism anthropology. Some of the topics highlighted here are the contribution of tourism to the economic development of destinations; the relationship between tourism and arts in urban renewal; the relationship between tourism, agriculture and fisheries; and finally the relationship between tourism and rural industries. In short, Selwyn's framework is a very positive one in terms of creating a structure with which to better understand tourism anthropology.

Naomi Leite and Nelson Graburn (2009) also focus on key expanding themes in tourism anthropology, such as research into places, people, movement, things and the global. In the first category, *places*, they integrate research into the production of places and their marketing as tourist destinations (image, process, power, performance, meanings). For this, the political economy and semiotics that analyse the identity and visibility of tourist destinations are important. The second category, *people*, integrates the study of the social agents of tourism, residents and local reactions to tourism. In *movement*, the third category, they analyse tourist trips from the structure of the experience and their relationship with pilgrimages; while in the fourth category, *things*, tourism anthropologists study museums, theme parks, souvenirs, photos and other objects as vehicles for tourist representations. Finally, in the fifth category, the *global*, anthropologists approach tourism as a global circulation of images and ideas in a world deeply interconnected by transnational and translocal travellers. In the latter part of their work, Leite and Graburn point to the future thematic directions of an already mature tourism anthropology: tourism and medicine, tourism and the media, tourism and power, tourism and activism, tourism and kinship.

Our work is informed by the varied theoretical contributions made by anthropologists to the study of tourism. It is linked to four major lines of inquiry in the anthropology of tourism: tourism as a socio-cultural exchange; tourism as a modern ritual experience; tourism as a practice of differential consumption; and tourism as an instrument of political-ideological power.

From individual to team tourism ethnographies

Ethnography is a method and a core technique in anthropology and in other social sciences such as sociology (Guasch 2002). Ethnography is what differentiates anthropology (Stocking 1992: 30). Ethnography is a methodology and method of socio-cultural research, a set of procedures and rules for producing and organising knowledge (Velasco and Díaz de Rada 1997). These procedures and rules have to do with a methodological position that implies strangeness, curiosity, 'thick' description (Geertz 1991), the translation and interpretation of the socio-cultural reality with which we deal. In this situation of meeting with others, we learn about their problems, their perceptions, their behaviour and their way of life in their own words, voices and looks.

Anthropologists do ethnography to examine unique and microscopic events to answer major universal questions. Seeing the universal in everyday life and the quotidian in the universal are tasks undertaken by anthropologists in their fieldwork, regardless of whether the field scenario is a small community, a transnational migrant population, a company or the global community. Doing fieldwork, anthropologists study human problems in contexts of cultural diversity. Their know-how is ethnography, a professional practice that can be considered a craft (Díaz de Rada 2011), since the anthropologist's field is his or her particular *atelier*, where young learners learn from experienced fieldworkers.

Ethnography is more than a technique or set of tools. Research techniques are the operational procedures and instruments for producing data (e.g. questionnaires, life histories, surveys, interviews). These data serve to understand phenomena, to capture the relations between phenomena and the intentionality of actions. In the words of Penelope Harvey (2008), 'Ethnography is a conscious ignorance'.

The ethnographic method converts the anthropologist into the main instrument for data collection, and is therefore an intersubjectivity between observer and observed. In this respect, decades after Clifford Geertz critically highlighted this concept in *The Anthropologist as Author* (1988), the influence of the rhetorical and stylistic resources of the authors of classic monographs is still that ethnography is an individualised social practice that silences the company and intervention of mates and research assistants during fieldwork. Thus, collaborative research and team ethnography pose a threat to the reputation of anthropologists in their academic field, where the value of individual work is overprivileged (see Lassiter 2005) compared with those who might be described as 'silent co-authors' found behind team ethnographies; for example wives, husbands, translators, colleagues and other collaborators.

The anthropologist's context, experience, personality and personal biases compose what has been called the 'personal equation' (López Coira 1991), in which objectivism is challenged when ethnography is understood as a personal experience. In Paul Rabinow's words: 'the ethnographer is a guy of flesh and blood, with his weaknesses, his miseries and yet with all his human greatness that tests his own person in trying to understand the other person' (Rabinow 1992: 16). But this does not necessarily lead to naïve, candid subjectivism. Through reflexivity as a method and the contextual analysis of constructed reality, the certainty – not absolute truth – of ethnographies – in a word, their quality – can be better controlled. Team ethnographies give new dimensions to ethnography's quality control. In the traditional control chain formed by the ethnographer, his/her supervisor, peers and the public, a new peer control is inserted that has been present in all stages of the process of producing anthropological knowledge.

According to Susan Tax Freeman (1991), ethnographic observation and self-awareness of the anthropologist's prejudices are the strengths of anthropological knowledge and what validates the anthropologists' work. She argues that this observation makes it possible to understand a culture in the intimacy of the local people, living with them, and taking into account the anthropologist's family condition, his/her residence, age, sex, personality, his/her relation to the social structure of the local culture, his/her biography and the distance needed to accomplish comparative analysis (ibid.: 130–135). Freeman also asserts that the anthropologist's understanding and observation are always incomplete and that no culture is fully understood; as a result, some anthropologists need assistance (Freeman 1991: 130).

The anthropological tradition emphasises the ethnographic method as a solitary initiation in prolonged direct contact with the Other, as a somehow mysterious process through which one learns the practice of the anthropological office of ethnographer. However, at present tourism ethnography (Frohlick and Harrison 2008) is changing the very notion of ethnography by converting it into a method of co-investigation, participatory research and co-authorship in some cases (Pereiro and De León 2007). Due to the complexity of the phenomenon, ethnography – and particularly tourism ethnography – increasingly requires ethnographic teamwork. This is also true due to the multi-situated and international character of tourism (see Hollinshead 2004: 63), its capacity to create world culture (Kirshenblatt-Gimblett 1998), the ability of tourism to create intercultural differences more properly researched by team research (Pereiro et al. 2012), and the need to plan tourism with more observation and participation (Hall 2010: 138). This is because reality is not individual, but social and relational, multiple and contextual (Decrop 2004: 160), all of which stimulates a multi-ethnographic approach.

Tourism ethnography has gone from being a single authorised voice representing the studied, to conversational and dialogical analyses in which it explores intersubjective experiences and integrates greater interdisciplinarity (Phillimore and Goodson 2004: 19). It attempts to improve the quality of anthropological research with attention to subjectivity, ethics, values and politics, without neglecting a multi-method triangulation approach, mixed approaches and systemic and post-positivist approaches to tourism. In this way, different researchers or anthropologists analyse the same type of data, or different data and contexts, viewing realities in common, or comparing them and constructing a more complex ethnographic bricolage richer in nuances and contrasts (Jordan and Gibson 2004: 215–235; Belsky 2004: 273–291).

Team ethnographies from the CPIS to Santiago de Compostela

'A tourist is half a pilgrim, if a pilgrim is half a tourist.'

(Turner and Turner 2011: 20)

From a classic disciplinary view, tourism was born in the nineteenth century as a product of industrialisation and new working conditions. From another point of view, however, the origin of tourism is linked to pilgrimage trips (Collins-Kreiner and Gatrell 2006; Margry 2008; Sharpley 2009). Journeys motivated by religious or spiritual considerations have become popular in recent times and represent an important segment of international tourism (Timothy and Olsen 2006; Margry 2008; Norman and Cusack 2015). According to the World Tourism Organization, nearly 330 million tourists visit the main religious shrines of the world every year (UNWTO 2014). They are notable for their plurality and the diversity of religions, creeds and contexts in which they practice. This relationship between religion and tourism was highlighted in the 1970s by MacCannell (1976) and in the 1980s by Horne (1984), who argues that contemporary tourists are modern pilgrims who carry tourist guidebooks as their devotional texts.

Our team research focused on the tourist usage and meanings of an ancient religious pilgrimage route, the Portuguese Inland Way to Santiago de Compostela (Caminho Português Interior de Santiago, CPIS), which is slowly being revitalised and touristified today. Its focus is a touristology of the motivations, post-experiences and meanings that tour pilgrims on this route attribute to this social practice, interpreted here as a collage of pilgrimage, religiosity, spirituality and tourism (unlike the interpretations of other authors such as Palmer et al. 2012).

The antecedents to the Way of St James (Camino de Santiago/Caminho de Santiago) are found in the old travellers to the 'end of the earth' in Galicia (Cunha de Magalhães 2005). In 44 AD, James the Apostle was martyred, and around the year 820 remains attributed to the saint were buried in a tomb in Compostela with the aim, according to some authors, of creating social and political Catholic cohesion vis-à-vis the Muslims (Brochado de Almeida 2011: 5). The Order of Santiago was founded around 1161 for the purpose of protecting the pilgrims on the Way of St James. After centuries of decline, at the end of the nineteenth century, Santiago de Compostela Cardinal and Archbishop Miguel Payá and historian Emilio López Ferreiro 'rediscovered' and reinvented the tomb of James the Apostle. In 1884, Pope Leo XIII issued a bull, *Deus Omnipotens*, recommending the pilgrimage to Santiago (see Mouriño 1997).

In the 1960s and 1970s, Father Elias Valiña (from Pedrafita do Cebreiro) fought to revitalise and research the French way to the shrine of Santiago de Compostela, invigorating the pilgrimage movement. In 1982 Pope John Paul II did the pilgrimage to Santiago de Compostela, and in the Holy Year of 1993 the Government of Galicia invested in the *Xacobeo*, a tourist and cultural promotion to celebrate the holy year of St James. Also in 1993, the French Way to Santiago was declared a World Heritage Site by UNESCO. All these factors greatly boosted the pilgrimage movement and the Santiago routes (cf. Álvarez Sousa 1999; Sánchez-Carretero 2015). In 1986 2,491 pilgrims arrived at Santiago (on foot, bicycle or horseback), in 1997 some 25,179 arrived, and in 2015, 262,459.[1] The various Ways of St James, the first declared European Cultural Route, which have inspired many other pilgrimage routes, are today a symbol of European identity as well as a strategy for local, regional, national and international tourism development (Lois González et al. 2014).

Before Portuguese independence in the twelfth century, 184 parishes in Portugal bore the name of Santiago, many of which later changed to the patron saint of São Jorge. The iconography of Santiago that prevails in Portugal is that of the apostle pilgrim with a book, a scallop and other symbols of pilgrimage, rather than Saint James the Moor-slayer (riding a horse and swinging a sword over Moor heads). In Portugal, the ancient Roman roads and transhumance trails used nowadays as Ways to Santiago de Compostela were used by pilgrims in the Middle and Modern Ages (Brochado de Almeida 2011: 15), through a terrain especially problematic to walk over in both the north and the centre. The Portuguese Inland Way (https://cpis.utad. pt) covers 205 kilometres from Viseu to Chaves in Portugal, and 180 kilometres from the border with the autonomous community of Galicia in Spain (in the village of Vilarelho da Raia) to Santiago de Compostela. In Verín,

Galicia, the Portuguese Inland Way converges with another way to Santiago, the Vía de la Plata (Silver Way). Like the Silver Way, which crosses western Spain from south to north, the CPIS differs from the other routes to Santiago, being a two-way route that allows pilgrims to walk to Santiago de Compostela (northern Portugal; Galicia, Spain) or Fatima (central Portugal). Its re-emergence as a pilgrimage route in the twenty-first century was inspired by a book by Arlindo Cunha de Magalhães (1995) on the history of the Portuguese Ways of St James as well as an exhibition on the Jacobean ways that was held in Vila Pouca de Aguiar in 2011.

The first official experience of walking along the Portuguese Inland Way to Santiago was in 2000, when a group of mayors and civil servants from the towns crossed by the trail walked from Cidadela de Aguiar to Sabroso de Aguiar. At this time, a very close collaboration began between the Portuguese municipalities along the route to create a product-experience of cultural tourism and pilgrimage, and the Portuguese Inland Way to Santiago de Compostela (Caminho Português Interior de Santiago, CPIS) officially opened to walkers in 2012. There are eight Portuguese municipalities involved in this project: Viseu, Castro Daire, Lamego, Peso da Régua, Santa Marta de Penaguião, Vila Real, Vila Pouca de Aguiar and Chaves. It is administered by the Câmara de Vila Pouca de Aguiar and its tourism councillors, notably Catarina Chaves. The first step in this inter-municipal and transnational cooperation project was to put signage along the route, and the second was the creation of 'hostels' to house the pilgrims every 30–35 kilometres. On 24 April 2012, the first official walk along this new stage of the route took place. Additionally, the CPIS project is part of an international cooperation network for the routes to Santiago.[2] In the words of one of the CPIS heads, 'The Portuguese Inland Way is a recent path [...] the goal is not to create a mass product [...] that is dangerous' (Catarina Chaves, personal communication, June 2016). This is a rarely taken route, with few pilgrims on it,[3] and is most often used in the spring and summer (March–September). The low number of pilgrims staying in the hostel[4] indicates how far the route is from overcrowding and how intimate the pilgrimage experience can be.

Team ethnography, or 'when two heads are better than one'

Under the auspices of the Cultour+ project,[5] a graphics and audiovisual ethnography team was developed over the course of a few months in 2016 and 2017 by the authors. We walked and observed some parts of the CPIS together, carrying out in-depth interviews with pilgrims, local development agents, walkers and pilgrim association founders, taking pictures, reflecting and writing field notes. We both conducted discussion groups with different stakeholders (hostel managers, walkers' associations, cultural heritage and tourism public managers, pilgrims, researchers) and recorded the debates along the route.[6] From the field to the desk, we discussed theoretical perspectives, shared updates on the state of the art and news in journals and articles, and worked together on publications, discussing them draft by draft.

The research was developed from academic positions and within the Cultour+ project framework between Xerardo Pereiro (Portugal, University of Trás-os-Montes and Alto Douro – UTAD) and Martín Gómez-Ullate (Spain, University of Extremadura). This helped to extend it to students and other academic activities such as the Cultour+ summer school, where the research results were shared and disseminated with all the international partners involved with the project. There was an intense exchange of initiatives, knowledge and perspectives, not only academic but also from entrepreneurs planning business projects based on the routes, tourism consultants and local development agents. A scientific meeting for knowledge dissemination was held in Vila Real, there was a walking tour by CPIS with university students in tourism and local stakeholders, and an exhibition about the route during April and May 2017 in UTAD). The summer school included a research visit to the Silver Way. A one-day journey departing from Caceres and ending in Baños de Montemayor allowed us to interact with expert guides and interpreters of cultural and natural landscapes and heritage, town authorities, hostel managers, entrepreneurs and so forth. In addition to the Silver Way's tourism highlights, relationships between 'tour pilgrims' and hostel and hotel owners were discussed, in particular the special competition between hostel managers to attract pilgrims and villages to become the ending/starting point of a stage in the journey. Some perspectives on distinctive parts of the route were debated in situ (at the Tourism Hostel of Hervás), such as the new Green Trail planned to replace the old railway between the cities of Plasencia and Béjar.

Between January 2016 and December 2017, the authors participated in discussion groups at anthropology and cultural tourism conferences and, most importantly, learned to work together as a team, negotiating differences and asymmetries. While as anthropologists we had many approaches in common, we had different theoretical and methodological influences, and also had to negotiate subjectivities found in anthropology, for example on the de-differentiation between tourism and pilgrimage (Palmer et al. 2012). We both developed methodological guides, observation scripts and interview protocols that were enriched by parallel experiences on both routes (CPIS and Silver Way). The authors' different backgrounds and life situations were important, especially our shared cross-border trajectories, being both Spanish (but one Galician and the other Castilian) with very close contact and experience with Portugal (one working and living in Portugal for 20 years, the other married to a Portuguese and spending long periods in his parents-in-law's house in Portugal). We both assumed the interpretive character of our field notes and auto-ethnographies (Creese et al. 2008) in addition to an awareness of the ethnographic, personal and critical character of ethnography. In particular, and above all, we discovered the need to work as a team and collaborate together as anthropologists on the one hand, and with other anthropologists and tourism researchers on the other. These tasks were not always easy, and while they had some advantages, they also had their limitations.

Doing tourism ethnography in teams means collaborating in ethnographic research and team ethnography (Clerke and Hopwood 2014), but it is important to differentiate between collaborative ethnography and team ethnography. In collaborative ethnography, the ethnographers share with their informants their ethnographic methods and writing, collective fieldwork and co-writing as research strategies. Also, several forms of ethnography involve multiple researchers. Collaboration refers to the relationship between a researcher and the researched. Here, collaboration is seen as the interactions between a researcher and the local people, the purpose of which is to co-produce insider knowledge about these communities. The keywords of collaborative ethnography are equity, co-writing and co-working, that is, how ethnography unfolds through our dialogic collaboration with our subjects (cf. Dietz and Álvarez Veinguer 2014a, 2014b).

Team ethnography is different from collaborative ethnography (cf. O'Reilly 2009: 201–208). Erickson and Stull (1998: 15) describe team ethnography as a cooperative and collaborative joint venture between researchers. Team ethnography reduces the loneliness, anxiety and self-doubt that can accompany traditional solo research. Moreover, diversity in membership enriches both the research and its outcomes. According to Erickson and Stull (1998), there are several levels or steps in team ethnography.

1   'Getting started'. This relates to team selection and management structure (hierarchical or egalitarian). In our case we constructed an egalitarian team ethnography, with distributing research tasks and cooperation within the project responsibilities.
2   'Getting there'. In fieldwork and research, team skills, capacities, interests and temperaments were negotiated as complementary and non-competitive aspects that improved the development of the project research.
3   'Fieldwork methods'. In this step, both ethnographers planned the fieldwork methods and interviews through a permanent dialogue and exchange (by mail, WhatsApp, Dropbox, telephone, etc.), reviewing the interviews done by each other and enriching the questionnaire for further interviews. Both authors speak Spanish, Portuguese and English, language skills that were important in this research project.
4   'Writing'. The most difficult level of team ethnography. Should the work be written with one voice? With polyphony or multivocality? The question is how to write as a member of a team. In our case we constructed two voices to articulate one case study (the CPIS) and different voices in a comparative perspective about the other case study in Spain (the Silver Way). Once the niches and research responsibilities were defined, we shared theoretical perspectives, literature, scientific reviews, field notes, photos, historical documents, documentaries, summer course programmes and ideas about the cultural routes studied.

According to Erickson and Stull (1998), all teamwork ethnography is asymmetrical. How did we negotiate asymmetries in our team research? First, we recognised and underlined the strong skills, valuable experiences and the right to be different of every research partner, and their roles in the project. Second, we recognised asymmetries and diversities as part of human life, trying to avoid tensions and conflicts, in addition to assuming that differences between researchers could enrich the anthropological projects. One example is how, at the beginning of the project, we decided to think in dichotomous, polarised terms about tourism and pilgrimage, while after reading, discussing and reflecting, we began to analyse tourism and pilgrimage as a more linked phenomenon: tour pilgrimage.

As anthropologists and social scientists more broadly know, tourism research is multidisciplinary; our effort was to use pedagogical strategies to explain the advantages of anthropology and tourism ethnography to tourism degree students. Furthermore, the longstanding friendship between the researchers, as in this case, provided a solid base for team ethnography in the tourism arena. Team ethnographies are a collective construction of anthropological knowledge, a process through which we found far more advantages than disadvantages.

Among the advantages is that team ethnography enables a more complex and multifaceted anthropological view, and so a deeper understanding of the field and object of study – in this case, the pilgrimage experience from all the involved agents' views. Ethnography provides access to different places of daily life due to the researchers' personal biases, so intercultural and inter-gender teams should be encouraged. Team ethnography reduces the traditional hierarchy between investigator and investigated; improves quality control through questioning the ethnographies (data and/or interpretation) of the other investigator and confirming or denying their validity; makes it possible to see through more eyes and feel through more senses allowing simultaneous related actions in different places reaching more units of analysis and observation; and confronts different research views and impressions questioning unilineal and univocal interpretations.

Among the disadvantages, the most relevant we identified is that if anthropology is a time-consuming discipline, team ethnography needs even more time and dialogue, from the first moment of negotiating field strategies. Also, it forces researchers to commit time to thinking about how to share the ethnographies, and the additional ethnographic information collected reduces the amount of time available to analyse the data.

Conclusion

This chapter has analysed the changes from individual to team ethnographies of tourism – a very important emerging trend for anthropology's theoretical and methodological progress – and presents a case study focusing on team ethnography from a cross-cultural and transnational perspective. The study highlights the differences between collaborative ethnography (ethnographies co-produced by researcher and researched) and team ethnography (research teams comprising multiple interdisciplinary members). Team ethnography challenges the traditional and hegemonic academic individualism awarded by university evaluations and rankings.

Our team ethnography is part of a larger multi-sited study with common fieldwork in one site in northern Portugal and ongoing fieldwork research on the Silver Way where it crosses Extremadura (Spain). The different professional and personal biographies of the researchers come together in the fieldwork, analysis and writing processes, producing work that is well informed by different insights and experiences in the field. We have cooperated to reduce potential conflicts, or competition, between us as field workers, and neither of the authors felt pressure to distinguish themselves from the other, or negotiated a narrative to account for personal and intellectual differences between team members. As our epistemological positions were aligned, there was no need to negotiate issues of anthropological knowledge. Asymmetry can be productively and ethically exploited in research teams.

The solitary and heroic anthropologist going into the field is embodied in the classic anthropology literature, for example in the works of Bronislaw Malinowski. New methodologies that draw on social networking and co-working facilities are emerging on a daily basis and challenge the stereotype of the 'loneliness of the long-distance runner' so common to some social sciences and humanities. The creation of a team ethnography, with all the complex negotiations and arrangements that it entails, offers a positive model because – crucially – it sets up a deliberative process that involves testing the work as it is being done, in turn improving control of both processes and outputs.

Notes

1 source: Pilgrim's Reception Office in Santiago, https://oficinadelperegrino.com/esta disticas/
2 see www.saintjamesway.eu
3 378 in 2015 according to data from the Pilgrim's Reception Office, https://oficina delperegrino.com/estadisticas/
4 Between January 2012 and July 2016, only 245 pilgrims slept in the hostel in Almargem, district of Viseu (data collected from the hostel's register).
5 A European Erasmus+ Strategic Partnership with the title 'Innovation and capacity building in higher education for cultural management, hospitality and sustainable tourism in European cultural routes', ref. 2015-1-ES01-KA203-016142, http://www.cultourplus.info/en/
6 For an example see https://www.youtube.com/watch?v=zP7yQXfItqE

Acknowledgements

The contribution of Martín Gómez-Ullate to this article comes from research funded by the Program Aimed at Attracting and Retaining Research Talent for inclusion in the Research Centers of the Autonomous Community of Extremadura (Government of Extremadura) [Ayudas destinadas a la retención y atracción de talento investigador para su incorporación en los Centros de Investigación de la Comunidad Autónoma de Extremadura] and by the Becas de Movilidad al Personal Docente e Investigador de la Universidad de Extremadura y de los Centros Tecnológicos de la Comunidad Autónoma de Extremadura en centros extranjeros de Enseñanza Superior y/o Investigación (Consejería de Educación y Empleo, Junta de Extremadura).

In the case of Xerardo Pereiro (UTAD), he is very grateful to CETRAD (http://www.cetrad.utad.pt) and the support of the European Structural and Investment Funds in the FEDER component, through the Operational Competitiveness and Internationalization Programme (COMPETE 2020) [Project No. 006971 (UID/SOC/04011); Funding Reference: POCI-01-0145-FEDER-006971]; and national funds through the Portuguese Foundation for Science and Technology (FCT) under project UID/SOC/04011/2013. Specifically, the research for this article was carried out under the auspices of the Cultour+ 'Innovation and capacity building in higher education for cultural management, hospitality and sustainable tourism in European cultural routes' project, an Erasmus+ project, under the leadership of the University of Extremadura (UNEX, Spain) in collaboration with the University of Trás-os-Montes and Alto Douro (UTAD, Portugal) and other European partners. The project was approved by the EU with financial support of €189,135. Contract number 2015-1-ES01-KA203-016142.

References

Álvarez Sousa, A. (ed.) (1999) *Homo peregrinus*. Vigo: Xerais.

Ateljevic, I., Pritchard, A. and Morgan, N. (eds) (2007) *The Critical Turn in Tourism Studies. Innovative Research Methodologies*. Amsterdam: Elsevier.

Atkinson, P. and Hammersley, M. (1994) *Etnografía: métodos de investigación*. Barcelona: Paidós.

Belsky, J. (2004) Contributions of qualitative research to understanding the politics of community ecotourism. In: J. Phillimore and L. Goodson (eds) *Qualitative Research in Tourism: Ontologies, Epistemologies and Methodologies*. Abingdon, UK: Routledge, pp. 273–291.

Brochado de Almeida, C. A. and Dias Brochado de Almeida, P. M. (2011) *Caminhos Portugueses de Peregrinação. O Caminho do Litoral para Santiago*. Maia: ISMAI-CEDTUR-CETRAD.

Burns, P. M (1999) *An Introduction to Tourism and Anthropology*. London: Routledge.

Bruner, E. M. (2005) *Culture on Tour. Ethnographies of Travel*. Chicago: Chicago University Press.

Carvajal, J. E. (1992) *La cara oculta del viajero. Reflexiones sobre antropología y turismo*. Buenos Aires: Biblos.

Chambers, E. (2000) *Native Tours. The Anthropology of Travel and Tourism*. Prospect Heights, IL: Waveland Press.

Chambers, E. (2005) Can the anthropology of tourism make us better travelers? *National Association for the Practice of Anthropology Bulletin*, 23(1): 27–44.

Clerke, T. and Hopwood, N. (2014) Ethnography as collective research endeavor. In: T. Clerke and N. Hopwood (eds) *Doing Ethnography in Teams. A Case Study of Asymmetries in Collaborative Research*. Dordrecht: Springer, pp. 5–18.

Collins-Kreiner, N. and Gatrell, J. D. (2006) Tourism, heritage and pilgrimage: the case of Haifa's Baha'i gardens. *Journal of Heritage Tourism*, 1(1): 32–50.

Creese, A., Bhatt, A., Bhojani, N. and Martin, P. (2008) Fieldnotes in team ethnography: researching complementary schools. *Qualitative Research*, 8(2): 197–215.

Crick, M. (1994) *Resplendent Sites, Discordant Voices. Sri Lankans and International Tourism*. London: Routledge.

Cunha de Magalhães, A. (1995) *Caminhos Portugueses de Peregrinação a Compostela. Itinerários portugueses [Identificação dos caminhos e coordenação da investigação]*. Santiago de Compostela/Porto: Xunta de Galicia/Centro Regional de Artes Tradicionais.

Cunha de Magalhães, A. (2005) O Caminho português: património e etnografia. In: X. Pardellas (ed.) *Turismo religioso: O Camiño de Santiago*. Vigo: Universidade de Vigo, pp. 49–84.

Decrop, A. (2004) Trustworthiness in qualitative tourism research. In: J. Phipplimore and L. Goodson (eds) *Qualitative Research in Tourism. Ontologies, Epistemologies and Methodologies*. London: Routledge, pp. 156–169.

Díaz de Rada, A. (2011) *El taller del etnógrafo. Materiales y herramientas de investigación en etnografía*. Madrid: UNED.

Dietz, G. and Álvarez Veinguer, A. (2014a) Etnografía colaborativa: coordenadas desde un proyecto en curso (InterSaberes). In: Universitat Rovira i Virgili (ed.) *Periferias, fronteras y diálogos: Actas del XIII Congreso de Antropología de la Federación de Asociaciones de Antropología del Estado Español*. Tarragona: Universitat Rovira i Virgili, pp. 3447–3471. http://digital.publicacionsurv.cat/index.php/purv/catalog/book/123

Dietz, G. and Álvarez Veinguer, A. (2014b) Reflexividad, interpretación y colaboración en etnografía: un ejemplo desde la antropología de la educación. In: C. Oehmichen Bazán (ed.) *La etnografía y el trabajo de campo en las ciencias sociales*. México: UNAM, Instituto de Investigaciones Antropológicas, pp. 55–89.

Erickson, K. and Stull, D. (1998) *Doing Team Ethnography: Warnings and Advice*. Thousand Oaks: Sage.

Freeman, S. T. (1991) Aproximación a la distancia: el juego entre intimidad y extrañeza en el estudio cultural. In: M. Cátedra (ed.) *Los españoles vistos por los antropólogos*. Madrid: Júcar, pp. 127–141.

Frohlick, S. and Harrison, J. (2008) Engaging ethnography in tourist research: an introduction. *Tourist Studies*, 8(1): 5–18.

Geertz, C. (1988) *Works and Lives. The Anthropologist as Author*. Stanford: Stanford University Press.

Geertz, C. (1991[1973]) *La interpretación de las culturas*. Barcelona: Gedisa.

Gmelch, S. B (2004) *Tourists and Tourism*. Long Grove, Il: Waveland Press.

Guasch, O. (2002) *Observación Participante*. Madrid: Centro de Investigaciones Sociológicas.

Gutiérrez Brito, J. (ed.) (2006) *La investigación social del turismo. Perspectivas y aplicaciones*. Madrid: Thomson.

Hall, M. C. (ed.) (2010) *Fieldwork in Tourism: Methods, Issues and Reflections*. London: Routledge.

Harvey, P. (2008) Relaciones experimentales: La antropología y la ciencia imprecisa de la ingeniería. In: M. Bullen and C. Díez Mintegui (eds) *Retos teóricos y nuevas prácticas*. Donostia: Ankulegui, pp. 29–54.

Hollinshead, K. (2004) A primer in ontological craft: the creative capture of people and places through qualitative research. In: J. Phipplimore and L. Goodson (eds)

Qualitative Research in Tourism. Ontologies, Epistemologies and Methodologies. London: Routledge, pp. 137–155.

Horne, D. (1984) *The Great Museum: The Re-presentation of History.* London: Pluto Press.

Jordan, F. and Gibson, H. (2004) Let your data do the talking: researching the solo travel experiences of British and American women. In: J. Phipplimore and L. Goodson (eds) *Qualitative Research in Tourism. Ontologies, Epistemologies and Methodologies.* London: Routledge, pp. 215–235.

Kirshenblatt-Gimblett, B. (1998) *Destination Culture. Tourism, Museums, and Heritage.* Berkeley: University of California Press.

Lassiter, L. E. (2005) *The Chicago Guide to Collaborative Ethnography.* Chicago: University of Chicago Press.

Leite, N. and Graburn, N. (2009) Anthropological interventions in tourism studies. In: T. Jamal and M. Robinson (eds) *The Sage Handbook of Tourism Studies.* London: Sage, pp. 35–64.

Lois González, R.Santos-Solla, X. M. and Taboada-de-Zuñiga, P. (eds) (2014) *New Tourism in the 21st Century: Culture, the City, Nature and Spirituality.* Cambridge: Cambridge University Press.

López Coira, M. (1991) La influencia de la ecuación personal en la investigación antropológica o la mirada interior. In: M. Cátedra (ed.) *Los españoles vistos por los antropólogos.* Barcelona: Júcar.

MacCannell, D. (1976) *The Tourist: A New Theory of the Leisure Class.* New York: Schocken.

Macleod, D. V. L. and Carrier, J. G. (eds) (2010) *Tourism, Power and Culture. Anthropological Insights.* Bristol: Channel View.

Margry, P. J. (ed.) (2008) *Shrines and Pilgrimage in the Modern World. New Itineraries into the Sacred.* Amsterdam: Amsterdam University.

Mouriño, E. (1997) *Vivir o camiño. Revivir a historia.* Vigo: Ir indo.

Nogués Pedregal, A. M. (2005) Etnografías de la globalización. Como pensar el turismo desde la antropología. *Archipiélago,* 68: 33–38.

Norman, A. and Cusack, C. M. (eds) (2015) *Religion, Pilgrimage and Tourism.* London: Routledge.

O'Reilly, K. (2009) *Key Concepts in Ethnography.* London: Sage.

Palmer, C. T., Begley, R. O. and Coe, K. (2012) In defence of differentiating pilgrimage from tourism. *International Journal of Tourism Anthropology,* 2(1), 71–85.

Pereiro, X. (2009) *Turismo cultural. Uma visão antropológica.* La Laguna (Tenerife): PASOS.

Pereiro, X. (2010) Ethnographic research on cultural tourism: an anthropological view. In: G. Richards and W. Munsters (eds) *Cultural Tourism Research Methods.* Wallingford: CABI, pp. 173–187.

Pereiro, X. (2013) Tourism and indigenous cultures in Latin America. In: M. Smith and G. Richards (eds) *Handbook on Cultural Tourism.* London: Routledge, pp. 214–219.

Pereiro, X. (2014) Tourism images and narratives of identification between the north of Portugal and Galiza (Spain) in tourism promotional literature. In: R. C. Lois-González, X. M. Santos-Solla and P. Taboada-de-Zuñiga (eds) *New Tourism in the 21st Century: Culture, the City, Nature and Spirituality.* Cambridge: Cambridge University Press, pp. 154–176.

Pereiro, X. (2015) Anthropological research on the impacts of indigenous tourism. In: W. Munsters and M. Melkert (eds) *Anthropology as a Driver for Tourism Research.* Antwerp: Garant, pp. 47–68.

Pereiro, X. and Fernandes, F. (2015) Antropologia e turismo: dos trilhos, atores e espaços à genealogia da turistificação da Antropologia em Portugal. *PASOS: Revista de Turismo e Património Cultural*, 13(2): 333–346.

Pereiro, X. and De León, C. (2007) *Los impactos del turismo en Kuna Yala (Panamá). Turismo y cultura entre los kuna de Panamá.* Madrid: Ramón Areces.

Pereiro, X.De León, C., Martínez Mauri, M., Ventocilla, J. and Del Valle, Y. (2012) *Los turistores kunas. Antropología del turismo étnico en Panamá.* Palma de Mallorca: Universitat de las Illes Balears.

Phillimore, J. and Goodson, L. (eds) (2004) *Qualitative Research in Tourism. Ontologies, Epistemologies and Methodologies.* London: Routledge.

Pinto, R. and Pereiro, X. (2010) Tourism and anthropology: contributions to a plural debate. *Revista Turismo & Desenvolvimento*, 13/14(1): 447–454.

Rabinow, P. (1992) *Reflexiones sobre un trabajo de campo en Marruecos.* Madrid: Júcar.

Richards, G. and Munsters, W. (eds) (2010) *Cultural Tourism Research Methods.* Wallingford: CABI.

Sánchez-Carretero, C. (ed.) (2015) *Heritage, Pilgrimage and the Camino to Finisterre.* New York: Springer.

Santana, A. (1997) *Antropología y turismo. ¿Nuevas hordas, Viejas culturas?*Barcelona: Ariel.

Selwyn, T. (2001) Bosnia-Hercegovina, tourists, anthropologists. *Anthropology Today*, 17(5): 1–2.

Selwyn, T. (2007) The Political economy of enchantment: formations in the anthropology of tourism. *Suomen Anthropologi*, 32(2): 48–70.

Sharpley, R. (2009) Tourism, religion and spirituality. In: T. Jamal and M. Robinson (eds) *The Sage Handbook of Tourism Studies.* London: Sage, pp. 237–253.

Simonicca, A. (2004) *Turismo e società complesse. Saggi antropologici.* Roma: Meltemi.

Stocking, G. W. (1992) *The Ethnographer's Magic and other Essays in the History of Anthropology.* Madison and London: University of Wisconsin Press.

Timothy, D. J. and Olsen, D. (eds) (2006) *Tourism, Religions and Spiritual Journeys.* New York: Routledge.

Turner, V. and Turner, E. (2011[1978]) *Image and Pilgrimage in Christian Culture.* New York: Columbia University Press.

UNWTO (2014) El primer Congreso Internacional de la OMT sobre Turismo y Peregrinaciones explora el nexo entre el turismo y las rutas espirituales. Madrid, Organización Mundial del Turismo. http://media.unwto.org/es/press-release/2014-09-16/el-primer-congreso-internacional-de-la-omt-sobre-turismo-y-peregrinaciones-

Velasco, H. and Díaz de Rada, A. (1997) *La lógica de la investigación etnográfica. Un modelo de trabajo para etnógrafos de la escuela.* Madrid: Trotta.

9 Everyone has a traveller's tale to tell

How oral history can contribute to tourism ethnography

J. M. Trapp-Fallon

Introduction

Using oral history for tourism research seems to fit well in an environment where social science is criticised for trying to predict and emulate the natural sciences. In particular, where there is a call for investigation into the local, national and global problems that we all experience, oral history can offer a useful tool for communicating and constituting findings from these investigations in ways that relate to our values and understanding of the world (Flyvberg 2001). The suggestion that tourism ethnography would benefit from more reflexivity and an incorporation of more of the local and advocacy is further evidence that there is room for an oral history approach. This is especially the case when there has been an intimation of a demand for short-term ways to intensively research mobile communities and to contextualise this research into the longer-term life ways of the participants (Graburn 2002). Back (2007: 7), too, says 'We need to find more ways to engage with the ordinary yet remarkable things found in everyday life.' Yet despite these views, oral history is a topic that is relatively unexplored in tourism ethnography. This chapter seeks to define and discuss the benefits of oral history in an attempt to address this imbalance.

What is oral history?

Oral history is defined as the facilitation of 'dialogue grounded in personal experience and interpretive reflections on the past' (Kerr 2016: 371). However, this does not comprehensively cover what oral history is, summed up simply by the Oral History Society (OHS) in the UK as the 'recording of people's memories, experiences and opinions' (OHS 2017). This definition is deliberately loose to prevent too many constraints on the research process, but fundamentally the intention of undertaking oral history research is to spend time listening to what people think and say over time and recording this information. It has been described by Thompson (2000) as the oldest form of history, and this is endorsed by many oral historians who point out that many documents have been taken from oral sources (Tonkin 1992). The OHS works for the collection, preservation and use of oral history recordings, and so the oral historian should be committed to a transparency in their research approach and make their interviews available through archives. Hearing the sound of voices directly is therefore essential to oral history, and was the motivation for the establishment of the OHS in 1973, where members were keen to record the voices of the everyday and retain memories of times past. Early on, it was discovered in the gathering of information that there was a need for complementary information too, for in conducting an interview these supplements may prompt and enrich the narrative; examples included photographs, newspaper reports and historical records (Roulston 2010).

Unsurprisingly, then, oral history interviewing is often described as the collection of narratives from ordinary people, and because of this description it has been given a range of other names, including life story, biography, personal narrative and memoir (Yow 2005). Some of these overlap, and attempts to categorise, however well meant, force unnecessary divisions. An example may be seen in the work of Roulston (2010), who is rare in that she discusses oral history but distinguishes oral history interviewing from feminist interviewing, where the latter is seen as using questions that are less structured and open-ended. This, she argues, is different from ethnographic interviewing, which she sees as finding meanings within cultures, oftentimes in the native language (ibid.). Another distinction may be that life story possibly concentrates on an individual, whereas oral history interviews may take place with more than one person. Nonetheless, this is a very fine distinction, because in both life-story and oral history interviews there is an expectation that the interviewer will take time with a person, allowing spontaneity and an interchange of dialogue not necessarily covered in a single interview. It may subsequently lead to multiple meetings to allow both interviewer and interviewee the opportunity to consider their dialogue, responses and reflections.

The training for oral history research by the OHS is for the interview to be a recording of the interviewee rather than the interviewer, so interviewers must restrain themselves from plugging gaps in the interview/conversation, often resulting in an interview having pauses or even longer silences. This research therefore takes time, but at its heart is the importance of listening. This is crucial for ethnography too: according to Gobo and Molle (2017) the ethnographer must be forever listening whilst in the field, for it is the interviews and informal conversations that help the researcher understand what is being observed and to uncover meanings. This commitment to engagement with the participant is what the anthropologist learns, and 'the opening up a sometimes very uncertain space of dialogue and encounter with people in the ordinary circumstances of their life' (Back 2007: 9) may cause discomfort and the need for time for recall, all of which the researcher should accommodate.

Speaking directly to informants in this way is at the heart of ethnography (Nash 2007). And yet this has been a thorny issue for anthropologists, who debate the importance of using the vernacular in their research. As Campbell (2006) notes, even if the anthropologist has spent time learning the language and avoids the use of a translator, the ability to translate and write up field-work in a manner that is transparent can be hugely challenging. The work of the ethnographer generally consists of describing their field observations in a way that is intelligible to their reader, and this often leads to some level of creativity and an inevitable alteration in meaning (Gobo and Molle 2017). Tape recordings – whether transcribed or not – offer the opportunity for those recorded to listen verbatim and approve what they hear, and in this way there is a shared account and a mutual responsibility.

The benefits of having a sound recording are substantial, as Craven (1973) illustrates when she pokes fun at herself in her fictional account of an encounter with an anthropologist:

> Mark said hastily 'I had trouble with that word too. It took me a month to learn it. The Indians pronounce it Kwacutals.'
>
> 'Young man [said the anthropologist] for the past century in England this band has been known as the Quackadoodles, and as the Quack-adoodles, it will be known forever.'

(ibid.: 103)

An exploration of many of these challenges and issues may be found in the *Oral History Reader* (2006) edited by Perks and Thomson, who are significant individuals in the understanding of and writing about oral history globally. They studied the evolution of oral history research, describing the period of time since 1945 as seeing four paradigm shifts in thinking about technique. Firstly, they see oral history from post-war memories as people's history; then they recognise post-positivist interpretations to memory and subjectivity in the 1970s; later the consideration of the objectivity of the interviewer as analyst in the 1980s; and fourthly the digital revolution at the end of the twentieth century to the present day (ibid.). These four phases show how oral history is both dynamic and challenging, forcing oral historians to think about memory as a historical resource, the psychology of the interviewer experience, and how technology can be used for transparency. What the outcome of these phases has meant for us today is that oral history has transformed public thinking about contemporary history in many countries because of its inclusion of perspectives other than those usually recorded representing the social and political elites (ibid.).

This extract from an oral history interview with Billy Kay is a recollection of when he went on a school trip to Russia in 1965:

> On that trip to Russia when I was 16, on board were Lanarkshire Lithuanians. I'd never heard there were any Lithuanians in Lanarkshire, but they were there, they were on their way home and I got to know them and took a mental note of that and that was one of the first programmes I broadcast as an example of an ethnic group hardly anyone knew about.

Even in Bellshill a lot of people didnae know about them because they changed their names a couple o' generations before.

(Interview with Billy Kay, 1980)

An example from the USA illustrating the first paradigm identified by Perks and Thomson (2006) which considers both tourism and landscape is in the work of Norkunas (1993). In this study, Norkunas sees a whole alternative history to the official history of Monterey, California, and in writing *The Politics of Public Memory* she addresses the absence of acknowledgment of 'Native Americans, Asians, Mexicans and southern Europeans, and it concerns an industrial economy and the working classes' (ibid.: 17). She sees a consistent lack of official recognition of different classes and social groups in three tourist sites, and yet knows that orally transmitted family stories reveal a very different history of specific cultural groups with a strong sense of identity and connection with place (ibid.).

Salazar has argued that 'contemporary anthropological scholarship recognizes that dominant imaginaries and discourses do not reflect the actual situation on the ground and often silence the voice of the powerless' (2013b: 692), and so in saying this, the author believes he is reinforcing the significance of undertaking oral history interviews, so that people's voices are heard and empowered. The bottom-up approach of oral history can address issues at so-called ground level, and in some situations provide the only way that the 'poor underprivileged' communities can have their opinions heard (Kakar 1998: 264). In his exploration of the problem of leprosy in India, Kakar revealed suppressed details of leprosy sufferers, and that myths about lepers abounded. In his pioneering work in seeking the voices of women and children sufferers in particular, Kakar (1998) addressed the bias in the reporting of treatments confined to the recording of male sufferers. At the same time as providing a more detailed picture of the opinions of sufferers and medical personnel through his recordings of oral history interviews, he was also able to publicise his findings and influence a change in policy to help address the issues he discovered (ibid.).

For the illustration of the second and third paradigms identified by Perks and Thomson (2006), the two ethnographic pieces written by Kaur (1999) and Gupta (2014) are included here. Kaur's (1999) experience of staying in Goa, India turns into an exploration of her own identity, given the reflexivity in her account of her own personal story and her connection with the place she is visiting (ibid.). This is exactly what Tonkin (1992: 2) purports when she says 'I argue that one cannot detach the oral representation of pastness from the relationship of teller and audience in which it was occasioned.' Kaur (1999) offers the reader an exposition on the difficulty of being a woman, a second-generation Indian in India, and a researcher. She chose to immerse herself in complete participation for her data collection, and concealed her role as researcher from those she observed or had conversations with, recalling and recording her conversations in her notes later. This auto-ethnographic approach revealed she had not expected her stay in India to be such a liminal experience. In her writing, she explains how she was perceived differently by those she met and, within these perceptions, she found herself in between lives, not quite fitting into the land of her parents' birth by the locals, but being seen as a local by other international visitors.

There is an indication here of the multiple perspectives taken in tourism, often cited as the 'tourist gaze' (Urry and Larssen 2012), but this can be seen in Kaur's (1999) work as the multiple interactions between hosts and guests. Separately, Gupta's (2014) ethnographic encounters during a 14-month stay in India represents what Crick (1996) describes as the combined roles of tourist and anthropologist. Gupta (2014) portrays Goa as a place of tensions where different groups are simultaneously experiencing and seeing Goa in a variety of ways. Her writing of separate vignettes of the rich Russian visitors, seemingly oblivious to the impact on the local people of being scantily clad; of the trance music party goers immersed in their own bubble of nighttime activity; of the Indian domestic tourists coming to gaze at Europeans at play; and about the environmental issues of a ship run aground polluting the water near the beach give readers rich insights into the complexities of the place as a shared space where the past mingles with the present, detailing host/guest relationships as well as the economic dependency upon tourism for the region.

Just as Gupta immersed herself to gain some understanding of tourism in Goa, Studs Terkel, who worked on American radio for many years and allegedly took his tape recorder everywhere with him, recorded his encounters resulting in extensive oral history research. He fits well into the American perspective on oral history where individuals are emphasised, as seen in the definition provided by the Institute of Oral History, Baylor University, Texas, which states:

> Through dynamic, recorded interviews, oral history preserves the stories of individuals who helped create the fabric of history and whose lives, in turn, were shaped by the people, places, events, and ideas of their day.
>
> (Baylor University 2018)

Terkel (1995) places himself centrally in the research process and sums up his particular approach in his memoir *Talking to Myself* by saying 'I have tried to capture the voices of others, so in this instance, have I sought out my own.' In this way, a fascinating account of conversations with people throughout his life alongside biographical information provides insight into American society in his lifetime, and his own perceptions and beliefs are juxtaposed with the words from his conversations.

The digital revolution as the fourth paradigm has made oral history accessible in a way never seen before. The Institute of Oral History's website offers access to 6,000 interviews online (Baylor University 2018), with downloadable interviews in different formats and a comprehensive instruction manual on how to be an oral historian.

Such extensive online resources, making interview recordings available to a wider audience through the world wide web, provide transparency and accessibility for anyone interested. This has been the aim of the British Library's Sound Archive, which has one of the largest sound collections in the world and a very large collection of oral history recordings (British Library n.d.), and is the reason for a number of different projects such as the BBC's Listening Project (BBC 2017). The Listening Project offers the opportunity to people around Britain to record conversations about any topics they choose; for example, a grandmother and grandson discussing winning a holiday is one of the most played (BBC 2018). The invitation is for two people known to each other to have a meaningful conversation on a topic that is important to them. These recordings are made in portable recording booths set up in different sites around the UK, such as at the Hay Literature Festival. The outcome of listening to these recordings brings wide-ranging voices and perspectives to the listener, often providing a moving and insightful record of British society as well as hearing how people choose to speak.

What makes oral history different?

The recordings found in many of the accessible archives online share a richness of meaning and interpretation in people's perceptions and experiences, and this is what Portelli (2006) believes is what makes oral history different. He states very specifically that the inherent non-objectivity of oral sources is that they are 'artificial, variable and partial' (ibid.: 38). Importantly, the content of the oral source also reflects the frame of reference of the interviewer, their questions, dialogue and personal relationship, and this is the reason why the informant should take priority and be allowed to speak, and should not be led. Oral testimony is never the same twice, and in this way, Portelli argues, it is impossible to exhaust the memory of the informant. Bharucha (2003: 2) offers some insight here after two years of interviewing his subject about Rajasthan, India:

> When a particular session with Komalda runs its course, one is never left with any conclusive argument or insight, still less a thesis. But one thing is clear: something has been learned along the way.

This notion of gaining some insight and perspective, which may possibly lead to a rewrite, is what MacMillan refers to when she states that history too is 'eternally under construction' (MacMillan 2016: x). This evolving nature of understanding and appreciation that comes from the immediacy of the voice and contact with the informant may well lead into different forms of interpretation (Portelli 2006). An example of this may be seen in Gurinder Chadha's 2017 film *Viceroy's House*, where she presents an interpretation (informed by her own family) of the events of 1947 and resulting partition in India. As with any personal perspective, the film is not without its critics, but this public declaration of the heartache of separation reinforces the point that dramatic events are far from isolated in time, but shape and form lasting impressions having wider ramifications in people's lives.

Ethnography and orality

The interpretation of interviews and the evolving perspectives on history led to Walsh calling ethnographers 'storytellers who create narratives of tragedy, irony and humour which make their writing a literary activity' (Walsh 2004: 227). However, he does qualify this statement by noting that the reflexivity that accompanies the collection of stories must be grounded in the social and cultural context in which the recording takes place; that is, there needs to be transparency about the where, when and with whom the oral history interview is recording. What is important to note here is that there is an interactivity in the ethnographic process in which the voice of the other becomes alive through the voice of the author, in what is described as the 'acoustical eye' (Denzin 1997: xiii). This epistemology is, according to Denzin, one that privileges sound, indeed one that he does not appear to favour, saying that 'some modernist qualitative researchers [mistakenly] place considerable faith in the primacy of voice over writing'. His opinion appears to be disparaging to ethnographers, saying that they collect and tell multiple versions of the truth, going as far as to say that the 'acoustical mirror always distorts' (ibid.: 35).

Such damning criticism has led researchers to defend themselves and think hard about how to present their analysis and findings. Cole (2005), after spending time researching communities in Indonesia, argues that different voices from outside sources often offer corroboration for differing viewpoints. Shostak (1998) also addresses Denzin's (1997) criticism in bringing together three different voices when researching the lives of women of the !Kung san (Bushmen) in Botswana. Rather like the work of Kaur (Kaur and Hutnyk 1999), the voices that Shostak (1998) connected were her interviewee and herself in two roles. The first-person narrative of the woman she interviewed extensively about her life during several visits to Botswana was linked with the second, which was the voice of herself as an anthropologist (who placed the first-person narrative in context), and thirdly with her own personal voice 'as a young woman experiencing another world' (ibid.: 404). This exploration of her own role both inside and outside helped her consider whether personal narratives could be viewed as ethnography. She struggled with presenting the voices alone, however, and for acceptability of her findings sought corroboration from outside sources, such as statistics about marriage ages, to verify the information told in interviews.

Shostak's uncertainty about presenting her ethnographic approach (ibid.: 412) was to some extent confirmed when she explained the difficulty in finding a publisher for her research because it was criticised for making the women in the Kalahari desert sound like the 'woman next door' in New York. Her significant achievement is, however, in identifying commonality in women's experiences from very different parts of the world, and this 'spirit of democratisation' (Black and MacRaild 2000: 88) is evident in her oral histories, thereby contributing to a much greater empathy and understanding of the wider world.

The importance of narratives like those of Shostak (1998) is that they support a much greater understanding of people and their experiences; as Bruner (2005) explains, there is much to be discovered in the routine, rather than the unexpected. In saying this, he is challenging the credibility of newsworthy soundbites and the need to be writing about the special and extraordinary, thereby inferring that the ordinary is without merit or interest (Thompson 2000). This is endorsed by Dann and Cohen's (1996) view that ethnomethodology (the rites and rituals of the everyday) was underexplored in the study of tourism. They emphasised that a great deal of research in anthropology has been about the discovery of strangeness and 'the other', whereas what is possible with oral history is an understanding of the everyday experiences of people. The recording and interpretation of the everyday shows there is much to find that is shared experience and common to many, leading to a much closer connection.

In her exploration, Shostak's (1998) achievement endorses the view of Monaghan and Just (2000: 23), believing that 'dialogue is the backbone of ethnography', an opinion shared by Cole (2005). She, when reporting her participant observations in Indonesia, demonstrates that her study led to detailed case studies of life and experiences, giving the reader a strong sense of community identity. This dialogue is achieved in using oral history and addresses the gap that Crick (1996) bemoaned in seeing an absence of attention to tourism by anthropologists and, in particular, the 'lack of the local voice' (ibid.: 19) in tourism research. Later, Andrews (2011) observed a lack of engagement in dialogue with tourists in much of the literature written by key theorists. This had been noted previously by Graburn (2002), who was prompted by a comment made by cultural historian colleague who, after reading MacCannell's seminal book *The Tourist* (1976), asked where he could find tourist ethnographies because although he had found the book a stimulating read, he did not find a single tourist in it.

Ethnographic research that does include the individual voice and explicitly includes oral history interviewing is evident in Urvashi Butalia's book *The Other Side of Silence*, where she explores the meaning of the 1947 Partition in India. Butalia (1998) believed that the oral narratives enriched history, but she acknowledges that she struggled with how to present these in her research. She clearly states that there 'is no way that we can begin to understand what Partition was about, unless we look at how people remember it' (ibid.: 13). Her meshing together of oral narratives and her own interpretations is an example of how narratives and personal stories help us see history differently from official narratives recorded in print from the time.

This very human presence is also absent from the early anthropological writings (see Pratt 2008), where there is a detachment in the writing as if the author is absent. In contrast, this has been successfully adopted in Feldman's (2007a) role as author/tour guide at visitor sites in Israel. His simultaneous exploration of the narratives of both past and present situated around guiding pilgrims/religious tourists in contested spaces makes personal voices distinct and clear, for example in the perceived separation of pilgrim and tourist experiences, and in so doing highlights 'the sides to travel stories that are rarely told and demand more attention' (Kaur and Hutnyk 1999: 5). Feldman's (2007b) work on guiding the visiting of memorials to the holocaust is also significant in that he does what Atkinson (1998) describes as the sharing of the information with the lived experience. In his role as guide, he is constantly with the visitors, and as such surpasses the issue that has been raised that tourists do not wish to spend time in lengthy discussions about their experiences, preventing research (Harrison 2008).What this means is that there is an experience of the here and now mixed with a feeling and connection with the past. By collecting information in the form of oral impressions and feelings at the time of the visit and afterwards, which may otherwise be unavailable, there is the possibility of gaining deeper insights about the ideas and beliefs of today often revealing a complexity that might not otherwise be understood.

Rose (2003) is a rare example of combining oral history, ethnography and memoir in her exploration of an understanding of community with her students, who interviewed steel workers in Steelton, Pennsylvania. Rose explains her thinking by saying she was following new social history, oral history and ethnography, and in this way let students discover the narratives of the people as well as those recorded in documents. She bravely developed a student class project that was not simply a history of Steelton, but an activity of knowing the residents in a way that would be useful to the community. In doing this, she found opportunities to explore interesting and relevant topics, such as contrasting perceptions of what happened and what is said to have happened, in order to explore the challenging complexities of race, gender and class in both the past and the present.

Overall, there are limited explorations in the wider body of knowledge, and this applies particularly to the connection between oral history and tourism (Trapp-Fallon 2003; Trapp-Fallon and Boughey 2007). So, in seeking evidence, Graburn (2002) selects Nancy Frey's work as an exemplar when discussing tourism ethnography, and refers to her in-depth and lengthy interviewing of pilgrims to Santiago de Compostela as 'personal ethnographies' (ibid.: 30). Frey's (1998) book represents her study over time, meeting many people often choosing to take the journey at a critical point in their lives; unsurprisingly given those motivations, this is a journey that has an impact that is felt for years to come. Such strong emotions fuel long-lasting memories, which augments Graburn's (2002) belief that it is not always essential to have been in the field, or to even to have been a participant, to achieve the rich, thick descriptions that are forthcoming in depth interviews. It is commonly seen in tourism ethnography that tourists are expected to recall experiences, usually being spoken to after an event or after their journeys (ibid.), and these demonstrate that their memories do live on (Frey 1998).

The issue of memory and recall that is often sought in tourist ethnographic investigations is evidenced in Gupta's (2014) description of the disenchantment of the expatriate community with present-day Goa. These feelings fit with Salazar's (2012, 2013a) description of tourism imaginaries, where the nostalgia and myth that was the place 'Goa' in the minds of those who chose to travel there and stay reflects a specific tourist demand. This notion of nostalgia and associated myth-like qualities formed much of Salazar's (2013b, 2014) exploration into the narratives that support tourism supply in Tanzania, in particular how these infiltrate the tourism information provided by local tour guides. He makes the forceful observation that, 'while tourism imaginaries are by nature elusive, it is in the practices and discourses that they become tangible' (Salazar 2014: 112), emphasising that in the main 'indigenous knowledge is almost completely absent in the training cycle of tour guides' (ibid.: 119). This distance between what is a local interpretation and understanding plus what is deemed fitting for tourists highlights the distance between perceptions and reality, straying into considerations of what constitutes an authentic and real experience. The role of different voices in the tourist experience shows too in the study of Kaspin (1997), who, like Salazar (2013a, 2013b, 2014), was in Africa when she found herself in a situation where her anthropologist's voice clashed with those of the Kenyan tourist industry officials. In her realisation that 'their voice cannot be her voice' and in her struggle to understand the differing perceptions of the situation (Kaspin 1997: 57) she reveals the value in undertaking recordings, and for these to be stored and interrogated or simply listened to for greater transparency.

The acceptability of the local or indigenous voice goes to the heart of the challenges for oral historians. There is a tendency to describe such voices as 'legend, fairy tales and beliefs' (Salazar 2014: 119) but, just as we have seen in the West, thinking has evolved. The development of 'ethnology' as a mix of 'social history and sociology' has halted the criticisms of folklore and allowed the shift from an amateur interest into a more serious academic pursuit (Thompson 2000: 71). So now each of the disciplines of folklore, sociology, history and anthropology all use in-depth interviews 'to understand the ways that the narrator attributes meaning to experience' (Yow 2005: 9), and this opens the door to oral history research.

Therefore the anthropologists' tool of ethnographic research including oral history interviewing can therefore contribute to a wider interpretation of tourism anthropology (Kaur and Hutnyk 1999) and also fits with a range of other disciplines. For example, the anthropologist David Geary's (2013) research into the 'Incredible India!' marketing campaign, which is designed to encourage international visitors who, it is hoped, will be also high spenders in India, raises some relevant points. He calls for the economic impacts to be judged and assessed in the narratives and 'lived experiences' of the people who are supposed to benefit from international tourism (ibid.: 57), and oral history interviews would fit well in this example.

Despite making the case for oral history research in tourism ethnography, it is understandable that potential researchers may be lost because of the lack of inclusion of oral history technique in mainstream research methods texts (for examples see Seale 1998; Smith 2016) or in texts about tourism anthropology (for examples see Badone and Roseman 2004; Burns 1999). There is also the time-consuming and laborious nature of listening to tapes many times and analysing the findings from abundant data. However, ethnographers are accustomed to managing large amounts of data from both participation and recorded interviews/dialogues, and so the analysis is ongoing throughout the fieldwork, as Frey (1998) demonstrated. Her analysis was formed by connections between her different sources and in developing a code to identify clusters and themes. However, the study of tourism reveals that it is highly likely that findings will differ because of the subjectivity of experiences, and so concerns about research replication do not fit. What is important is to gain permissions and to be transparent. Tonkin (1992: 4) suggests the use of a unified model of research that uses both 'social cognition and historical production', giving an opportunity to understand people in a particular time and space. Collins-Kreiner (2016), in recognition of the limitations of the different disciplines in coping with the dynamic nature of the tourism ethnographer's experience, has called for post-disciplinary research and synthesis in writing about tourism. In making this request she endorses what can be seen in many places nowadays: that an open and interdisciplinary research approach is used in the form of oral history involving speaking directly to sources that is not confined to the research of academics, but includes artists, the media and museum services, where sound, image and text are combined in displays of history and memory (Perks and Thomson 2006). Indeed, in 2017, it appears that oral history is central to many current UK television programmes and radio broadcasts.

Conclusion

Cole (2005) has said that the anthropological interpretation of tourism and acknowledgement of the role of oral history have been slow to develop. She is not wrong, and yet there is evidence for an acceptance that the voices of the everyday are required in academic research. There is also the belief that tourism contributes to world relations and international understanding, yet this too is under-researched (Brown 2009). Where substantive effort is being made in the practice of oral history is in the libraries and sound archives of projects, but these resources do not appear to focus on tourism, neither do they have the input of the anthropologist to interpret their findings. So in this chapter there is an encouragement for tourism ethnographers to engage in oral history research. To do this, the chapter includes definitions of oral history highlighting the simplicity of the definition produced by the OHS, and an explanation of the four paradigms of oral history posited by Perks and Thomson (2006), with examples, as well as the issues and challenges that oral history poses. These observations and examples reveal a sometimes confusing mix of terminologies and some misplaced academic elitism, both in the way that the individual voice is heard and in the recording of the everyday experience. By addressing the use and interpretation of oral history, for example in Butalia's (1998) and Shostak's (1998) work there is evidence of how research may be enhanced by different voices, whether they be tourists themselves or researchers in their mixed anthropologist/tourist role. As Shostak puts it, 'No more elegant tool exists to describe the human condition than the personal narrative' (ibid.: 413).

References

Andrews, H. (2011) *The British on Holiday: Charter Tourism. Identity and Consumption.* Bristol: Channel View.

Atkinson, R. (1998). *The Life Story Interview.* Thousand Oaks, CA: Sage.

Back, L. (2007) *The Art of Listening.* Oxford: Berg.

Badone, E. and Roseman, S. (2004) (eds) *Intersecting Journeys: The Anthropology of Pilgrimage and Tourism.* Champagne, IL: University of Illinois Press.

Baylor University (2018) Institute for Oral History. Available at https://www.baylor.edu/oralhistory/index.php?id=931318 (accessed 11 November 2017).

BBC (2017) Listening Project. Available at http://www.bbc.co.uk/programmes/b01cqx3b (accessed 11 November 2017).

BBC (2018) Listening Project. Available at https://sounds.bl.uk/Oral-history/The-Listening-Project?_ga=2.55203554.837145912.1517854099-1428934080.1517854099 (accessed 5 February 2018).

Bharucha, R. (2003) *Rajasthan, An Oral History: Conversations with Komal Kothari.* New Delhi: Penguin Books India.

Black, J. and MacRaild, D. M. (2000) *Studying History,* 2nd edn. London: Macmillan.

British Library (n.d.) British Library Sounds. Available at https://sounds.bl.uk/ (accessed 5 February 2018).

Brown, L. (2009) Using an ethnographic research approach to understand the adjustment journeys of international students at a university in England. In: A. Woodside, C. M. Megehee and A. Ogle (eds) *Perspectives on Cross-Cultural, Ethnographic, Brand Image, Storytelling, Unconscious Needs, and Hospitality Guest Research.* Bingley: Emerald.

Bruner, E. M. (2005) *Culture on Tour: Ethnographies of Travel.* Chicago: University of Chicago Press.

Burns, P. M. (1999) *An Introduction to Tourism and Anthropology.* London: Routledge.

Butalia, U. (1998) *The Other Side of Silence: Voices from the Partition of India.* New Delhi: Penguin.

Campbell, J. R. (2006) Who are the Luo? Oral tradition and disciplinary practices in anthropology and history. *Journal of African Cultural Studies,* 18(1): 73–87.

Cole, S. (2005) Action ethnography using participant observation. In: B. W. Ritchie, P. Burns and C. Palmer (eds) *Tourism Research Methods: Integrating Theory and Practice.* Wallingford, UK: CABI.

Collins-Kreiner, N. (2016) The life-cycle of concepts: the case of 'Pilgrimage Tourism'. *Tourism Geographies*, 18(3): 322–334.

Craven, M. (1973) *I Heard the Owl Call my Name*. New York: Buccaneer Books.

Crick, M. (1996) Representations of international tourism in the social sciences: sun sex, sights, savings and servility. In: Y. Apostolopoulos, S. Leivadi and A. Yiannakis (eds) *The Sociology of Tourism: Theoretical and Empirical Investigations*. London: Routledge.

Dann, G. and Cohen, E. (1996) Sociology and tourism. In: Y. Apostolopoulos, S. Leivadi and A. Yiannakis (eds) *The Sociology of Tourism: Theoretical and Empirical Investigations*. London: Routledge.

Denzin, N. K. (1997) *Interpretive Ethnography Ethnographic practices for the 21st Century*, Thousand Oaks, Sage.

Feldman, J. (2007a) Between Yad Vashem and Mt Herzl: changing inscriptions of sacrifice on Jerusalem's 'Mountain of Memory'. *Anthropological Quarterly*, 80(4): 1147–1174.

Feldman, J. (2007b) Constructing a shared Bibleland: Jewish Israeli guiding performances for Protestant Pilgrims. *American Ethnologist*, 34(2): 351–374.

Flyvberg, B. (2001) *Making Social Science Matter: How it Fails and How it can Succeed Again*. Cambridge: Cambridge University Press.

Frey, N. (1998) *Pilgrim Stories, On and Off the Road to Santiago*. Berkeley: University of California Press.

Geary, D. (2013) Incredible India in a global age: the cultural politics of image branding. *Tourist Studies*, 13: 36–61.

Gil, G. J. (2010) Ethnography among 'experts': notes on collaboration and sabotage in the field. *Qualitative Research*, 10(1): 49–69.

Gobo, G. and Molle, A. (2017) *Doing Ethnography*, 2nd ed. London: Sage.

Graburn, N. (2002) The ethnographic tourist. In: G. M. S. Dann (ed.) *The Tourist as a Metaphor of the Social World*. Wallingford, UK: CABI.

Gupta, P. (2014) Frozen vodka and white skin in tourist Goa. In: D. Picard and M. A. Di Giovine (eds) *Tourism and the Power of Otherness: Seductions of Difference*. Bristol: Channel View Publications.

Harrison, J. (2008). Shifting positions. *Tourist Studies*, 8: 41–59.

Kakar, S. (1998) Leprosy in India: the intervention of oral history. In: R. Perks and A. Thomson (eds) *The Oral History Reader*. London: Routledge.

Kaspin, D. (1997) On ethnographic authority and the tourist trade: anthropology in the house of mirrors. *Anthropological Quarterly*, 70(2): 53–57.

Kaur, R. (1999) Parking the snout in Goa. In: R. Kaur and J. Hutnyk (eds) *Travel Worlds: Journeys in Contemporary Cultural Politics*. London: Zed Books, pp. 155–172.

Kaur, R. and Hutnyk, J. (eds) (1999) *Travel Worlds: Journeys in Contemporary Cultural Politics*. London: Zed Books.

Kay, B. (1980) An interview describing the genesis of the Odyssey radio series. Available at http://www.billykay.co.uk (accessed 18 February 2018).

Kerr, D. R. (2016) Allan Nevins is not my grandfather: the roots of radical history practice in the United States. *Oral History Review*, 43(2): 367–391.

MacCannell, D. (1976) *The Tourist: A New Theory of the Leisure Class*. Berkeley: University of California Press.

MacMillan, M. (2016) *History's People: Personalities and the Past*. London: Profile Books.

Monaghan, J. and Just, P. (2000) *Social and Cultural Anthropology: A Very Short Introduction.* Oxford: Oxford University Press.

Nash, D. (ed.) (2007) *The Study of Tourism: Anthropological and Sociological Beginnings.* Oxford: Elsevier.

Norkunas, M.K. (1993) *The Politics of Public Memory: Tourism, History, and Ethnicity in Monterey.* Albany, NY: State Unversity of New York Press.

Oral History Society (2017) available at http://www.ohs.org.uk/ (accessed 5 February 2018).

Perks, R. and Thomson, A. (eds) (1998) *The Oral History Reader.* London: Routledge.

Perks, R. and Thomson, A. (eds) (2006) *The Oral History Reader,* 2nd edn. London: Routledge.

Portelli, A. (2006) What makes oral history different? In: R. Perks and A. Thomson (eds) *The Oral History Reader,* 2nd edn. London: Routledge.

Pratt, M. L. (2008) *Imperial Eyes: Travel Writing and Transculturation.* New York: Routledge.

Roulston, K. (2010) *Reflective Interviewing: A Guide to Theory and Practice.* London: Sage.

Rose, S. (2003) Community studies: the pedagogical uses of ethnography, oral history, and memoir. *Transformations,* 19(2): 21–44.

Salazar, N. B. (2012) Tourism imaginaries: a conceptual approach. *Annals of Tourism Research,* 39(2): 863–882.

Salazar, N. B. (2013a) *Envisioning Eden: Mobilising Imaginaries in Tourism and Beyond.* Oxford: Berghahn Books.

Salazar, N. B. (2013b) Imagineering otherness: anthropological legacies in contemporary tourism. *Anthropological Quarterly,* 86(3): 669–696.

Salazar, N. B. (2014) Seducation: learning the trade of tourist enticement. In: D. Picard and M. A. Di Giovine (eds) *Tourism and the Power of Otherness: Seductions of Difference.* Bristol: Channel View Publications.

Seale, C. (1998) *Researching Society and Culture.* London: Sage.

Shostak, M. (1998) 'What the wind won't take away': the genesis of Nisa – the life and words of a !Kung woman. In: R. Perks and A. Thomson (eds) *The Oral History Reader.* London: Routledge.

Smith, S. L. J. (2016) *Practical Tourism Research,* 2nd edn. Wallingford, UK: CABI.

Thompson, P. (2000) *The Voice of the Past: Oral History,* 3rd ed. Oxford: Oxford University Press.

Tonkin, E. (1992) *Narrating Our Pasts: The Social Construction of Oral History.* Cambridge: Cambridge University Press.

Trapp-Fallon, J. (2003) Searching for rich narratives of tourism and leisure experience: how oral history could provide an answer . *Tourism and Hospitality Research: The Surrey Quarterly Review,* 4(4): 297–306.

Trapp-Fallon, J. M. and Boughey, J. (2007) Making the memory come alive and active: using oral history. In: A. G. Woodside (ed.) *Advances in Culture, Tourism and Hospitality Research,* Vol. 1. Oxford: Elsevier.

Urry, J. and Larssen, J. (2012) *The Tourist Gaze 3.0.* London: Sage.

Walsh, D. (2004) Doing ethnography. In: C. Seale (ed.) *Researching Society and Culture,* 2nd edn. London: Sage.

Yow, V. (2005) *Recording Oral History: A Guide for the Humanities and Social Sciences,* 2nd edn. Walnut Creek, CA: Altamira Press.

10 Growing me growing you

Collaborative student fieldwork in tourism research

Diana Loutfy, Karolin Stuke and Desmond Wee

Introduction

It is hard not to find this tune by Abba familiar – 'Knowing Me, Knowing You' – even though you might not have been around when they released their single in 1977. This catchy song marks a bleak circumstance of a romance that had to end, based on a knowledge of how the self and the other have come to be. Yet knowing the other, or the subject of research and its contingency, and being involved as reflexive and performative researchers (Clifford and Marcus 1986; Fabian 2014) may culminate in the beginnings of a 'growing me, growing you'. The story continues and develops alongside various nuances of cultural representation. Crick (1985), for example, emphasised the blurring of boundaries between what it meant to be an anthropologist and a tourist. But Crick was speaking as an anthropologist who could have been potentially a tourist. What would it mean to begin as tourists, or students on a 'tour' of contextualised spaces doing ethnographic research?

Let us begin by situating the anthropologist and the tourist in a modern or global space, and in so doing, ask ourselves what Arjun Appadurai and the late John Urry have in common, aside from the fact that they were both born some years apart in the 1940s. Appadurai's sense of modernity was about a social imaginary based on global cultural flows, beginning first with mediation of all sorts, and then movement involving migrations, or in other words, 'modernity is an elsewhere, just as the global is a temporal wave that must be encountered in *their* present' (Appadurai 1996: 9; emphasis in original). Urry positioned the tourist place as a reflexive process about being a part of the global world order, beyond the entrapment of the tourist gaze, for which he was better known. His idea of mobilities involved imaginative travel of not only symbols and images, but materialities that transformed the social as society into mobility (Urry 2000). But what does it mean when an encounter is in its *present* and how does this exist in terms of its *materiality*?

Ironically, *global* mobilities are not enough to encapsulate a more local order of the sensuous, such as smell. In fact, both Appadurai and Urry were obsessed with smells. Appadurai (1996) recounted himself 'smelling' modernity during his stint in America, which expresses, among many other axioms, varied nuances of how we could envisage this modernity in which we live. In a similar way, Urry (1999) described how the distinctive smells of towns and particular streets, imagined or otherwise, had the propensity to become place markers. But do these smells change over time, and if so, is it happening more quickly than before? Do different people smell different things? Conversely, and more importantly, does 'modernity' contain a myriad of smells, which could be experienced in similar ways? This reflexive embodiment requires enveloping oneself in corporeal movement that produces physical proximities, being bodily in the same space as a discrete landscape. A co-presence is hence created involving sensing, of which smelling a particular space is also a part of the world order in producing meanings of place. Hence, modernity is filled with 'sensescapes' (Rodaway 2002) in which bodies circumnavigate the globe. On a more intimate level, these bodies engage vibrant spaces, and even flirt with them (see MacNaghten and Urry 2000; Crouch 2005) to produce meanings that are practised and performed.

The field(s) of anthropology are becoming increasingly fluid, based in large part on global mobilities, but also on its combination with an academia ready to navigate through emergent meanings in an understanding of culture that is contingent. Who is the contemporary anthropologist or tourist? Could they be one and the same? If so, would the spaces of everyday practice need to be reframed to provide for alternative interpretation? If our understanding of the 'field' should consist of various roles on a continuum incorporating the researcher (anthropologist or the like), the research of the subject in space (local) and its vicarious consumer (tourist), then we need to allow a *potentialis* for such roles and spaces to conflate in dynamic ways.

The transformation of self in relation to tourism mobilities is not new (Crick 1985; Graburn and Jafari 1991; Nash and Smith 1991; Galani-Moutafi 2000; Bruner 2005), yet this self is usually singular, and much 'smaller' than the other. In research following discussions around the lonely anthropologist (Forge 1967) and beyond (Gottlieb 1995), what is instrumental is a collaborative framework involving diverse engagement. This chapter proposes engaging students in a collaborative field, as reflexive researcher-student straddling the role of the anthropologist, the tourist and the local, and using contemporary technologies such as modern mobilities and new social media to build on cultural knowledge. This collaboration, rather than tending towards a research end, is constitutive of developing and evolving 'fields' that encompass multiple actors and provide a mediation between self and other.

Engaging the field(s)

The mediation between self and other is experiencing the other and learning from the other. It is also a reflection of how the self is practised through an intermediary, juxtaposed in relation to the other across modern spaces. More specifically, how does the student, as intermediary, contribute to an evaluation of the other, especially if we consider Smith's (1989) notion of host and guest?

Bruner (2005: 17) in *Culture on Tour: Ethnographies of Travel* described the 'borderzone' as a 'meeting place between the tourists who come forth from their hotels and the local performers, the "natives," who leave their homes to engage the tourists in structured ways in predetermined localities for defined periods of time'. This performative interaction between tourists and locals, rather than being a linear impartation of culture, was an emergent one in which 'both locals and tourists engage in a co-production: They each take account of the other in an ever-shifting, contested, evolving borderzone of engagement' (ibid.: 18). This playful engagement is further illustrated in the core argument of Bruner's (2001) 'Tourism in the Balinese borderzone', where he accentuated that tourism not only shaped Balinese culture, but has become so much a part of Balinese culture that it could even be said that tourism is a part of Balinese culture.

The example of Bali echoes the case of the modern city, in which the materialities of the city are informed by tourist flows. Becoming a tourist place is a reflexive process about being a part of the global world order as circulating images, people, objects and other symbolic capital further reinforce this transient sense of spaces around the globe (Selwyn 1996; Lury 1997; Franklin 2003). What needs to be considered is how the various modes of mobilities that are meshed into the mobile self, the mobile other and the mobile place converge in ways that might require new ways of understanding.

Tourism and ethnography is usually discussed in terms of ethnographies of touristic practice (Graburn 1983; Smith 1998). This chapter, however, attempts to elucidate a pedagogical framework for teaching tourism by incorporating an ethnographic component to reflexive tourist practice in the field. In other words, if tourism modules are usually taught (like most other modules at the university) within the classroom, how do we take students out of the classroom to learn about tourism through 'experiencing' tourism? Arguably, it would be hard to find students of tourism (or any students for that matter) who have not engaged in some form of tourism before beginning their studies. The impetus is to create an environment for involving students to think about tourism in critical ways. This implies that the subject of research is not only prone to interpretation and change, but (re)produces, at the same time, a framework for understanding cultural phenomena in the selected field.

> [W]e *have* begun to recognize the field endeavour as a site occupied by a group of interacting, positioned actors – the anthropologist and various 'others' – whose attempts at a conversation are inevitably shaped by mutual images, suspicions, assumptions, and histories. Perhaps not surprisingly, we have been even more reluctant to take the critical next step: to problematize the different sets of social and intellectual relations that, in one way or another, we often bring with us to the field, or in which we become intricately enmeshed while in the field, as members of a professional and/or personal team.

Gottlieb (1995: 21) was making an important point, but she was referencing mainly collaboration across colleagues and partners in terms of co-authorship. Here we premise the rather ambitious (or even outrageous) possibility to engage a group of researchers in the form of students across various backgrounds, with little or no experience in ethnographic research. And even though more is not necessarily better, it is important to emphasise that the more people in the anthropological team, the less the increasing problem of trying to be as invisible as possible and ascertaining the 'real truth' of the culture 'out there' (Gottlieb 1995: 22). To emphasise this, Bundgaard and Rubow (2016) iterate that the classic fieldwork too often fails to support the learning process when fieldwork is squeezed into the time frame of the curriculum, and they advocate that cooperative reflection during fieldwork can improve the quality of the empirical material and the analytical process significantly.

'Culture, markets and consumption': a reflexive student ethnography

'Culture, markets and consumption' is a Master's level module taught at Karlshochschule International University that seeks to describe, understand and analyse the economy as a cultural phenomenon. Students who participate in this module (usually comprising a large number of international students) discuss how markets are more of a 'conversation' (Levine 2011) rather than a simple economic structure to be calculated, with the focus on people and how they consume goods and services while acting on the 'inside' of the market. The underlying argument supports the notion that if the common values that a culture shares are loosely settled upon by members of the community, then these values are also embedded in the market itself (Sahlins 2000). Through cultural conditioning based on various notions of mobilities, adaptabilities and acclimatisation, people react differently to situations based on their different backgrounds (Kastanakis and Voyer 2014). Rather than looking at cultures as fixed, this module is based on a platform that approaches culture as contingent. Hence, markets are conceived of as socially constructed and 'not merely technical accomplishments [but] are cultural intentions that are inculcated, enacted, and that must (their audiences) engross' (Wherry 2012: 3). The relationship between markets and culture can be explored through new ways of consuming in terms of creation and reproduction of social practices. It is pertinent then to consider the 'appropriation of spaces in which these practices are being forged, creating new identifications of consumption and commodification processes through the reappraisal of public spaces' (Sonnenburg and Wee 2016: 325).

Before fieldwork proper, the Master's students attended a series of lectures to ground their theoretical knowledge of consumption theory and ethnographic practices. They were then tasked with identifying various cultural arenas within the locality of Amsterdam (picked by the students) and began preliminary secondary research. After which, the students, comprising two groups of four and two groups of three, participated in a five-day field trip in Amsterdam by analysing the spaces they had selected (in situ in Amsterdam) and derived a theoretical framework based on their observations.

The first group explored the idea of locality and identity through street food consumption; the second group analysed the meaning of creative and collaborative work spaces through incubator projects; the third group related the historical underpinning of waterways and the construction of modern identity for residents; and the fourth group researched the feasibility of sustainable living through a model community established for this specific purpose. The students were accompanied by their lecturer as well as an external coach. The group stayed on a 150-year old, three-mast Clipper for the five days, and this experience contributed immensely to the experiences in the field. The ship was both a subject of study and the accommodation for the group. The week-long schedule was as follows: the first and last days were booked for observing the cityscape, while the three days in between were distributed amongst the four groups. Each group was responsible for its own cultural arena in the city and prepared an itinerary for either a full or a half day, in which the entire class would visit the location of their project and help to 'conduct' the research. At the end of the day, all groups gathered on board the ship, ate together, and stayed till late collating all their observations and experiences from the day. The final results were then collated in a presentation format to be presented as part of the module examination back in Germany at the Karlshochschule.

Group 1: What is local? A study on consuming street food in Amsterdam

One group was intrigued by the cultural diversity of Amsterdam and questioned what *local* could mean in a cosmopolitan space. They chose to explore food culture by researching and analysing the relations between street food consumption and the habituation of people visiting 'fast food' vendors through various ritualised processes. These included 'Maoz', 'Vleminckx', 'Wok to Walk' and 'Febo'. At the core of the group's research was a statement by Bell and Valentine (1997: 168), 'The history of any nation's diet is the history of the nation itself, with food fashion, fads and fancies mapping episodes of colonialism and migration, trade and exploration, cultural exchange and boundary making.' The other class members were assigned interview questions exploring what motivated people to eat in particular places on a selected street in Amsterdam. The questions ranged from quality of street food to price ranges, as well as the type of food. The group members themselves visited multiple street food vendors and observed encounters at each site. Multiple characteristics were observed, such as type of food ordered, menus, lighting, space, design, duration of stay, time of day, etc.

Although it was difficult for the group to relate a deep sense of cultural heritage to how 'local people' defined street food, one interesting observation was that the emergence of a street food culture in Amsterdam combined aspects of the many nationalities residing there to form one new 'comprehensive' culture. Their framework of analysis took them back to Geertz (1973), in which they approached culture as semiotic and based their research on symbols that shifted into connections and relationships amongst different street food vendors. In a way, culture could be understood only because people have given it meaning and that the 'webs of significance' were created by humans themselves (Geertz 1973). The group realised that these inter-relations between multiple cultures produced a melting pot of differences in which the *opposite* of globalisation has occurred: 'foreigners' became locals and localised their cultures, to fit into local Amsterdam. In a way, 'no rule' was the rule. Adaptation to preconceived rules and rituals related less to a particular culture, but more towards the making of a modern city. It was about the 'culture of a city' and the agglomeration of the spaces within a global city.

Group 2: Space and creativity – Startup Village in Amsterdam

Another group focused on *space and creativity,* and explored a new 'Startup Village' in Amsterdam, an initiative by ACE Venture Lab, a high-tech and science-based incubator that helps startups grow. The idea of the village is the creation of a new community working space at the Amsterdam Science Park, where new high-tech and science startup businesses can be hosted. It comprised a colourful array of containers stacked on top of each other. A common social space is also being built so that members of each company can network with one another.

The focus of this group was to understand the spatial dimensions of community growth: how could the negotiation of space facilitate the interaction of 'creative' communities within the village? In other words, how did the 'Startup Village' support the purpose it was built for? As the class was visiting the village, they were each given a list of questions by the coordinating group that tackled topics such as colours, light, texture of the containers, neighbouring atmosphere, senses, etc. Each student then wandered off on their own and absorbed the feel of the place before attempting to answer the questions. The results of the questions as well as the group's observations of the place, alongside discussions with some residents of the Startup Village, helped the group develop six dimensions of analysis: 'temporality/mobility'; 'beyond the space'; 'visual representation'; 'distinction/authenticity'; 'materials/colours'; and 'community/individuality'. Amongst the various milestones and findings, the group discussed how the allocation of space (containers) contributed to 'opening up' the imagination of the occupants as well as visitors. Another important aspect was the social aspect of the community and the multiple usage of space as both workplace and community space. Implicit expectations about encounters were about random social interactions that constituted space as opposed to structure. There was a burgeoning sense of the 'liminoid' (see Turner 1983) based on the transitory aspects of the space and the liminal nature of atmosphere, since 'innovative and creative' processes have become a continuous process of production and reproduction.

Group 3: Interrelations between the ship, the sail and the sea – waterways in Amsterdam

This group was inspired by the fact that Amsterdam, also known as the 'Venice of the North', is surrounded by water, not only in terms of its physical geography, but also in how water is inherent in cultural discourses and everyday practices. The city is built on 90 islands and around 1,500 bridges link more than 100 kilometres of canals (bMA 2002), with houseboats decorating the landscape. The seventeenth-century Canal Ring Area of Amsterdam inside the *Singelgracht* is designated as world heritage (UNESCO World Heritage Centre 2010) and exemplifies Amsterdam's waterways as part of the city's culture. The flow of water, as manifested in terms of energy, resources and transportation within the urban environment, provides a vital means of subsistence to both citizens and tourists. This was used as a starting point to analyse the interrelation between culture (symbolised by the water), markets (embodied by the sail) and consumption (represented by the boat) in the context of waterways in Amsterdam.

First, the group started researching the city's canals and harbours alongside the shipyards. The students were impressed by the NDSM, a neighbourhood in the Amsterdam-Noord borough built on and using the industrial structures on the former land of the Nederlandsche Dok en Scheepsbouw Maatschappij (NDSM) shipbuilding company. It used to be Europe's largest shipyard dating from the fifties—which developed after its bankruptcy in 1984 (NDSM 2012) into a colourful cultural hotspot. The group decided to focus on Amsterdam's inventiveness in transforming water and heritage into other meanings of consumption. Around the NDSM wharf is the Amstel Botel, a floating hotel with 175 hotel rooms, in stark contrast to the geWoonboot, a sustainable houseboat venue for meetings and training courses that is entirely self-sufficient. What seemed to be a central part of the discourse at NDSM wharf, through media and other forms of representation, was the assumption of a successful development of the area, albeit a gentrified one. With this in mind, the group started to rethink their translation of water and heritage through symbolic appropriation by investigating the Amsterdam 'Coat of Arms', a ubiquitous symbol in the city marked by three crosses (XXX) dotting the entire landscape on lamp posts, government institutions and brothels. Notwithstanding its inscription on the iconic phallus, the XXX is thus situated as part of an 'economy of signs' (Lash and Urry 1994) in which global mobilities negotiate the flow of human and non-human capital.

The group examined different interpretations of the XXX to address it holistically, concentrating on the 'power' of water. On the one hand, they stressed the narrativised relation of the St Andrew crosses, which depicted the biggest dangers for Amsterdam's citizens: fire, flood and the black death (de Joseph 2016). On the other hand, the power of water also denoted the historical Hanseatic trade and transportation as an economic driver. A deep relationship of Amsterdam's citizens to 'water' was established, something that shaped the city's culture and identity. In fact, it was not only a culture symbolised by water: the economic possibilities for Amsterdam also meant a hoisting of sails and the creation of new markets of consumption embodied by what it meant to sail, to trade, but also to conquer. The simplification and exclusion of the colonial enterprise, and the selection of a temporal focus, is also at once the construction of a particular self–other relationship and the imposition or negotiation of a power relationship (Clifford and Marcus 1986). Hence, the power expressed is as much a process of consumption of which the 'ship' became a part, both as a metaphor and as the practice of staying in one.

Group 4: Exploring a sustainable living area – the GWL Terrein

Perhaps it is no secret that the Netherlands is a frontrunner in sustainable business practices (Balch 2013). But how do the citizens integrate sustainability into their daily life processes? The fourth group of students decided to investigate a sustainable living area, the Gemeente Waterleiding (GWL) Terrein, which used to be the city's former municipal water board. They asked the following questions: How is sustainability 'lived' within a sustainable living area? To what extent does this sustainable community contribute to the making of culture? And if so, what culture? By considering the 'Sustainability Triangle' with the three co-equal aspects of 'economic', 'environmental' and 'social' (Baumast and Pape 2013), the group started to explore the GWL Terrein and its sustainability-based habitation. The six-hectare enclosure was established in 1989 by the Westerpark Municipal District Council and developed into a car-free, environmentally friendly residential area nested in a 'melting pot' of interested and committed people with various backgrounds (Westerpark Municipal District Council 2000). As the aspects of the 'Sustainability Triangle' were discussed on the Council's homepage, the group was eager to find a relation between the justification for sustainability and its everyday practice. A guided tour with a resident of the GWL Terrein was organised for the entire group.

After isolating the different observed elements of how spaces are constituted around the GWL Terrein in terms of what sustainable practice entailed, finding relationships between them, and characterising the concept of sustainability according to the observed symbols, it soon became apparent that the expectations of an innovative and holistically sustainable living area were not fully met. Instead, the group observed that the focus was on the social dimensions of sustainability, especially since GWL is characterised by its diverse community, for example, the possibility to share food, services and opinions. The ecological approach was dated and the economic dimension was rarely addressed. It felt as if the heyday of the community has moved on and been replaced by a dystopic wasteland, with ideals set only on paper.

Nevertheless, what was an interesting discovery for the group was that GWL is still an area of accommodation that is sought after by residents of Amsterdam, whether the implements of sustainability are adhered to fully or otherwise. Finally, the group reflected, based on this experience, on how a more holistic implementation of the sustainability approach could be introduced to allow the emergence of a culture held together by a kind of organic solidarity (Durkheim 1898) based on democratic principles.

Reflections of collaborative fieldwork

Reflections were collected through meta-research both during and after fieldwork. In the evenings during fieldwork, the group in charge of the day would lead a discussion with the rest of the group, drawing out diverse experiences of place. This was an intense experience as there were contributions across cultural spheres and implicit learning, heightened by the fact that all this took place on board a rocking ship. The results were especially meaningful for the third group, investigating waterways, as they realised that their research was embodied into their practices.

After the fieldwork in Amsterdam, focus groups were established back at the Karlshochschule amongst the students to consolidate their experiences over time, on how they understood the framework of their research and their accompanying roles. A particular aim was to re-create the atmosphere on the ship and provide a context that could simulate the field experience. The moderators were also students from the class, but worked reflexively to distance themselves from influencing the results of the focus groups. The focus groups were designed to encompass five phases (see Pfeiffer and Jones 1983) to reflect on the questions that were being asked, as this was what constituted the framework for the ethnography. The first phase was analysing the experience itself as it occurred – the field trip to Amsterdam, and how the students spent five days on a sailing ship while studying the culture and markets of the local city. It was about what constituted the experience, but it also became clear that the ship the students stayed on was the highlight, as both discourse and embodied experience. It was an ethnography on (and of) a ship.

Secondly, the sharing phase consisted of guiding the participants to discuss their feelings, reactions and observations. The questions guided the participants to debate their personal experiences and thus focus on their individual journeys. Thirdly, the processing phase took place by analysing and re-reading the data collected from the previous phase. The questions were directed towards other participants' answers and encouraged discussions within the groups. The fourth stage was the generalising stage, in which the questions asked guided the participants to take a broad view and create abstract themes from the conversations that took place. The participants were encouraged to think about the experiences they had as a whole and relate them to other similar (or different) experiences they had in their lives. Finally, the last stage of the focus group design was the application phase, in which participants were asked questions that were relevant to the direct implications or utilisation of what they had learned in their everyday lives. These were relevant to what they had learned concretely both as individuals and as a group. The aim of this stage was to create a concrete outcome of the learning experiences and provide opportunities to apply it to real-life situations.

Discussion

It seemed almost as if the subject of research within the spaces of Amsterdam was 'lost' in terms of what it meant to do tourism ethnographies. Instead, the focus was directed towards the experience of the self: as students or tourists and the multiple roles played while performing both. In fact, the reflections of the focus groups demonstrated that the subject of experience gravitated from a study of the context to a study of self-experience within the context. In a way, this was a deviation from the original task, but by allowing the obfuscation of the self–other, it also became almost inevitable that the research of the other became inherently a reflexive experience of self or a kind of autoethnography.

One reflection that surfaced was about the use of spaces and the rituals performed by students within these newly acquired and temporal spaces. Many had fluid roles and jumped from one responsibility to the other, resulting in minimal conflict during the field trip. Living on a sailing ship instead of being in separate hotel rooms forced everyone to be accommodating towards each other. A simple example of this was 'shower time'. The group was made up of 15 people who had to negotiate a shower schedule that did not take more than an hour every morning or evening. A certain rhythm, perhaps through a delicate and particular kind of consensus (see King and Cowlishaw 2009), overtook the group as they went through the five days without any apparent conflict. Each day had different 'leadership' and the team quickly adjusted to following different people every day. It was clear that the main outcome of the trip was less about the projects themselves, but the group dynamics (or the group spirit, as it was described) that created a bond amongst the students, helping them to become closer and understand each other better.

The students realised that everywhere they went, they discovered different kinds of shared social spaces and gained extraordinary (learning) experiences while engaging these spaces. The most intense experience was on board the ship, where the students not only slept, but also cooked, ate and drank, washed the dishes, studied, played games and reflected every evening about the day's experience. It was more than a 'unique' accommodation, but a space where thoughts, ideas, memories and experiences were shared, allowing the possibility for 'in-between' learning (Bachmann-Medick 2017: 37). This special spatial layout affected the place of each individual and transformed these spaces into meaningful inter- and intra-spaces of being. The ship was conceived as, and became, a symbol for a growing alliance of diverse people.

These intricate spaces also extended beyond the ship onto the street on which the ship was docked, *Javakade*, which on one hand was reminiscent of the colonial era of the Dutch East Indies, and on the other was a social arena of diversity, cultural encounters and symbolic exchange. Even though the ship was docked, the students were indeed embodying the waterways, as the third group described above, and they were indeed 'sailing' around the city of Amsterdam.

The ship was not only the focal point of navigation across spaces, but it was also connected to the students' sense of collective memory. The experience on the ship and their travels around Amsterdam triggered old memories of the past as many of the students had already been on school trips previously. The fact that the ship was devoid of internet also added to a rooted sense of presence, as opposed to a virtual one. The lack of technology contributed unwittingly to a 'return to tradition' and created greater solidarity among the group. This sense of nostalgia was also evident in the ways the students chose to express their memories, in particular through the sharing of stories, showing pictures and videos to each other and recalling colours, scents and sounds. Hence, nostalgia needs to be understood as an affect of collectivity in which memories are recalled by 'performing, narrating, and styling an evocative and embodied present' (Prasad 2015: 212).

This brings to mind Bruner's (1991) notion of narrative retelling, how personal identities are indeed built on not only incisive memories, but transient ones as well. It is no wonder that upon the end of the field trip in Amsterdam, the students' nostalgic feeling of wanting to return to the simple and special past was also, at the same time, the wish to organise a similar trip together, to be able to construct new memories, *once again*. In other words, this nostalgia was also a tool for picturing and identifying the future the people involved would like to pursue (Cho et al. 2014). It was not only a longing for the past, but a projection (see Pfeiffer and Jones 1983), a translation into the future, and what happens to the 'you' (as opposed to the 'I').

Conclusion

When asked about the smell of 'Amsterdam', one of the students commented that it smelled of water, then another agreed and said it smelt of canals. And when asked about the kind of water it smelt like, the response from the first student was that it was 'water that had been there for a long time'. We asked if this water was still or was it moving, and she said, 'neither'. Another student interjected and said, 'it really depends on where you are walking'.

This walking around, through sailing and smelling was about students moving around Amsterdam. On the one hand they were observing, but on the other hand they were also being observed, by themselves. When seeking to understand the construction of self, it is important perhaps to be conscious of being 'looked at' *as tourists*, as much as 'looking' and trying to understand the world around. In a way, they were embellishing through movement and observation: looking while moving, and moving while being looked at, the adage that 'cultures do not stand still for their portraits' (Clifford and Marcus 1986: 10). The ephemeral nature of the project through the involvement of multiple locales and liminal time frames was closer to a poesis based on temporality rather than prolonged exposure in the 'field'. Hence, this reflexivity is not about a soaking into thick description (Geertz 1973) through prolonged exposure in a particular context, but a rendering of the *thin*, in situ, as a hallmark of this modernity that has been well encapsulated by Appadurai (1996) and Urry (2000).

A common quote that the students kept reproducing in their final presentations was their understanding of culture according to Geertz (1973) as a historically transmitted pattern of meanings, shared by a group of people and learned by new members as they became part of the group. A 'culture' was in this sense literally created as the kaleidoscopic student 'ethnographer' who explored the cosmopolitan and shifting spaces in Amsterdam was also the basis of the group that came from multiple backgrounds (German, Lebanese, Russian, Mexican, Venezuelan, Philippina, Greek, Singaporean). Also, the fact that all of them, with the exception of the accompanying lecturer, were Master's students highlighted a flattening of hierarchies, not only in terms of institutional structure, but also in terms of student agency. This agency is localised, especially when thought of by Appadurai (1996: 7), 'where there is consumption there is pleasure, and where there is pleasure there is agency'. If consuming pleasure is the epitome of tourism, then the pleasure of consumption has to be where anthropology feeds in, to understand even further the agencies involved in the imagination. In a way, we were a kind of 'displaced' people informed by an everyday cultural practice through which the work of the imagination is transformed.

The fact that the students had to 'return' to the ship in the evening seemed like a de-colonising impetus, one that stood in contrast with the disembarkation of the *Conquistador* in search of greater glory. It created yet another space of analysis, and through reflexive discussions of their experiences of the day, they were engaging each other and 'extracting' stories not only of the subject of research within a particular space, but of the many interpretations of place based on cultural subjectivities of multiple voices. These inputs created an infinitely ongoing project, a kind of fieldwork which stems as a 'never-to-be-completed-task' (Watson 1999: 2) based on spatial, temporal and embodied modalities of experience. Yet this contingent task also brought about four different stories that converged in how students understood the spaces within and across the field(s) of Amsterdam. Hence the subject becomes less about the cultural arena per se, or even the encounters within the arena, but the experiences of the space through various modalities of seeing.

The success of this trip in terms of achieving the learning outcomes, as well as the student satisfaction of the module in terms of greater experiential and life-long learning, may serve as a 'pre-test' for deeper investigation into which students employ ethnographic methodologies in and out of the classroom.

Ideally, Master's students (and, more ambitiously, even Bachelor's students) using ethnographic approaches may be given more time (for example an entire semester) to conduct fieldwork as a group, and under the tutelage of an instructor, in a contextual setting in which various cultural arenas may be engaged. By revisiting the empty house in 'Knowing Me, Knowing You', in the old familiar rooms, cultural memory may grow rather than stagnate in emptiness. 'Knowing' could be 'growing' and giving credence to a transformation of both self and other, in creative ways.

References

Appadurai, A. (1996) *Modernity at Large: Cultural Dimensions of Globalization.* Minneapolis: University of Minnesota Press.

Bachmann-Medick, D. (2017) Cultural turns. A matter of management? In: W. Küpers, S. Sonnenburg and M. Zierold (eds) *ReThinking Management. Perspectives and Impacts of Cultural Turns and Beyond.* Wiesbaden: Springer, pp. 31–51.

Balch, O. (2013) Going Dutch: why the country is leading the way on sustainable business. *The Guardian* [online] Available at: https://www.theguardian.com/sustaina ble-business/blog/dutch-companies-leading-sustainable-business [Accessed 24 April 2017].

Baumast, A. and Pape, J. (2013) *Betriebliches Nachhaltigkeitsmanagement.* Stuttgart: Eugen Ulmer Verlag.

Bell, D. and Valentine, G. (1997) *Consuming Geographies: We Are Where We Eat.* London: Routledge.

bMA (2002) Amsterdam heritage. Introduction. Amsterdam Municipal Department for the Preservation and Restoration of Historic Buildings and Sites. [online] Available at: https://web.archive.org/web/20080208132713/http://www.bmz.amsterdam. nl/adam/uk/intro/intro.html [Accessed 20 March 2017].

Bruner, E. (2001) Tourism in the Balinese borderzone. In: S. Lavie and T. Swedenburg (eds) *Displacement, Diaspora and Geographies of Identity.* Durham: Duke University Press.

Bruner, E. (2005) *Culture on Tour: Ethnographies of Travel.* Chicago: University of Chicago Press.

Bruner, J. (1991) The narrative construction of reality. *Critical Inquiry,* 18: 1–21.

Bundgaard, H. and Rubow, C. (2016) From rite of passage to a mentored educational activity: Fieldwork for master's students of anthropology. *Learning and Teaching,* 9(3): 22–41.

Cho, H., Ramshaw, G. and Norman, W. C. (2014) A conceptual model for nostalgia in the context of sport tourism: re-classifying the sporting past. *Journal of Sport & Tourism,* 19(2): 145–167.

Clifford, J. and Marcus, G. E. (1986) *Writing Culture. The Poetics and Politics of Ethnography.* Berkeley: University of California Press.

Crick, M. (1985) 'Tracing' the anthropological self: quizzical reflections on field work, tourism, and the ludic. *Social Analysis,* 17: 71–92.

Crouch, D. (2005) Flirting with space: tourism geographies as sensuous/expressive practice. In: C. Cartier and A. Lew (eds) *Seductions of Place: Geographical Perspectives on Globalization and Touristed Landscapes.* Abingdon: Routledge.

Durkheim, É. (1898) L'Individualisme et les intellectuels. *Revue Bleue,* 10: 7–13.

Fabian, J. (2014) *Time and the Other: How Anthropology Makes its Object*. New York: Columbia University Press.

Forge, A. (1967) Lonely anthropologist. *New Society*, 10(255): 221–223.

Franklin, A. (2003) *Tourism: An Introduction*. London: Sage.

Galani-Moutafi, V. (2000) The self and the other traveller, ethnographer, tourist. *Annals of Tourism Research*, 27(1): 203–334.

Geertz, C. (1973) *The Interpretation of Cultures*. New York: Basic Books.

Gottlieb, A. (1995) Beyond the lonely anthropologist: collaboration in research and writing. *American Anthropologist*, 97(1): 21–26.

Graburn, N. (1983) The anthropology of tourism. *Annals of Tourism Research*, 10(1): 9–33.

Graburn, N. and Jafari, J. (1991) Introduction: tourism social science. *Annals of Tourism Research*, 18(1): 1–11.

de Joseph, K. (2016) What does the triple X (XXX) in Amsterdam mean? [online] Available at: http://goamsterdam.about.com/od/Basic-Facts/f/What-Does-The-Triple-X-Xxx-In-Amsterdam-Mean.htm [Accessed 25 Apr. 2017].

Kastanakis, M. N. and Voyer, B. G. (2014) The effect of culture on perception and cognition: a conceptual framework. *Journal of Business Research*, 67(4): 425–433.

King, A. J. and Cowlishaw, G. (2009) Leaders, followers and group decision-making. *Communicative & Integrative Biology*, 2(2): 147–150. [online] Available at: https://www.ncbi.nlm.nih.gov/pmc/articles/PMC2686370/ [Accessed 15 March 2017].

Lash, S. and Urry, J. (1994) *Economies of Signs and Space*. London: Sage.

Levine, R. (2011) *The Cluetrain Manifesto: The End of Business as Usual*. New York: Basic Books.

Lury, C. (1997) The objects of travel. In: C. Rojek and J. Urry (eds) *Touring Cultures: Transformations of Travel and Theory*. London: Routledge, pp. 75–95.

MacNaghten, P. and Urry, J. (2000) Bodies in the woods. *Body & Society*, 6(3/4): 166–182.

Nash, D. and Smith, V. (1991) Anthropology and tourism. *Annals of Tourism Research*, 18(1): 12–25.

NDSM (2012) History. [online] Available at: http://www.ndsm.nl/en/thema/historie/ [Accessed 20 March 2017].

Pfeiffer, J. and Jones, J. (1983) *Reference Guide to Handbooks and Annuals*. San Diego: University Associates.

Prasad, P. (2015) Paradiso lost: writing memory and nostalgia in the post-ethnographic present. *Text and Performance Quarterly*, 35: 202–220.

Rodaway, P. (2002) *Sensuous Geographies: Body, Sense and Place*. London and New York: Routledge.

Sahlins, M. D. (2000) *Culture in Practice: Selected Essays*. New York: Zone Books.

Selwyn, T. (1996) *The Tourist Image: Myths and Myth Making in Tourism*. Chichester: John Wiley and Sons.

Smith, V. (1989) Introduction. In: V. Smith (ed.) *Hosts and Guests: The Anthropology of Tourism*, 2nd edn. Philadelphia: University of Pennsylvania Press.

Smith, V. (1998) War and tourism: an American ethnography. *Annals of Tourism Research*, 25(1): 202–227.

Sonnenburg, S. and Wee, D. (2016) An introduction to touring consumption. *Journal of Consumer Culture*, 16(2): 323–333.

Turner, V. (1975) *Dramas, Fields, and Metaphors: Symbolic Action in Human Society*. Ithaca: Cornell University Press.

Turner, V. (1983) Liminal to liminoid, in play, flow, and ritual: an essay in comparative symbology. In: J. C. Harris and R. Park (eds) *Play, Games and Sports in Cultural Contexts.* Champaign: Human Kinetics, pp. 123–164.

UNESCO World Heritage Centre (2010) Seventeenth-century Canal Ring Area of Amsterdam inside the Singelgracht. [online] Available at: http://whc.unesco.org/en/list/1349/indicators/ [Accessed 20 March 2017].

Urry, J. (1999) Sensing the city. In: D. R. Judd and S. S. Fainstein (eds) *The Tourist City.* New Haven, CT: Yale University Press, pp. 71–88.

Urry, J. (2000) *Sociology beyond Societies: Mobilities for the Twenty-first Century.* London: Routledge.

Watson, C. (1999) Introduction: the quality of being there. In: C.W. Watson (ed.) *Being There: Fieldwork in Anthropology.* London: Pluto Press, pp. 1–24.

Westerpark Municipal District Council (2000) Eigentijdse ecologie. [online] Available at: http://www.gwl-terrein.nl/files/artikelen/GWL_terreinbrochure_eigentijdse_ecologie_2000.pdf [Accessed 20 March 2017].

Wherry, F. (2012) *The Culture of Markets.* Malden: Polity.

11 The postmodern turn in tourism ethnography

Writing against culture

Burcu Kaya Sayari and Medet Yolal

Introduction

Postmodernism has evoked radical thoughts in the realm of cultural studies. It did not take long for the influential book *Writing Culture* (Clifford and Marcus 1986) to initiate new debates on the anthropological discourse and power relations within the ethnographic process. This era initiated a radical change in culture studies. Culture has traditionally been considered to have attributes such as boundedness, homogeneity, coherence and stability (Rosaldo 1989; Gupta and Ferguson 1992). However, these hallmarks were not seen to overlap with the social reality which is characterised by variability, inconsistencies, conflict, change and individual agency (Brumann 1999). Consequently, these debates triggered the movement of 'writing against culture' as suggested by Fernandez (1994: 161). Since the concept of culture inevitably constructs hierarchies between observer and observed (Abu-Lughod 1991), debates in the book have also influenced thoughts about fieldwork and the ethnographic representation.

The existing literature in the realm of tourism anthropology has contributed to revealing dominant discourses, gender bias and asymmetrical power relations (Veijola and Jokinen 1994; Aitchison 2001; Botterill 2003) through the arguments of Spivak (1985), Said (1978), Clifford (1983) and other pioneer authors. Since all these discussions have their roots in the notion of culture, there is still a need for critical studies that focus on solutions rather than problems for doing ethnography and writing outside the demarcations of discourse.

Writing Culture, which grasped the 'poetics and politics of ethnography', initiated the fourth of the eight moments of Denzin and Lincoln's (2011) classification of 'breaking points' in qualitative research. The fourth moment's stance is highly critical to positivist approach and its extensions, which comprise objectivity and value-free reality. The authors of *Writing Culture* have illuminated the ways in which participant observation in writing distorts the subjective/objective balance (Clifford 1986: 13). The arguments of the book were followed by repercussions on the suppression of agency and conducting ethnographic work (Risjord 2007: 416). The book provided vivid background for the diffusion of colonialism to ethnographic practices and writing. Even though the book did not represent a paradigm shift, it drew attention to a self-conscious and critical anthropology (Collins and Gallinat 2010: 3). In a short time, the discussions and debates exceeded the book itself, and concepts such as reflexivity of scholars, ethnographic authority, importance of critique and modes of writing have centred on ethnographic studies in the globalised, fragmented world that characterises the postmodern era.

Collins and Gallinat (2010) summarise the further developments occurring at different phases that have a diverse range of logic, such as the movement towards an experimental style of ethnographic writing, the treatment of ethnographic texts as 'texts', and mining works of literature for ethnographic data, which came to be regarded as fieldwork 'in fiction'. Even though these phases correspond to different perspectives, the importance of the work is that it paved the way for more 'experience-near accounts and cultural critique' (Collins and Gallinat 2010: 8). Since most of the anthropological work has strong links with tourism (Nash and Smith 1991), it is essential to discuss the impacts of the debates around and critics of *Writing Culture* in the context of tourism. Thus, this chapter aims to discuss ways to overcome representation problems that occur as an extension of the notion of culture that 'anthropological distinction between self and Other rests on it' (Abu-Lughod 1991: 471). Abu-Lughod's study provides the framework for this chapter, aiming to overcome some of the problems that ethnographic representation can raise. The chapter starts with representation problems that occur in tourism and the approaches developed in response to them. Further, 'forms of others' encountered as a consequence or a trigger of tourism activities are discussed. Finally, the chapter offers a framework that may help researchers to prevent negative connotations of culture, through Abu-Lughod's (1991) suggestions, and developments in tourism studies.

Representation problems

The contributors of *Writing Culture* (1986) focused on the problems encountered in trying to represent the so-called 'natives' point of view', which has been the aim of anthropology since Malinowski (1961[1922]). However, the question of how it is going to 'be expressed so that it is comprehensible, and yet still foreign' has been raised while reporting the natives' point of view (Risjord 2007: 417). Moreover, 'the crisis of representation' shifted attention to the multiplicity of ontological, epistemological and axiological revolutions (Mura and Pahlevan Sharif 2015: 831) in a way that is just compatible with the crumbling nature of postmodern reality. This was also a turning point for the objectification of cultures, which had been the dominant method in the field:

> In the course of history, colonialism, religious missions, ethnographic research, and tourism have provided ample outlets for the quest for self-

representation; in the face of modernity's inherent qualities of individualism, mobility and fragmentation, such a quest has been motivated by a
nostalgia for ideal, integral communities. The end result of this process
has been the objectification of cultures, societies, and geographies.

(Galani-Moutafi 2000: 220).

Besides the multiplicity of voices and differences, the crisis of representation
also triggered debates regarding structure and agency (Ateljevic 2000). In this
regard, Ateljevic (ibid.: 372) underlines two major issues: first, reinforcing
strategies to revive approaches by finding inspiration from new sources while
resisting the rigid confines of disciplinary discourse; and second, redefining
methodological strategies while realising theoretical strategies. These reflexive
strategies include not only the researcher, but also 'self, teller, listener and
recorder, analyst and reader' (Westwood et al. 2006: 35).

Deconstructive and critical methodologies provided a fruitful basis for
empirical research, while interpretive approaches enabling the researcher and
the subjects have their voices in studies (Ateljevic 2000: 372). The emphasis
on giving the voices of social actors in ethnographic studies gave rise to a
detailed examination of the ability of these studies to set forth the experiences
of the agents (Low 1996: 862). Therefore, the way for 'packing' the 'native
point of view' has been found by giving place to voices of all parts and
transmitting them to the texts. This point of view also affected human geography studies, shifting their attention to grasp the construction of realities
and experiences in the context of spatialisation of culture (Low 1996: 862).

This dialogic approach objected to the idea of culture as a 'bounded and
contained concept', as a part of Clifford's approach vigorously defended the
polyphonic attributes of culture and multiplicity of voices (Makagon and
Neuman 2009: 8). Yet this stance has also been subject to criticism. Pasquinelli (1996: 68) argues that the idea of dialogical anthropology is only realistic
for complex societies under study. She suggests that otherwise, it is not possible for the anthropologist to be both observer and observed. However,
Feld's (1982) study proves that Pasquinelli's argument is not valid for all
occasions. In his ethnographic study *Sound and Sentiment: Birds, Weeping,
Poetics, and Song in Kaluli Expression* (1982), Feld scrutinises how natural
and human sounds are meaningfully situated in the ethos, or emotional tone,
of Kaluli expression. In 1987, he returned to Papua New Guinea. Benefitting
from 'dialogic editing', he conducted a new study that focused on Kaluli
people's thoughts about their expressions in 1982 and Feld's explication (Feld
1987). This method shows that it is possible to carry voices of both parts to
the text regardless of societies' formation.

As a part of postmodern writing, recognition of multiple realities is central
for this approach since it implies a clear shift from modernist dichotomies to
multiplicity. Moreover, attempts to divorce ourselves from the observed on
the basis of a single difference result in the ignorance of other inherent
hierarchies:

Forms of difference in human social life – gender, class, race, culture, history, etc – are always experienced, constructed and mediated in relation with each other. If we establish a priori dominance or significance of one particular form of difference in our theoretical frameworks, then we automatically run the risk of ignoring others.

(Moore 1988: 196)

These debates also found reflections in criticisms about the tourist typologies that modernist approaches have elaborated:

Rather than having ethnographic accounts speak of cultural complexity, these typologies have done little more than splitting the Tourist into halves and ascribing these different motifs that do not ultimately contest MacCannell's unitary Tourist – they all dwell in a culturally barren landscape of modernist construed universality.

(Alneng 2002: 123)

In the same vein, Risjord (2007: 418) argues that the ethnographer's objectivity, univocality and generalisation of *the culture* to all subjects are rooted in the rhetorical techniques that construct the ethnographer's authority. Although the practice of speaking for others can ascribe hierarchy in various ways (Alcoff 1991: 29), it is not always easy for the ethnographer to abandon authority, which is portrayed as inevitable in some cases. It is the fieldwork conditions that sometimes place the ethnographer as 'the authority on the spot', as being a source of information about the world outside and answering the questions of locals (Salazar and Graburn 2014: 6).

Inscribing 'voices' on the texts without neutrality is an inseparable element of critical studies, and this move created a significant difference between anthropology and anthropology of tourism. Reflexivity of the researcher in a balance with the representation of multiple voices is just compatible with the nature of contemporary tourism activities as well. This approach also links the theory with practice. Today, tourists are active players even in the destinations' promotions, and they are reflexive players in the reproduction of images (Rickly-Boyd et al. 2016: 22). Moreover, Tribe (2005: 5) posits the emergence of more reflexivity in tourism research as a sign of it reaching maturation. He also suggests that this results in widening of the research boundaries, which goes beyond the applied business field. This shift in tourism research has also changed the way self and 'other' are positioned in ethnographic research in tourism.

Telling 'other' tales of the field

The debate on universality and particularity is still current as a part of the controversy between the heritage of the Enlightenment and Romanticism (Platenkamp and Botterill 2013: 113). Likewise, the retrospective stance and homogenised point of view of evolutionist ideas are challenged by the cultural relativism. The pastoral tendency of ethnographer 'as a reverence for a simplicity "we" have lost' (Rosaldo 1986: 97) also creates Others and constructs the hierarchies of dichotomies as 'civilized and primitive, West and "non-West", future and Past' (Clifford 1986: 113):

> the hypothesis implies the thought that our modern Western European civilization represents the highest cultural development toward which all other more primitive cultural types tend, and that therefore retrospectively we construct an orthogenetic development towards our modern civilization.
>
> (Boas 1920: 312)

Clifford questions the assumption that 'the other society is weak and needs to be represented by outsider' (Clifford 1986: 113) and for him, the attempt to save the disappearing object is just a textual construction that legitimates a representational practice (ibid.: 112). The same assumption is also valid for tourism. Källén (2015) reveals that when tourists travel to the land of the 'primitive', just as in a time machine, they feel like they set foot in a world that belongs to the past. Further, she demonstrates that tourism can adopt the same guises of benevolence and philanthropy with colonialism by assuming that someone 'needs' help or protection. This hierarchy constructed by tourism activities is considered to be the main agent that creates the Other in critical studies. Benevolent tourism activities, as allied to broader strategies and politics, are evaluated as bringing together 'the consumption behaviour and the lives of Others "in need"' (Baptista 2017: 15), or prolonging colonially created power asymmetries through performance of 'being indigenous' as a part of an economic mechanism (Giblin 2017). While the ethnographer tries to capture the nostalgia in the quest for the authentic and undistorted form of a society, tourism undertakes the role of protector of the authentic form of cultural practices or constructs it by itself again, asserting hierarchy.

Bloch (2017) suggests that the Othering process does not always trigger from 'the outside' or under colonial effects. He vividly portrays that Hindu leaders' religious nationalism discourses unleash severe actions of 'the authorities against even their own citizens' in the case of heritage tourism (Bloch 2017: 73). Further, he demonstrates that discourses on tourism may function as an 'Othering' element that focuses on the residents involved in tourism activities, since the religious leaders interpret these activities as a part of 'Western capitalist economy, modernisation processes and anti-environmentalism', which results in constraints on the individual agency of the Hampi villagers. However, Silverman (2015: 145) demonstrates that tourism and ideological formations should not always contaminate relations or create 'others'. A national branding campaign in Peru succeeded in building a strong sense of identity and support for the nation at home. The campaign managed to intermingle 'the official discourse of national identity [...]

constructed around past glory [...] with popular culture' by enfolding existing ideologies (Silverman 2015: 141). Further, he indicates that contextual and historical approaches become valuable tools for the academic study of nation-branding, since these activities are essentially rooted in a 'political, ideological, economic, social, cultural, technological, and environmental milieu' (Silverman 2015: 145). While tourism can entail Othering or assembling practices, it may choose to stay 'neutral', as Pahre (2015) also reveals. He demonstrates that, in order to prevent controversies, national historic sites are restored and reconstructed in a value-neutral way by obscuring actual history. However, he criticises this, saying that 'interpretation should put events in contexts, discussing political differences [...] the consequences [...] and the events associated with them' (Pahre 2015: 78).

Even though tourism sometimes triggers 'Othering', the power intrinsic to the Other creates tourism occasionally, as Badone (2015) reveals. Badone demonstrates that touristic representations of Les-Saintes-Marie-de-la-Mer, which includes gypsies, converts the prevalent stereotype into an alluring tourist element. Even though the gypsy pilgrimage causes some undesirable consequences for the local people, such as 'garbage in the streets, drunkenness and drug use during the pilgrimage', theft, fights and closure of some stores and restaurants (Badone 2015: 174), the romantic portrayal of the gypsy image contrasts sharply with the widespread stereotype in contemporary Europe and Les-Saintes-Marie-de-la-Mer. Yet the representations of Les-Saintes-Marie-de-la-Mer promise 'the nostalgic, pastoral image of the "gypsy" uncontaminated by industrial civilization' (Badone 2015: 176).

Since tourism activities strongly comprise cross-cultural elements and 'gazing at the Other', they produce discourses and are fed with them in turn. The distinctions that imply divisions in tourist typologies and create the tourist–Other dichotomy are parts of the critique of the structural perspective and the effort of deconstruction of tourism. Yet the question remains: How can we integrate these practices into research?

Writing against culture in tourism

In her influential study, Abu-Lughod (1991) argues that if 'culture, shadowed by coherence, timelessness, and discreteness, is the prime anthropological tool for making "other", and difference, as feminists and halfies – people whose national or cultural identity is mixed by virtue of migration, overseas education, or parentage – reveal, tends to be a relationship of power, then perhaps anthropologists should consider strategies for writing against culture' (Abu-Lughod 1991: 466). She discusses three modes of writing as discourse and practice, connections, and ethnographies of particular. In the first strategy, she argues that discourse and practice are functional notions that can compensate for the absence of the culture concept when it is discarded. As a second strategy, she suggests connections that underpin tracing historical, national and transnational connections as well as placing them in context. As the final strategy, drawing upon Geertz (1975, 1988), she suggests writing ethnographies to 'bring closer the language of everyday life and the language of the text' as a 'mode of making other is reversed' (Abu-Lughod 1991: 474). In the rest of this chapter, the correspondence between the methodological and theoretical basis of these tools and tourism will be scrutinised by considering the current situation of the field.

Discourses and master narratives

Abu-Lughod (1991) argues that there are variant mechanisms that enable discourses and structures of power to operate in the field. Building on Foucault, she grasps discourse as a concept that is 'meant to refuse the distinction between ideas and practices or text and world that the culture concept too readily encourages' (ibid.: 472). She points to 'the social uses by individuals of verbal resources'. From this viewpoint, our attempt is to reveal different power structures that operate within the tourism realm which prevent us from reaching individual narratives and experiences that may enable us to capture real practices. In this attempt, the evaluation of tourism as a neo-postcolonial activity that is also an important part of imaginaries (Salazar and Graburn 2014: 6) depicts only one angle of this whole picture. Bruner (2005a) argues that the narratives constructed by colonial governments and intellectuals of anthropology and the tourism industry have the power to affect 'actions, tourist behaviours, [and] selection of the cultural elements for display'. Therefore, he interprets them as 'not only stories of meaning but of power' (Bruner 2005a: 3). Moreover, 'the dominant discursive narratives of any historical era' are prevalent at any level of tourism activities. These activities are supported with master narratives that pervade in society through various channels. Therefore, one can easily find these constructed stories in the brochures at tourism agencies without any further attempt at digging out the diffuse power structures (Bruner 1991: 248). Then one needs to be careful about the distance between discourse and the experience, since these constructed narratives provide a base for individual dreams. Apart from these master narratives that point to power structures, narratives of individuals are also essential components in shedding light on individuals' inner worlds. Like master narratives, 'even post hoc tourist narratives are "constructed" (by individuals) and their analysis can be revealing' (Graburn 2002: 31). Since one of the advantages of anthropology and ethnographic studies is the fact that they enable us to grasp groups of people in their sociological contexts and temporalities (Salazar and Graburn 2014: 6), this feature is also helpful in gaining a deeper understanding of such narratives of tourism activities, which are temporal in their very nature.

As another important element of discourse creation, issues about writing and style are still intrinsic to publishing in the field of tourism, and they actively shape the tourism discourse. It can be argued that not only the writing style, but also the whole publishing process exert different hierarchies, stretching the distance between discourse and practice. First-person writing breaks the barriers generated by the post-positivist tradition and gives rise to the subjective positionality of the researcher (Westwood et al. 2006), and the importance of reflexivity is recognised in qualitative tourism research (Ateljevic et al. 2007; Wilson and Hollinshead 2015). However, issues about writing and style still display the barriers to moving beyond the second moment in qualitative tourism research, as writing in the third person pushes the author to the backstage of the text construction (Riley and Love 2000).

Moreover, geographical and linguistic differences coexist with barriers of writing and style. Mura and Pahlevan Sharif (2015) focus on some of the Asian countries affected by British, Dutch and French colonial powers. They assert that Anglo-Saxon dominance and 'English language as the lingua franca of academic life' is transparent in most of the Southeast Asian countries (ibid.: 833). Therefore, it is not inconceivable from the incidences of the acceptance of the superiority of 'Western education styles [...] (to) Eastern systems', scholarships for degrees in Western countries, or requests for branches of Anglo-Saxon universities in Asia that the effect of the created vision and image also grips the countries themselves, and they hold the same beliefs that were created by colonial powers (ibid.: 833). As Das (1994: 134) asserts, education is a major component in having an 'authentic voice', owing to its unique powers to shape ideas, beliefs and stances:

> The danger for the Indian anthropologist is that she is vulnerable to the charge of being either 'defensive' or 'chauvinistic'. The educated Hindu cannot speak with an authentic voice on matters pertaining to caste or religion since she is condemned to seeing the institutions of her society from a Western point of view.
>
> (Das 1994: 134)

This is a fruitful discussion. In order to capture the particularities, 'authentic voices' are essential. Yet for the people who are not native English speakers, these voices may not remain the same.

In pointing out the geography of the dominant knowledge, Winter (2009) shows that almost all key concepts of the field allude to social changes occurring in either Western Europe or North America. He cites the notable examples of the Grand Tour of Northern elites, the Parisian *flâneur*, the Thomas Cook package tour, the mass tourism of Victorian Britain's working class, and MacCannell's (1976) American tourist (Winter 2009: 23). These 'ready already' concepts not only served as a basis for the analysis of the other countries, but also they became the 'tool bag of theories' that hides 'their cultural and historical roots' (Winter 2009: 23). This is also a valuable discussion that needs to be touched on in the tourism realm. Clifford's (1988: 266) criticism of Said and Orientalism could be fruitful in this discussion. Clifford criticises Said for ignoring 'a wide range of Western humanist assumptions'. Moreover, he argues that Said confines the Orientalist discussions to the Arab Middle East, ignoring the Far East, India, the Pacific and North Africa (ibid.: 267). Reflecting on these criticisms, it can be argued that the positive improvements provided by Western Europe or North America should be recounted as well. Moreover, as the countries that are not in Europe and did not experience direct colonisation, we should also participate in the discussion and provide other partial views to Mura and Pahlevan Sharif's (2015) discussions in order to reach a complete picture. And, while having these discussions, we need to underline that we are obliged to discuss all these arguments through the English network, which points to 'the dilemma of how to better integrate non-English scholarship, whether it emanates from Europe, Asia or Africa, into the English language academy' (Winter 2009: 30). Last, but not least, we need to be careful about the tendency of these discussions to fix the differences, as Abu-Lughod (1991: 470) warns.

Connections in the mobile world

In the scrutiny of connections, Abu-Lughod stresses the power of history and contextual background in revealing underlying structures. Pels (1997) emphasises that we need to deconstruct the concept of culture as a tool that is favoured by colonial settings as well as history, and points to the fieldwork and allegorical modality of empirical methods that colonial circumstances affected. He argues that, under the auspices of the cultural classifications and historiography, colonial governmentality developed an ontological base (Pels 1997: 167). He further points out that we need not only to grasp the concurrent developments of modernity and colonialism together, but also to elucidate the 'reflexively blurred boundaries' between them (Pels 1997: 178). On the other hand, Asad (1979: 93) asserts that it is wrong to evaluate social anthropology as mainly aiming to serve the colonial administration in the colonial era, or that it was a sole 'reflection of colonial ideology'. He links social anthropology's composed approach to itself as just one part of 'bourgeois consciousness', which 'has always contained within itself profound contradictions and ambiguities – and therefore the potentiality – for transcending itself' (Asad 1979: 93). Therefore, he underscores the need for scrutiny of 'the historical power relationship between the West and the Third World' in order to reveal not only these contradictions, but also assumptions and intellectual representations of non-European humanity (ibid.: 93).

History and context are essential elements, not only in discussions about colonialism. In travel writing, as Santos (2006: 638) reveals, when the situation is illustrated without specific socio-cultural and historical contexts, it calls forth the reproduction of dominant Western notions as another angle of power assertion. Providing a context in a proceeding history saves us from the frozen points of view that inscribe static ideas. Moreover, by the 'cultural turn', it is realised that economic, cultural and social layers of geographies are intertwined inherently (Ateljevic 2000: 372), and context is a vital element in following the changes occurring in these layers in response to each other:

We thus need an explicit strategy to counterbalance the emphasis on social systems change and, at the same time, better understand the process that enables them to remain relatively stable over time. A historical analysis that interprets current ideas and practices within the context of the unfolding sequence of action and meaning that has led to them provides this balance.

(Yanagisako and Collier 1994: 199)

Then, how can we create an approach that has a non-static nature? With the introduction of the mobility paradigm, after its precedents in which arose sedentary theories and nomadic metaphors, a new perspective has arrived (Mavric and Urry 2009: 647–648) as another agent which plays an important role in the examination of connections. This point of view grasps all the destinations and tourist places as the product of interrelations and networks. Mobility is also evaluated as a metaphor that provides a non-static point of view:

In the last several years, the metaphors of mobility have proven useful for deconstructing anthropology's fixed and ethnocentric categories such as those of self and Other, the familiar and the exotic. More important, the advance of self-reflexive anthropologies, which involve an awareness of oneself and of the importance of giving due credit to the voice of the Other, lies in their contributing to reduce the problems of subjectivity in participant observation.

(Galani-Moutafi 2000: 220–221)

With this new research paradigm, the research technique that is seen as fruitful has been multi-sited ethnography (Mavric and Urry 2009: 650–652). It is the ethnography that 'moves from its conventional single-site location, contextualised by macro-constructions of a larger social order, such as the capitalist world system to multiple sites of observation and participation that cross-cut dichotomies such as the 'local' and 'global', the 'lifeworld' and the 'system' (Marcus 1995: 95). Yet, by some authors, it is also evaluated as 'not practically feasible' and cannot be conducted since there cannot 'be such a thing as a multi-sited ethnography' (Hage 2005: 463). Moreover, Clifford evaluates conducting multi-sited ethnography as lacking depth of interaction (Marcus 1998: 245). Here, Marcus (ibid.: 246) underscores 'the depth' as 'interpretations of cultural experience'. Moreover, Marcus points out the difficulties of conducting multi-sited research since both the ethnographers and the objects of study are becoming more transcultural regarding their demography, which turns into a huge burden for the ethnographer. He warns that 'only cosmopolitan fieldworkers with fluency in more than one language and who are at home, or at least familiar with several culturally distinct places through their autobiographies can meet the challenge of developing a satisfying sense of depth of ethnography in the trend of second projects' (ibid.: 247).

Both historical analysis and providing context and linkages are vital for the critical approach to tourism practices. Only such an analysis can enable the development of a critical point of view in grasping the representations of 'hosts' and tourists:

> A critical analysis of tourism representations must recognize the political linkages between tourism discourses and technologies of power to uncover the ideologies and practices that structure touristic relations. One needs to examine how the ways tourists are enmeshed within webs of significance and taken-for-granted assumptions created by the world of tourism representations constitute the meanings they have and constitute them as political subjects.
>
> (Mellinger 1994: 776)

Ethnography of particular and individual tourist experiences

The personal significance and the richness of individual experiences that are not uniform are well informed discussions in the tourism literature (Ryan 2002: 1; Sharpley and Stone 2010: 2). These points of view about experiences are not evident in the field; on the contrary, they require a detailed process. Therefore, it is not always easy to catch the gist of these experiences. Graburn (2002: 32) states that 'as with the study of any modern peoples on the move, role labels (international, domestic, married, short-term, female, target worker) of today's tourists and travellers sometimes do not reflect accurately either their inner realities or even their own initial expectations'. More importantly, in the same vein as Cohen (1979) and Bruner (1994), Nash (2001: 494) argues that tourists and travellers come in various forms, and we should clarify the types rather than homogenising them. This will ensure that we not only illuminate the distinctive features of tourist experience, but also raise minor voices. As one of the essential tools, narratives have the ability to uncover constructed truths of the participants which differ from the objective truth (Westwood et al. 2006: 37). Narratives such as oral histories are powerful tools that may reveal the meaning inscribed to an experience, and their subjective nature may provide richness and multi-vocality to the text.

As an instance of these studies, Naidu (2016), drawing upon Abu-Lughod's (1991) term 'ethnographies of the particular', scrutinises the lived contexts and social realities of the Black South African women in her study. She reveals that tourism in South Africa is 'less about preserving cultural heritage, and possibly more about re-creating or reifying cultural identities as products that have found a supply in global tourism consumption' (Naidu 2016: 51). Even though young Zulu women are sometimes fine with dancing, in their narratives they assert that they feel uncomfortable with their dresses, or what Naidu refers to as 'un-dressiness' because, as she explains, the tourism imaginary of Zulu often incorporates topless young female virgins. Further, when Zulu-speaking young women are 'interviewed about what they thought of tourists, the consumption of female "cultural" bodies reveals that the issue of *what is cultural*, and *for whom* is complex and tiered with layered understandings' (Naidu 2016: 51). Therefore, we need the points of view of particular individuals not only to obtain deeper personal experiences, but also to illuminate what is paradoxically both evident but hidden.

Naidu's (2016) study also provides an example of a cultural heritage aspect that is constructed especially for the tourist experience. These experiences that tourists seek (Bruner 2005b) can also be entirely constructed in order to create identity and distinctiveness (Walton 2009: 116): what Hobsbawm and Ranger (1983) describe as an 'invention of tradition'. Therefore, it is essential to provide history and context to these practices as well. Nevertheless, practitioners are sometimes insensitive to the discipline and the context, and tourism promotional purposes can cause histories to be reduced to just 'a scattering' of the background of historical and cultural elements, as Walton (2009) argues. Tourism marketing, modernity and history can therefore seek to 'sanitize and manipulate the Other' (ibid.: 116). Even though we acknowledge globalisation and homogenisation, distinctive cultural elements have always been crucial and valuable elements in tourism. This has two ramifications for regions or countries: either they 'invent' cultural elements to attract tourists, or unique cultural features gain more importance and protection (Richter 2009: 192). Richter further asserts that 'ethnic minorities or marginal cultures' are seen as more valuable since they also function as core elements in tourism promotion, therefore eliminating 'the homogenization of society and suppression of minority groups' (ibid.). The problematic link between globalisation and the homogenisation of culture has been grasped in events settings as well. Quinn (2009) argues that large-scale events can diminish regional differences and jeopardise vital distinctive features, or may entail global commonalities.

As a stance against an extension of variant barriers in the academy, ethnographies of the particular approach may enable the ethnographer to escape the authoritative discourses that assert hierarchy:

> The very gap between the professional and authoritative discourses of generalization and the languages of everyday life (our own and others') establishes a fundamental separation between the anthropologist and the people being written about that facilitates the construction of anthropological objects as simultaneously different and inferior.
> (Abu-Lughod 1991: 471)

Conclusion

In this chapter, we have discussed the ways to overcome representation problems that occur as an extension of the coherence, timelessness and discreteness that the notion of culture proposes as the prime anthropological tool for making 'other'. The general effects of tourism on culture have long been under scrutiny. There have been variant scenarios that change with the broad range of consequences, which include contributing to the degeneration of the culture, fake folklore produced to meet tourist demand, or revitalisation of culture (de Kadt 1979: 14–15). Yet, with postmodern critics, we realise that the culture concept itself has more effects on tourism, and even on the process of unravelling and demonstrating the relations between culture and tourism. While culture shapes writing and discourse, sometimes it becomes the discourse itself in this process.

In tourism studies, we still have a lot of ground to cover in order to attain level eight of Denzin and Lincoln (2011) and avoid the connotations that the concept of culture implies. On the other hand, from Abu-Lughod's framework, there are also some steps we can follow in the field. We need to advance interpretive studies, which are valuable tools for gaining a deeper understanding, as tourism and heritage studies reveal, by illuminating historical patterns in the social, economic and political context in order to elude the static connotations that the culture concept itself implies. Moreover, as Abu-Lughod points out, gaining individual understanding can lead us to uncover power structures linked to the micro-levels as well as to shed light on multiple practices and experiences. It will also enable us to link the voice of academy with daily life.

Postmodern discussions encourage us not only to reveal multiple differences but also to make room for them. Therefore, the cutting-edge research requires us to 'open up our understanding to the multifarious discourses and practices of tourism' (Chambers 2007: 243). While we are focusing on de-centring in the anthropology, we need to move forward and integrate such an open vision in regard to caveats in style, balancing gender and geographies in publishing, and other academic activities. This move will not only be coherent with the arguments in our publications, but also will link our thinking and practice. Moreover, we need more attention in mobility and multi-sited fieldwork discussions to particularities and interactions in the global age.

We have attempted to evaluate the current view of ethnographic studies in tourism through debates about representation and the notion of culture. Although the concept of culture has some negative underpinnings, discarding the term is a case of 'the glass half-full and half-empty', as Abu-Lughod also admits (Brumann 1999: 15). Yet theoretical and methodological discussions about these shortcomings of the concept can still elevate our approaches.

References

Abu-Lughod, L. (1991) Writing against culture. In: R. G. Fox (ed.) *Recapturing Anthropology*. Santa Fe: School of American Research Press, pp. 137–162.

Aitchison, C. (2001) Theorizing other discourses of tourism, gender and culture: can the subaltern speak (in tourism)? *Tourist Studies*, 1(2), 133–147.

Alcoff, L. (1991) The problem of speaking for others. *Cultural Critique*, 20: 5–32.

Alneng, V. (2002) The modern does not cater for natives: travel ethnography and the conventions of form. *Tourist Studies*, 2(2): 119–142.

Asad, T. (1979) Anthropology and the colonial encounter. In: G. Huizer and B. Mannheim (eds) *The Politics of Anthropology: From Colonialism and Sexism Toward a View from Below.* The Hague: Mouton Publishers, pp. 85–94.

Ateljevic, I. (2000) Circuits of tourism: stepping beyond the 'production/consumption' dichotomy. *Tourism Geographies*, 2(4), 369–388.

Ateljevic, I., Pritchard, A. and Morgan, N. (eds) (2007) *The Critical Turn in Tourism Studies.* Oxford: Elsevier.

Badone, E. (2015) Seduction in the 'gypsy pilgrimage' at Les-Saintes-Maries-de-la-Mer. In: M. Di Giovine and D. Picard (eds.) *The Seductions of Pilgrimage: Sacred Journeys Afar and Astray in the Western Religious Tradition.* Farnham: Routledge, pp. 169–186.

Baptista, J.A. (2017) *The Good Holiday. Development, Tourism and the Politics of Benevolence in Mozambique.* New York: Berghahn.

Bloch, N. (2017) Barbarians in India. Tourism as moral contamination. *Annals of Tourism Research*, 62, 64–77.

Boas, F. (1920). The methods of ethnology. *American Anthropologist*, 22(4), 311–321.

Botterill, D. (2003) An autoethnographic narrative on tourism research epistemologies. *Loisir et Société*, 26(1), 97–110.

Brumann, C. (1999) Writing for culture: why a successful concept should not be discarded. *Current Anthropology*, 40(1): 1–27.

Bruner, E. M. (1991) Transformation of self in tourism. *Annals of Tourism Research*, 18(2): 238–250.

Bruner, E. M. (1994) Abraham Lincoln as authentic reproduction: a critique of post-modernism. *American Anthropologist*, 96(2): 397–415.

Bruner, E. M. (2005a) The role of narrative in tourism. Paper presented at On Voyage: New Directions in Tourism Theory, October 7–8, Berkeley conference. Available at www.nyu.edu/classes/bkg/tourist/narrative.docBruner, E. M. (2005b). *Culture on Tour: Ethnographies of Travel.* Chicago: University of Chicago Press.

Chambers, D. (2007) An agenda for cutting-edge research in tourism. In: D. Airey and J. Tribe (eds.) *Developments in Tourism Research.* Oxford: Elsevier, pp. 233–246.

Clifford, J. (1983) On ethnographic authority. *Representations*, 2: 118–146.

Clifford, J. (1986) On ethnographic allegory. In: J. Clifford and G. Marcus (eds) *Writing Culture: The Poetics and Politics of Ethnography.* Berkeley: University of California Press, pp. 98–121.

Clifford, J. (1988) *The Predicament of Culture: Twentieth Century Ethnography, Literature and Art.* Cambridge, MA: Harvard University Press.

Clifford, J. and Marcus, G. E. (eds) (1986) *Writing Culture.* Berkeley: University of California Press.

Cohen, E. (1979) Rethinking the sociology of tourism. *Annals of Tourism Research*, 6 (1), 18–35.

Collins, P. and Gallinat, A. (2010) The ethnographic self as resource: an introduction. In: P. Collins and A. Gallinat (eds) *The Ethnographic Self as Resource: Writing Memory and Experience into Ethnography.* New York: Berghahn Books, pp. 1–24.

Das, V. (1994) The anthropological discourse on India: reason and its other. In: R. Borofsky (ed.) *Assessing Cultural Anthropology.* New York: McGraw-Hill, pp. 133–144.

Denzin, N. K. and Lincoln, Y. S. (eds) (2011) *The Sage Handbook of Qualitative Research.* Los Angeles: Sage.

Feld, S. (1982) *Sound and Sentiment: Birds, Weeping, Poetics, and Song in Kaluli Expression.* London: Duke University Press.

Feld, S. (1987) Dialogic editing: interpreting how Kaluli read sound and sentiment. Cultural *Anthropology*, 2(2), 190–210.

Fernandez, J. W. (1994) Culture and transcendent humanization: on the 'dynamics of the categorial'. *Ethnos*, 59: 143–167.

Galani-Moutafi, V. (2000) The self and the other: traveler, ethnographer, tourist. *Annals of Tourism Research*, 27(1), 203–224.

Geertz, C. (1975) Thick description: toward an interpretive theory of culture. In: C. Geertz (ed.) *The Interpretation of Cultures*. London: Hutchinson, pp. 3–30.

Geertz, C. (1988) *Works and Lives: The Anthropologist as Author*. Stanford: Stanford University Press.

Giblin, J. (2017) Performing 'Indigenous; for international tourists who tour the rural poor. In: C. Hillerdal, A. Karlström and C. Ojala (eds) *Archaeologies of 'Us' and 'Them': Debating History, Heritage and Indigeneity*. London: Routledge, pp. 241–257.

Graburn, N. (2002) The ethnographic tourist. In: G. S. Dann (ed.) *The Tourist as a Metaphor of The Social World*. Wallingford, UK: CABI, pp. 19–39.

Gupta, A. and Ferguson, J. (1992) Beyond 'culture': space, identity, and the politics of difference. *Cultural Anthropology*, 7(1): 6–23.

Hage, G. (2005) A not so multi-sited ethnography of a not so imagined community. *Anthropological Theory*, 5(4): 463.

Hobsbawm, E. and Ranger, T. (eds) (1983) *The Invention of Tradition*. New York: Cambridge University Press.

de Kadt, E. (ed.) (1979) *Tourism – Passport to Development?* New York: Oxford University Press.

Källén, A. (2015) *Stones Standing: Archaeology, Colonialism, and Ecotourism in Northern Laos*. Walnut Creek: Routledge.

Low, S. M. (1996) Spatializing culture: the social production and social construction of public space in Costa Rica. *American Ethnologist*, 23(4): 861–879.

MacCannell, D. (1976) *The Tourist: A New Theory of the Leisure Class*. Berkeley: University of California Press.

Makagon, D. and Neuman, M. (2009) *Recording Culture*. Los Angeles: Sage.

Malinowski, B. (1961) *Argonauts of the Western Pacific*. New York: Routledge.

Marcus, G. (1995) Ethnography in/of the world system: the emergence of multi-sited ethnography. *Annual Review of Anthropology*, 24: 95–117.

Marcus, G. E. (1998) *Ethnography Through Thick and Thin*. Princeton: Princeton University Press.

Mavrič, M. and Urry, J. (2009) The new mobilities research paradigm. In: T. Jamal and M. Robinson (eds) *The Sage Handbook of Tourism Studies*. London: Sage, pp. 645–657.

Mellinger, W. M. (1994) Toward a critical analysis of tourism representations. *Annals of Tourism Research*, 21(4): 756–779.

Moore, H. L. (1988) *Feminism and Anthropology*. Oxford: Blackwell Publishers.

Mura, P. and Pahlevan Sharif, S. (2015) The crisis of the 'crisis of representation' – mapping qualitative tourism research in Southeast Asia. *Current Issues in Tourism*, 18(9): 828–844.

Naidu, M. (2016) Local contexts, local theory. In: J. Etim (ed.) *Introduction to Gender Studies in Eastern and Southern Africa*. Rotterdam: Sense Publishers, pp. 41–64.

Nash, D. (2001) On travelers, ethnographers and tourists. *Annals of Tourism Research*, 28(2): 493–496.

Nash, D. and Smith, V.L. (1991) Anthropology and tourism. *Annals of Tourism Research*, 18(1): 12–25.

Pahre, R. (2015) Material falsehoods: living a lie at this old fort. In: M. Robinson and H. Silverman (eds) *Encounters with Popular Pasts*. London: Springer International, pp. 61–80.

Pasquinelli, C. (1996) The concept of culture between modernity and postmodernity. In: V. Hubinger (ed.) *Grasping the Changing World: Anthropological Concepts in the Postmodern Era*. London: Routledge, pp. 53–73.

Pels, P. (1997) The anthropology of colonialism: culture, history, and the emergence of western governmentality. *Annual Review of Anthropology*, 26(1): 163–183.

Platenkamp, V. and Botterill, D. (2013) Critical realism, rationality and tourism knowledge. *Annals of Tourism Research*, 41: 110–129.

Quinn, B. (2009) Festivals, events and tourism. In: T. Jamal and M. Robinson (eds) *The Sage Handbook of Tourism Studies*. London: Sage.

Richter, L. K. (2009) Power, politics, and political science: the politicization of tourism. In: T. Jamal and M. Robinson (eds) *The Sage Handbook of Tourism Studies*. London: Sage, pp. 188–202.

Rickly-Boyd, J. M., Knudsen, D. C. and Braverman, L. C. (2016) *Tourism, Performance, and Place: A Geographic Perspective*. London: Routledge.

Riley, R. W. and Love, L. L. (2000) The state of qualitative tourism research. *Annals of Tourism Research*, 27(1): 164–187.

RisjordM. (2007) Ethnography and culture. In: S. P. Turner and M. W. Pisjord (eds) *Philosophy of Anthropology and Sociology*. Amsterdam: Elsevier, pp. 399–428.

Rosaldo, R. (1986) From the door of his tent: the fieldworker and the inquisitor. In: J. Clifford and G. E. Marcus (ed.) Writing Culture: The Poetics and Politics of Ethnography. Berkeley: University of California Press, pp. 77–97.

Rosaldo, R. (1989) Imperialist nostalgia. *Representations*, 26: 107–122.

Ryan, C.Ed. (2002) *The Tourist Experience*. London: Continuum.

Said, E. (1978) *Orientalism*. New York: Vintage.

Salazar, N. B. and Graburn, N. H. (eds) (2014) *Tourism Imaginaries: Anthropological Approaches*. Oxford: Berghahn Books.

Santos, C. A. (2006) Cultural politics in contemporary travel writing. *Annals of Tourism Research*, 33(3): 624–644.

Sharpley, R. and Stone, P. R. (eds) (2010) *Tourist Experience: Contemporary Perspectives*. Abingdon: Routledge.

Silverman, H. (2015) Branding Peru: cultural heritage and popular culture in the marketing strategy of PromPerú. In: M. Robinson and H. Silverman (eds) *Encounters with Popular Pasts*. London: Springer International, pp. 131–148.

Spivak, G.C. (1985) Can the subaltern speak? Speculations on widow-sacrifice. *Wedge*, Winter/Spring: 120–130.

Tribe, J. (2005) Editorial: New tourism research. *Tourism Recreation Research*, 30(2): 5–8.

Veijola, S. and Jokinen, E. (1994) The body in tourism. *Theory, Culture and Society*, 11: 125–151.

Walton, J. K. (2009) Histories of tourism. In: T. Jamal and M. Robinson (eds) *The Sage Handbook of Tourism Studies*. London: Sage, pp. 115–129.

Westwood, S., Morgan, N. and Pritchard, A. (2006) Situation, participation and reflexivity in tourism research: furthering interpretive approaches to tourism enquiry. *Tourism Recreation Research*, 31(2): 33–41.

Wilson, E. and Hollinshead, K. (2015) Qualitative tourism research: opportunities in the emergent soft sciences. *Annals of Tourism Research*, 54: 30–47.

Winter, T. (2009) Asian tourism and the retreat of Anglo-Western centrism in tourism theory. *Current Issues in Tourism*, 12(1): 21–31.

Yanagisako, S. J. and Collier, J. F. (1994) Toward a unified analysis of gender and kinship. In: R. Borofsky (ed.) *Assessing Cultural Anthropology*. New York: McGraw-Hill, pp. 190–201.

12 Afterword

Less than easy tourism research in a world of fun

Pamila Gupta

When Hazel Andrews invited me to write this afterword, I was honoured to take up the challenge. We had previously co-edited a special-issue journal together. We had both felt compelled by certain ethnographic encounters from the field as female anthropologists developing tourism research projects in Spain and India, respectively (Andrews and Gupta 2010). Issues of gender and reflexivity had come up for each of us in profound and prosaic moments; we wanted to open up a dialogue on how perceptions of self and other structured the production of knowledge both in the field and during the write-up phase. In this afterword I am in some sense picking up where we left off, and continuing our collaboration and conversation, only eight years later, and from our different positionalities in the here and now.

It was a pleasure to read through this group of exciting and timely essays that open up a series of debates and challenges onto the contemporary land-scape of tourism research across a variety of settings. With a focus on data collection and the role of the anthropologist, this edited volume suggests that, despite associations of fun, tourism research is less than easy – rather, it raises relevant anthropological questions of method, practice, reflexivity and ethical dilemmas – yet we persevere, for it is enriching at the same time. Hence my title: 'Less than easy tourism research in a world of fun', one which serves as a framing device for this afterword.

I raise three themes that came out of my reading of these contributions: what I want to call here 'wild zones', 'the ongoing epistemic' and 'team research'. I posit these themes in order to show their relevance, and their potential for paving the way for future tourism research.

Wild zones

First, rather than thinking about these tourist encounters as 'contact zones', a concept coined by Mary Louise Pratt (1992) that has productively made its way into tourism research, I want to posit instead a theme of 'wild zones' to amplify the issues at stake in the contributions by Jonathan Skinner and Danielle Kelly. These two chapters open up the worlds of suicide tourism in the UK and drug use during nightlife tourism on the party island of Ibiza

(Spain), respectively. Skinner's chapter pushes us to think of the role of the accidental or serendipitous – in this case an actual suicide that takes place off the cliffs of Beachy Head during fieldwork that then becomes part of his dark tourism research. Unfortunate events are often not discussed, yet they play an affective role in shaping how we think about and develop our projects. More often than not, they are commonly left out of our ethnographies or presented as if we had planned these research happenings. Skinner also shows the site of the neoliberal university as constraining our sometimes 'wild' research ideas such that they don't receive ethical clearance or funding, as was the case for his failed project on suicide tourism. Kelly's chapter pushes us to think about when, or at what time rather, and under what circumstances we undertake research. We often think of fieldwork as 'work' that takes place during the day. Instead, her chapter shows that the bulk of her field research took place at nighttime (amidst a 'wild' nightlife scene in Ibiza) and with people wildly intoxicated by alcohol, drugs or both. Just as Johannes Fabian's (2000) work on late nineteenth-century European travelogues reminds us that many travellers were often high on alcohol or opiates when they recorded their views of the other – in this case on Africa – perhaps the same could be said for many an anthropologist, past and present. It is an underdeveloped area of research that Kelly's chapter reflects upon, including her self-reflexive choice to not participate in drinking alcohol or ingesting drugs with her informants. What sorts of ethical issues are raised here and how do they shape fieldwork encounters, whether one partakes in these substances or not? The idea of 'wild zones' takes on many guises here that I want to offer as a fruitful theme for rethinking contact zones between anthropologists and tourists in the field as less contained, as spilling out, as having rough edges, as encompassing the unexpected and unprecedented.

The ongoing epistemic

A second theme raised by this set of contributions is what I want to call here the 'ongoing epistemic'. The chapters by Bakas, Koot, Dolezal, Fallon, and Loutfy, Stuke and Wee all attend to epistemological issues that are at the difficult centre of tourism research. Similarly to the continuing theme of the blurred boundary between what constitutes an anthropologist versus a tourist, a point first raised by Malcolm Crick (1985) in his seminal essay, these concerns remain unresolvable at one level, yet they need to be continually and gently probed in relation to specific fieldwork encounters in order to gain a sense of their nuanced contours. Perhaps these slight inflections show how it is not a static epistemological field, but rather a dynamic one, that is changing in relation to new sites, different sets of questions and a next generation of anthropologists. While Koot discusses the importance of auto-ethnography as a research method, he also shows the role of 'unawareness', 'memory' and white paternalism through a long engagement (19 years) with community-based tourism research in Namibia. His is a unique positionality that shows the pertinence of these ongoing issues in shaping the fieldwork encounter.

Bakas brings gender to the fore of her analysis on craft-making in touristic Greece, both her own and that of her informants; she also adds the intriguing experience of 'busyness' as attached to female roles; it is that which makes research amongst a group of Greek crafters difficult in the face of their intensive labour, with little spare time to chit-chat with her. It is only when she too is engaged in busy work alongside them that she is allowed access to their thoughts, ideas and (gendered) worlds. Her essay shows the very real constraints of gaining access in the field, and what we do in the field as anthropologists to gain that access, an epistemological reality that is not often discussed. Dolezal takes us on a less fun tour of fieldwork in Bali, showing how fieldwork is fundamentally constituted by ideas of work, using terms such as 'impact', 'facts', 'failures in the field' and 'findings'. Yet she also wants to show the subjective side of fieldwork, that is, the emotional experiences that shape our encounters. It is a fine balance between the two that becomes in some sense our written ethnographies.

Trapp-Fallon brings oral history back to the centre of our tourism ethnographies, suggesting both that anthropology's inherent reflexivity provides room for oral history, and that it is a methodology that is relatively unexplored in tourism research. She also points out that many tourism ethnographies suffer from a lack of engagement with actual tourists, as they are often focused on the place and purpose of touristic practices. Oral history, then, could help fill in portraits of those often missing tourists. That is, a return to the methodology of conducting life-histories in the field with a range of tourists might prove useful for both tourism understandings and theory making. Her argument may seem like an obvious point – one that shows we are mostly busy being participant-observers of tourism rather than spending time with tourists – but his plea for a return to oral history strikes me as relevant and timely. Lastly, Loutfy, Stuke and Wee raise two important epistemological issues that I believe should be continuing concerns for tourism research, and which I point to in order to conclude this second theme of the 'ongoing epistemic'. First, Loutfy, Stuke and Wee discuss the role of the sensorial in shaping our fieldwork encounters, an area first taken up by anthropologist Paul Stoller (1989) that remains curiously undertheorized in tourism research. A second point raised by Loutfy, Stuke and Wee is that of the deep entrenchment of tourism in particular cultures (following the work of Ed Bruner in Bali, 2001), such that it becomes part of culture. It is something that I have seen take place in Goa (India), where I have conducted tourism research for the past 25 years. In the context of the increased importance of tourism economies the world over, this is an important epistemological point that often fails to be addressed in our ethnographies precisely because it gets at the complexity of the culture concept which lies at the heart of anthropology.

Team research

A third and final issue that comes to the fore in these contributions is that of the changing nature of what I call here 'team research'. Anthropologists no longer conduct fieldwork in isolation from larger global frictions. Rather, as we face increased monetary crises at the level of the university and the state, we have had to think more creatively and with less research funding at our disposal. As well, the nature of what constitutes tourism research is also always changing, and is increasingly open to multidisciplinary approaches. I was struck with the potentiality of good team research reflected in the jointly authored chapters by Fernandes and Ramos, Pereiro and Gómez-Ullate, and Kaya Sayari and Yolal. These case studies show that two anthropologists working together can fruitfully combine their areas of expertise, vulnerabilities and positionalities. Terms such as 'methodological flexibility' and 'deep reflexivity' used by Fernandes and Ramos in their chapter can be reconfigured when there are multiple anthropologists working side by side. More generally, collaborative research and writing (or "team ethnographies," a term employed by Pereiro and Gómez-Ullate in their jointly authored chapter) appears less as a hindrance but rather as a productive tool that gives rise to the future landscape of tourism research more generally. These same authors also make a strong case for suggesting that anthropology can potentially provide ethical support for sustainable tourism development policies and practices: in other words, they show the importance of applied anthropology for tourism. Lastly, the contribution by Kaya Sayari and Yolal raises important issues concerning the nature of multi-sited ethnographies and comparative work, both of which are important and underdeveloped aspects of tourism research.

I hope that my brief tour through the various tourism landscapes presented in this timely new publication highlights the less than easy aspects of tourism research in a supposed world of fun created by tourism itself.

References

Andrews, H. and Gupta, P. (2010) Introduction. *Journal of Tourism Consumption and Practice*, 2(2): 1–14.

Bruner, E. (2001) Tourism in the Balinese borderzone. In: S. Lavie and T. Swedenburg (eds) *Displacement, Diaspora and Geographies of Identity*. Durham: Duke University Press, pp. 157–180.

Crick, M. (1985) Tracing the anthropological self: quizzical reflections on fieldwork, tourism, and the ludic. *Social Analysis*, 17: 71–92.

Fabian, J. (2000) *Out of Our Minds: Reason and Madness in the Exploration of Central Africa*. Berkeley: University of California Press.

Pratt, M. L. (1992) *Imperial Eyes: Travel Writing and Transculturation*. New York: Routledge.

Stoller, P. (1989) *The Taste of Ethnographic Things: The Senses in Anthropology*. Philadelphia: University of Pennsylvania Press.

Index

For Product Safety Concerns and Information please contact our EU
representative GPSR@taylorandfrancis.com
Taylor & Francis Verlag GmbH, Kaufingerstraße 24, 80331 München, Germany